Roger Maynard

HarperCollins*Publishers*

HarperCollins*Publishers*

First published in 2009
by HarperCollins*Publishers* Australia Pty Limited
ABN 36 009 913 517
www.harpercollins.com.au

Copyright © Roger Maynard 2009

The right of Roger Maynard to be identified as the author of this work has been asserted by him under the *Copyright Amendment (Moral Rights) Act 2000*.

This work is copyright. Apart from any use as permitted under the *Copyright Act 1968*, no part may be reproduced, copied, scanned, stored in a retrieval system, recorded, or transmitted, in any form or by any means, without the prior written permission of the publisher.

HarperCollins*Publishers*
25 Ryde Road, Pymble, Sydney, NSW 2073, Australia
31 View Road, Glenfield, Auckland 0627, New Zealand
1–A, Hamilton House, Connaught Place, New Delhi – 110 001, India
77–85 Fulham Palace Road, London, W6 8JB, United Kingdom
2 Bloor Street East, 20th floor, Toronto, Ontario M4W 1A8, Canada
10 East 53rd Street, New York NY 10022, USA

National Library of Australia Cataloguing-in-Publication data:

Maynard, Roger.
 Hell's heroes: the forgotten story of the worst P.O.W. camp in Japan / Roger Maynard
 ISBN: 978 0 7322 8523 4 (pbk.)
 Includes index.
 World War, 1939-1945 – Prisoners and prisons,
 Japanese Prisoner of war camps – Japan – Naoetsu-shi.
 Prisoners of war – Australia
 Prisoners of war – Japan – Naoetsu-shi.
 Naoetsu-shi (Japan) – History.
940.547252

Cover design by Matt Stanton
Cover images: (left) informal portrait of Snowy Collins by Australian War Memorial, Negative Number P03849.042; (middle) informal portrait of Don Alchin by Australian War Memorial, Negative Number P03849.021; (right) image of Kevin Timbs, courtesy of his family; barbed wire by Shutterstock.com.
Photos in picture section courtesy of the families of the Naoetsu veterans; other photos are from the Australian War Memorial or the author's collection.
Map of Singapore courtesy of Hilary Paterson, reproduced from *Singapore And Beyond* by Don Wall, by kind permission of Richard Wall.
Typeset in 12/15.5pt Bembo by Letter Spaced
Printed and bound in Australia by Griffin Press
70gsm Classic used by HarperCollins*Publishers* is a natural, recyclable product made from wood grown in sustainable forests. The manufacturing processes conform to the environmental regulations in the country of origin, Finland.

*This book is dedicated to John Cook
and the men of the 2/20th Battalion*

CONTENTS

Introduction		1
PART I		
Chapter 1	Heeding the Clarion Call	9
Chapter 2	Destination Malaya	29
Chapter 3	Battle Stations	49
Chapter 4	Unprepared and Under Fire	67
Chapter 5	Prisoners of the Japanese	103
PART II		
Chapter 6	Welcome to Hell	131
Chapter 7	Death, Diarrhoea and Dog Wallopers	153
Chapter 8	When Food is the Only Fantasy	179
Chapter 9	Living Under the Shadow of Death	213
Chapter 10	'Kill Them and Leave No Trace'	241
Chapter 11	'My God, What Have We Done?'	253
PART III		
Chapter 12	Liberation	263
Chapter 13	'Hang the Bastards'	279
Chapter 14	Searching for Watanabe	299
Chapter 15	The Rope-Maker Awaits His Fate	307
Epilogue		321
Naoetsu Roll Call		333
Sources and References		340
Map of Singapore		349
Naoetsu Boys		350
Acknowledgments		352
Index		354

INTRODUCTION

Hell's Heroes is the story of the camp that never was, so dubbed by one old soldier because the atrocities that happened there went largely unreported at the time. While the Burma–Thai Railway, the Bataan death march, Changi and many other parts of Asia have since become synonymous with Japanese brutality, most of the POW camps which were set up to provide slave labour for the enemy military machine were slowly forgotten in the aftermath to World War II.

Perhaps the scale of misery which had engulfed the rest of the world from 1939 to '45 had simply eclipsed the many other smaller tales of man's inhumanity to man.

Yet the experiences of those who found themselves imprisoned in Japan itself were equally appalling, providing a measure of horror that would match some of the world's most notorious war crimes. From late 1942 until the end of hostilities in August 1945, nearly 36,000 servicemen, including British, Dutch, Americans and Australians, were held as prisoners of war in Japan; it is no exaggeration to say they lived in the most horrific conditions.

The Naoetsu camp — nestled by the riverside in the west coast town of the same name — was almost too cruel to comprehend. Some 300 Australian soldiers, collectively known as C Force, spent nearly three years of their life there after being taken prisoner in Singapore in February '42 and enduring a spell at the notorious

Changi barracks complex. Most of them were from the 2/20th Battalion, but there were also men from other units within the New South Wales-raised 22nd Infantry Brigade, such as the 2/18th. Sixty of the 300 died in captivity, more men per capita than any other POW camp in Japan. After the war eight guards were executed for their reign of terror at Naoetsu, more than from any other camp in Japan.

At one stage there were as many as 130 POW camps in Japan, but few were so brutal as Camp-4B. It was here that the men of the 2/20th Battalion of the Eighth Division's 22nd Infantry Brigade were sent after the fall of Singapore, where they sustained nearly 500 casualties.

Most of them were volunteers who'd joined up from their homes in rural New South Wales, Sydney, Newcastle and the north coast. They were ordinary blokes who came together shortly after the 2/20th Battalion was formed in July 1940.

It was to be the adventure of a lifetime. Most had never left New South Wales, let alone Australia. The army might have turned them into a fighting force but they were essentially innocents abroad whose knowledge of the world was limited and experience of war was nil.

Blissfully unaware of the death and bloodshed to come, they looked to the future with the optimism of youth, untroubled by fear or personal doubt.

At the time of writing only ten old diggers from the 2/20th and one from the 2/18th are alive. Their memories are horrific, inspiring and occasionally funny. The use of black humour was a constant feature, if only to deal with the catalogue of tragedy and adversity.

Some who did not survive the ordeal, and others who lived to tell the tale, were forward thinking enough to record their everyday life in secret diaries or later in personal memoirs. It was against camp regulations to keep an unauthorised diary and the fear of discovery only added to the daily stress.

Their recollections make compelling reading, but more than that they provide incontrovertible proof of a strength and inner determination that seems impossible to comprehend today. How could they endure such physical deprivation and discomfort for so long? What happens to men when death is all around them? How do they keep hope alive?

From the day they arrived in the old wooden building that formed the first Naoetsu camp, the men began to fall ill as the eighteen-hour work shifts, lack of hygiene and extreme weather conditions began to take their toll.

If the illness and lack of food wasn't enough to strike them down, the men also had to put up with the punishments handed out by the guards, who would beat them with a wooden club known as a dog walloper. While all this was going on, the victims were often made to stand to attention outside for hours in freezing temperatures with little or no clothing.

What they also didn't realise was that the Japanese had no plans to release them if the war was lost. The intention was to slaughter them en masse.

I first stumbled across this largely forgotten slice of wartime history on 16 February 2006, the day after a ceremony was held in Sydney's Martin Place to commemorate the sixty-fourth anniversary of the fall of Singapore. Attendances at the annual gathering had declined in recent years, as many of the old soldiers who had witnessed the Allied forces' capitulation to the Japanese were either dead or too frail to be present.

The only veteran of the battle for Singapore to make it was John Cook, who was in his early eighties and determined to honour the memory of his fallen comrades. Much to his embarrassment, his presence was reported alongside a photograph of the service in the following day's edition of the *Sydney Morning Herald*, which included a reference to his spell in Naoetsu. I had never heard of the camp but a journalistic sixth sense stirred my interest.

John hated publicity and was reluctant to be interviewed. 'I don't want my name mentioned,' he warned when I approached him afterwards. However, he softened over the following months, helping enormously with my research and directing me to key contacts and interviewees. It was soon apparent that there was a much bigger story to be told. The more I spoke to John and the remaining survivors of C Force — strong-minded Kevin Timbs and tough-as-nails Joe Byrne; gentlemanly Jack Mudie; country boys Don Alchin, Snowy Collins and Henry Dietz; city-smart George Daldry and Herb Lamb; and others — the more I uncovered.

But it was the diaries that revealed the true extent of the pain and unremitting gloom. One which took me almost two years to track down had remained undisturbed in a cardboard box since the end of the war. When I opened it to digest the contents it was as though the very smells of Changi and Naoetsu wafted from the flimsy, pencilled pages.

Over the past few years I have travelled thousands of miles to track down and interview the survivors and those Japanese who still remember the camp. It was a journey that took me from New South Wales country towns to Singapore, Malaysia, Tokyo, Yokohama war cemetery and finally the ancient port city of Naoetsu. There I was able to retrace the footsteps of the men whose brutal incarceration is still recalled by elderly locals, and even the children of the guards who inflicted such cruelty on their charges.

The Naoetsu boys were little more than kids when they set sail from Sydney in 1941. Most were hardly out of their teens when they joined up. Over the next few years they would flower in a world where death was a daily visitor and where courage knew no bounds. Their story is a microcosm of war, revealing how an assortment of working-class men were thrown into the jaws of hell and survived against all odds. Sick, beaten, starved, traumatised and finally freed, their experience would influence the rest of their lives.

This is a simple but enthralling account of how the human will can triumph over adversity, a personal drama seen through the eyes of ordinary people who became extraordinary men. And how half a century later a move to reconcile old hatreds threatened to reignite them.

Their indomitable spirit provides an insight into a world that has long since disappeared but the qualities that inspired them are as relevant today as they were more than six decades ago.

Australia owes an enormous debt to the men of the 2/20th and the other units who had the misfortune to be held at Naoetsu. Theirs was a terrible yet amazing experience, one that history might easily have overlooked. This is their story. They are the unsung heroes of a living hell which took them from the gently lapping waters of Sydney Harbour to the jungles of Malaya, bloody street battles in Singapore, imprisonment in Changi and the horror that was Camp 4-B. No matter how they tried, they would never forget their struggle for survival and their mates who didn't make it. Even in old age they would be enslaved by the nightmares of the past. Only those who were there could fully appreciate the terror. Though in retrospect there was also fun and farce. Even in the darkest hours men can laugh. What a crazy time it was.

※ ※ ※

PART I

CHAPTER 1

HEEDING THE CLARION CALL

Australia was ill-prepared for conflict when Britain declared war on Germany on 3 September 1939. Even so, Prime Minister Robert Menzies was quick to support the Mother Country and soon committed thousands of soldiers, sailors and airmen to the European theatre.

By early the following year members of the 6th Division of the Australian Imperial Force (AIF) were on their way to the Middle East for training and from June 1940 Australian fighter pilots were daily risking their lives in the Battle of Britain. Come January 1941 the diggers got their first taste of serious action when they captured Bardia in Libya from the Italians and would go on to play a key role in the battle of Tobruk.

While London burned and much of Europe and North Africa was occupied by enemy forces, Australia remained largely untouched by the flames of war. Only those mothers, wives and girlfriends whose menfolk had already enlisted knew the frisson of fear of having a loved one serve overseas. And as the days went by, more and more young men were heeding the call to join up. But for most Australians, life continued as normal.

There were no bombs or blackouts to contend with, beer and

food were plentiful, and there was no shortage of entertainment. In Sydney the Hoyts Plaza was showing *The Great Dictator* with Charlie Chaplin. Greer Garson and Laurence Olivier starred in *Pride and Prejudice* at the Liberty Cinema, and at St James, *Night Train to Munich* featured Margaret Lockwood and Rex Harrison. Luna Park provided 'a thousand rides, slides and glides' with 'hair raising adventures, sparkling lights and laughing crowds'. For the young and agile, there was ice skating at the Glaciarium in Railway Square, and the Sydney Harbour Showboat offered an afternoon voyage for three shillings.

And there was plenty of work for those who had left school but were too young to enlist. Sixteen-year-old boys could earn £1/9s/3d a week in factories and seventeen-year-olds were paid a pound extra. What's more they didn't have to work on Saturdays. The smart lad or aspiring professional could buy a made-to-measure suit from Murdoch's for £5/18s/6d, as advertised in the *Sydney Morning Herald*; while for the same price, housewives could banish domestic drudgery with a Lehmann non-electric washing machine.

But the outside world was creeping in during the Australian summer of 1941. The newspapers also contained reports of the threat from Japan, a situation that had been escalating over the previous decade, first with that country's invasion of Manchuria in 1931, then with the brutal war against China six years later. More recently, in July 1940, Japan's overpopulation problems had led to the proclamation of its Greater East Asia Co-Prosperity Sphere — benevolently titled, it seemed, but in reality an aggressive foreign policy designed to transform the region as far afield as India, Australia and New Zealand, if not beyond. To cap it all in the mind of many Australian observers, Japan had then signed an agreement of mutual assistance, the Tripartite Pact, with the Axis powers of Germany and Italy.

Under the headline 'ALARM OF JAPANESE MOVES', the *Herald* of 4 February carried a despatch from its Washington correspondent noting 'the seriousness of Japan's gains in the southern Indo-Chinese territories' and the 'likelihood' of Japan establishing a naval base in the Vietnamese deep-water port of Cam Ranh Bay. More alarmingly the newspaper reported: 'The Chinese insist that Japan's moves presage an attack on Singapore. The Imperial garrison in Malaya is being strengthened and now includes Indian, Australian and New Zealand troops.'

It was a reminder that some Allied forces were already in place, ready to protect Crown interests in South-East Asia, although this time the Australians in particular saw their responsibilities differently compared to previous conflicts. Unlike during World War I, when they ended up becoming cannon fodder at the behest of their largely unappreciative imperial masters, now their own country's future could be at stake.

The terrible loss of life on the Somme and at Gallipoli had demonstrated Australia's courage and unswerving loyalty to Britain. But the experience of the Great War had left many servicemen disenchanted with the British military machine, its officer class and the general standard of soldiery. Come 1939–40, while Australians had volunteered to defend king and country, they feared a repeat performance in what now promised to be a truly global conflict.

Not that this was the official government line, of course. Prime Minister Robert Menzies had been swift to follow Britain's lead by declaring war on Germany within two days of Hitler's invasion of Poland in September 1939. Over the next six years almost a million Australians would heed the clarion call to war, serving in the army, navy, air force and merchant marine.

While the nation's collective sense of duty towards the Commonwealth could not be faulted, there was no hiding the fact that Australia was hopelessly unready for war, despite the clamour of warning bells emanating from both Europe and the north Pacific. The same disillusion that the Great War diggers had felt towards the military machine had been reflected in the polling booths during the ensuing decades, as a war-weary and Depression-affected electorate inadvertently kept Australia's defence spending at a perilously inadequate level. In 1939 the country had a permanent military force of only 3000 troops, and munitions amounted to leftovers from the 1914–18 conflict. But there were another 80,000 reservists at least, known as the Citizen Military Force or Militia, although their participation overseas would be strictly controlled for too long perhaps.

Still, Menzies had promised Neville Chamberlain, Britain's prime minister, a division of troops and, in an initial wave of patriotic fervour, his citizens duly flocked to recruitment offices throughout the land. The Second Australian Imperial Force, 6th Division, was the result. Led by Major General Thomas Blamey, the 20,000-plus Aussies received a glorious send-off as they departed from Sydney on 9 January 1940.

But it wasn't until after the fall of France, in May 1940, that widespread recruitment got under way. Hitler's Blitzkrieg through Europe that northern spring marked the end of the so-called 'phony war', and that together with the ever-growing threat from Japan galvanised Australia into a second recruitment drive. Within a matter of months, the AIF was able to form three new divisions. The 7th and 9th were to be sent to the Middle East to fight German, Italian and Vichy French troops, while the 8th Division was bound for Malaya — although no one knew it then.

※ ※ ※

By July 1940, recruitment centres in country towns and cities throughout the nation were handling thousands of men, as the 8th Division's three infantry brigades and their supporting units were being raised. The first of these was the 22nd Australian Infantry Brigade, made up almost entirely of servicemen and volunteers from New South Wales. Within this brigade, the 2/18th and 2/20th battalions took men from mostly Sydney, Newcastle and the north of the state, while the 2/19th constituted recruits mainly from the Monaro and Riverina regions of southern New South Wales. During the same period, the 23rd Australian Infantry Brigade's three battalions were raised in Victoria and Tasmania, while Western Australians, Queenslanders and South Australians joined up to form the 24th Brigade. As it transpired, however, only the later raised 27th Brigade would complete the 8th Division's strength in Malaya.

The call to arms had been so successful, in fact, that army recruitment centres had difficulty handling the huge numbers of young men who turned up. Accommodation was in such short supply that every inch of space at the Sydney Showground was utilised. It was a similar story elsewhere in New South Wales. In the major metropolitan centres the military introduced day training for young men who lived nearby. They became known as 'day boys'.

Many lied to beat the minimum enlistment age of eighteen. A few who were discovered and told to go home changed their name and returned to have a second go. They were usually successful. But not all the recruits were young men, by any means. Their ages ranged from sixteen to forty-five, with fathers following their sons and vice versa. The one fact that united them was their army prefix: all New South Wales volunteers were given the letters NX in front of their service number.

Brigadier Harold Taylor had been made commander of the 22nd Infantry Brigade back on 23 June, and Penrith-born Lieutenant Colonel William Jeater was duly appointed head of the 2/20th Battalion shortly afterwards. Other senior officers who would later figure prominently in the battalion's exploits included Majors Ronald Merrett and Andrew Robertson and Captains Archibald Ewart, John Fairley, Charles Moses (the ABC chief) and Roderick Richardson.

The second of these majors, **Andrew Esmond Robertson**, would become one of the most popular officers in Malaya, Singapore and Japan during C Force's early days at Naoetsu. Born in London in June 1906, he emigrated to Australia with his parents as a child and married his Scottish-born girlfriend Christina in March 1933. They had two children, John and Marjorie. Apart from his family, Andrew's twin loves were cricket and the army. He joined the Citizen Military Force, which he fitted in while working as an accountant on Sydney's north shore. In July 1940 he swapped his office for a tent and began full-time training. Over the next two years, Lieutenant Colonel Andrew Robertson (as he would become) proved himself as a courageous soldier and a great leader of men.

Harry Woods was twenty-two when he joined the 2/20th. He was born at Narrabri, in the north of the state, and grew up at Inverell. Harry left school to carve out a career for himself in the bank. After a few years as a teller he was slowly climbing the corporate ladder when he decided to volunteer. The recruiting officers who interviewed him at Mudgee clearly saw some potential in the young man and earmarked him for future leadership at the rank of acting sergeant. He was not to disappoint them. Harry was later made a lieutenant and went on to lead his men out of several close calls, especially in Singapore. Like so many of the men who arrived at Wallgrove Army Camp in the second half of 1940, he could have had no idea of how he would suffer at the hands of the Japanese.

Jack Mudie had too much to live for to even contemplate an early death. He had a girl waiting for him in Australia, as well as a good job. He'd seen his parents suffer too much during his childhood to consider manual work. Jack's father, William, and his mother, Eva, had a wheat and sheep farm at Gilgandra, north of Dubbo, in the central west of New South Wales, but successive droughts had forced the bank to foreclose on them. The Mudies headed to Sydney, where William toiled away as a stonemason in a quarry. It was hard yakka for a man who was intelligent and well educated but who fell victim to the twin impacts of climate and recession.

Jack, who was born in April 1907 at Windsor, on the outskirts of Sydney, had three brothers and a sister. They grew up in a close and loving family, often sitting around the fire at night playing puzzles and listening to their father reading poems and extracts from Shakespeare. The Bard clearly inspired Jack, who did well at school and won a scholarship to Fort Street Boys' High in the city. From there he went to teacher training college and, after passing his exams, gained a job in a country school in the south of the state.

Jack taught at Queanbeyan, where he met an attractive young woman by the name of Neno, who was the daughter of his landlady. He was in his early thirties and looking forward to married life in Naremburn, on Sydney's north shore, when war clouds started gathering. At first he joined the Militia as an army reservist but eventually enlisted on 3 July 1940. Older than most of the other men, Jack was another to instantly receive NCO status, and kept a fatherly eye on his charges. Seven months later, Jack would leave Australia at the rank of lieutenant.

Like Major Robertson, **Theo Lee** was non-Australian by birth. He was born in Dunedin, at the bottom of New Zealand's South Island, on 29 March 1919. Twenty-one years later, Theo found himself at Paddington enlistment office, in inner Sydney, where he joined the 2/20th at the rank of private. He'd been planning to marry Joy, his fiancée, but that would have to wait. Later, as a lieutenant, Theo Lee would play a crucial role in the battalion's overseas deployment, but it would be another half a century before the true measure of his worth emerged.

Over the next few years, Woods and Lee forged strong friendships with three other officers who would subsequently figure prominently in daily life at Naoetsu. Albert Yates (from Glen Innes), Jim Chisholm (of Inverell) and Alex 'Sandy' Barrett (who had studied as a doctor at Sydney University) all enlisted during the middle of 1940. Chisholm and Barrett were 2/18th men but imprisonment created a bond among this cadre of officers that would remain unbroken for the rest of their lives. Barrett's medical experience would play a key role in the survival of those unlucky enough to be incarcerated in Camp 4-B.

Herb Lamb also signed up at Paddington that July. Twenty-four years of age and fit as a fiddle, Herb was welcomed by the 2/20th with open arms and was soon on the short list of potential NCOs. Staff Sergeant NX52556 had always kept himself in trim. It was a hangover from his schooldays in Dubbo, where he loved athletics and became champion high jumper. He could also handle himself in a fight, which might be useful in the years ahead. 'My uncle taught me — he was a pretty good old stousher who also showed me how to box. I learnt never to give in.' Herb Lamb would remember those survival skills in years to come when his and many other lives would hang by a thread.

George Daldry had always been close to his brother Charles. They'd grown up as tough kids, never afraid of a fight and always ready to protect their interests in the back streets of Sydney. Charles was less than a year older than George, so there was little difference in age. Their close bond ensured they always looked out for each other, but within a couple of years that brotherly insurance would tragically unravel.

George signed up just a week after his brother at the enlistment office in Paddington. He was 5 feet 9 inches tall and fighting fit — 'I was in the local boys' club and I soon learnt how to throw a straight left and not to leave my head open.' The fact that he had joined the Militia at fourteen also helped. He'd done plenty of part-time training and was used to the demands of military life.

He was also underage, though even today his army records offer no hint of that. While his service record suggests he was twenty-one when he enlisted, George claims he was only seventeen. 'I shouldn't have been accepted because of my age, but there were others younger than me,' he reveals.

Ken 'Bluey' Firth was born in Sydney but grew up in Coonamble, in the central west of New South Wales. Known to all as 'Bluey', he was working behind the counter of the local general store when he signed up in June 1940, just two weeks after his twenty-first birthday. He too began his military life as a private but rose to become an NCO, in his case a corporal. Strong and tall with green eyes, auburn hair and a fair complexion, Bluey Firth was a larrikin at heart and liked a drink. He also enjoyed gambling and the feel of money in his pocket.

It was a trait common to most servicemen, including **Jimmy Houston**, who was thirty-seven when he joined the 2/20th. Older than most of the men, Jimmy was born in Scotland and grew up in the back streets of Glasgow until migrating to Australia before the war. A thick-set bear of a man with blue eyes and brown hair, he worked as a wharfie. Jimmy was a clever bloke, but hadn't had much of an education. Even so, he had a natural ability to write. It was a skill that would ultimately produce one of the most detailed POW diaries of the war.

Harold Julian had trained in the building industry after leaving school. Born in Lismore to Stephen and Muriel Julian in October 1917, he wasn't yet twenty-three when he signed up. Small but physically strong, Harry survived on his wits, like so many men of that time. The war offered the sort of travel and adventure that he'd never experience in northern New South Wales. Harry Julian enlisted on 16 July 1940 and joined the 8th Corps of Signals, learning Morse code and becoming a telegraph assistant.

Eric Richardson also joined up midway through 1940, but not as a member of the 2/20th. Twenty-year-old Eric, who grew up in Punchbowl in Sydney's west, joined the 2/18th Battalion, but as time went by, the lives of men from the two battalions would intersect, both on the battlefield and as POWs within C Force.

Dudley Boughton was another member of the 2/18th who fitted in this category. Dudley signed up at the Paddington enlistment office a fortnight before he turned twenty-six. He'd been educated at Sydney Boys High School, which he attended with his elder brother John. They were clever kids and keen sportsmen. He also had a younger brother, and twin sisters. Dudley was married by the time he left for overseas, to Mary — or 'Molly', as he often refers to her in his diary — a Manly girl.

Dudley Boughton was someone who didn't suffer fools gladly; he was well read and likeable, but could court controversy at times. Though he worked as a labourer, he had a strong academic bent, which encouraged him to record his experiences in a most illuminating manner as the war progressed.

Another 2/20th man, **Kevin Timbs** enlisted late in 1940, yet still made it in time to join the first convoy, the following February. Born in April 1919, he grew up a tall, dinky di Aussie in the New England region of New South Wales, near Glen Innes. There were twelve children in his family: nine boys and three girls. Kevin's parents, devout Catholics Patrick and Kate, had a property called Ferndale in the heart of what was known as 'Black Tommy country' — named after an Aboriginal outlaw who was accused of murder and horse stealing in 1876 and later shot to death by local constables. The area had a reputation as bushranger territory, attracting the likes of Thunderbolt Fred Ward.

Kevin left school and was put to work as a drover in the harsh and wild country around Glen Innes. Barely out of short pants, he spent the next few years herding cattle and taming the land. The Timbs family was still suffering from the effects of the Depression and money was tight. It was a familiar theme in the Australia of the late 1930s and early '40s. Joining up was an attractive proposition: it offered a regular wage, security, travel and maybe a little danger on the way. Risk could be a tempting option for a young man who sought adventure, and there would be many tales of heroism and daring before the war was over.

* * *

The volunteers were a motley crew when they began arriving at Wallgrove Army Camp, west of Sydney, at the end of July. First to set up headquarters there had been Lieutenant Colonel Duncan Maxwell's 2/19th Battalion on 13 July, followed two days later by both the 2/18th, led by Lieutenant Colonel Arthur Varley, and Jeater's 2/20th.

Largely unfit and ill-disciplined, many of the men needed weeks of intense exercise and instruction before they would even start to resemble soldiers. In this area at least, reservists like Jack Mudie and George Daldry had some sort of a headstart. Still, there were encouraging signs after just a week, judging by the 2/20th Battalion's war diary: 'already shows great improvement' was the verdict on the morning parade of 6 August.

Living conditions at dusty Wallgrove left a lot to be desired, with eight men to a tent and often unpalatable army rations, which contrasted sharply with Mum's home cooking. Herb Lamb,

Harry Julian, Bluey Firth and the other country boys were no strangers to doing it tough, but there could be no denying that winter on the open plains near Blacktown was a rough baptism into military life.

Rougher still was the attitude adopted by the commander of the 2/20th Battalion. In *Singapore and Beyond*, the battalion's official history, author Don Wall would write of Lieutenant Colonel William Jeater's 'unreasonable attitude' towards his junior officers at Wallgrove and then Ingleburn, and note: 'Jeater was demanding in his training procedures. He seemed able always to find harder ground full of rocks for trench digging …' No doubt lieutenants-in-the-making Woods and Mudie were subject to the CO's hostility, but not for nothing did the last of the pair earn the moniker 'Happy Jack'. 'First one up the hill gets an ice cream,' Sergeant J.V. Mudie would sometimes joke while training with his charges in C Company. The tough kids from the bush used to poke fun at the former school teacher, but if Jack was annoyed he never showed it.

Respite from the windswept bleakness of Wallgrove arrived in two forms during August 1940. First came the battalions' combat equipment — the most urgent, Don Wall intimates, being field kitchens (in the hope that the general standard of tucker might step up a notch, of course). Better still, from midway through the month, the brigade was on the move.

The new camp, at Ingleburn, near Liverpool, was a sure sign that the war was now being taken seriously at home. Purpose-built for the training of AIF infantrymen, construction on the site began in early October 1939, four weeks after which the first troops arrived there prior to embarkation with the 6th Division. Despite its infantry focus, however, signallers like Harry Julian, as well as army engineers and transport personnel, all received specialist training at Ingleburn during the course of the war.

The benefits were immediately obvious to members of the newly arrived 22nd Brigade, even after the long route march there. The camp was much cleaner than Wallgrove, the accommodation more comfortable — no question. In addition, Ingleburn offered easier access to the city: a visit home to see loved ones, when leave permitted, for Sydneysiders like the Daldry brothers, Eric Richardson, Jimmy Houston and Dudley Boughton; a chance to catch the bright lights and blow off some steam for Harry, Bluey and the other blokes from the country. But with the potential bonuses came the necessary stepping-up in the recruits' training regimen.

Within Colonel Jeater's 2/20th Battalion, the men still trained in their companies — A Company led by Major Ron Merrett, B Company by Captain Arch Ewart, C Company by Captain John Fairley, and D Company by Captain Charles Moses — and endless route marches continued to be a regular occurrence, on top of the specialist training in warfare. The difference now was that the 900-odd 'other ranks' would also be learning how to operate as a unified battalion.

Morale at Ingleburn was high as the spring wore on. The volunteers had long been fed up with learning about the war in Europe and elsewhere via newspapers, and Wallgrove had simply taken them further away from the action — but this was more like it. They were beginning to look, feel and think like a fighting force at last.

Over in the 2/18th Battalion, Punchbowl-born Eric Richardson turned twenty-one on 31 October, a week after which the three units were transferred to Bathurst Army Camp in preparation for deployment overseas. Like Ingleburn, this facility had been purpose-built for AIF training, but in the case of the Bathurst camp (actually located near Kelso, a few kilometres east of town), the original plan had been to create a tank base for the 1st Armoured Division. Concerns from neighbouring farmers put paid to that idea, and when the 22nd Infantry Brigade arrived by train, they replaced the camp's only previous occupants, troops from the Middle East-bound 7th Division.

Those volunteers who originated from the state's central west — Harry Woods, Herb Lamb and Bluey Firth among them — would have been right at home here, but then the citizens of Bathurst made a point of making all AIF personnel feel most welcome. Many solid friendships were formed during the three-month stay on the state's central tablelands, and correspondence between locals and diggers would continue throughout their time in Malaya.

It seems the feelings of bonhomie weren't necessarily shared by the 2/20th's commanding officer, though. On 19 November, with the much-anticipated Battalion Ball just a day away, Colonel Jeater saw fit to have the men camp out overnight at the scene of a recent bushfire, so leaving them somewhat worse for wear the following evening. Compounding the issue, he also ordered that a number of officers return to Kelso after the big do, at the Trocadero in town; all married men, they had no choice but to leave their spouses behind in Bathurst.

A glorious summer was under way as the 2/18th, 2/19th and 2/20th battalions set about brigade training and manoeuvres. Photographs taken at the time show men comfortable in each other's company, seemingly well settled into military life. The fact that they're dressed in desert fatigues betrays a cruel omen, however: the 22nd Brigade infantrymen were being trained for the dry terrain of North Africa and the Middle East, a far cry from the conditions they'd ultimately experience in the Malayan jungle.

Soon the volunteers' first Christmas as servicemen had arrived, along with a seasonal greeting from their divisional commander, Major General Henry Gordon Bennett:

> Though we are impatient to set out on the task for which we enlisted, we are fortunate that we are able to spend this Festive Season among relatives and friends in sunny Australia, rather than among the discomforts of alien land.
>
> May the year 1941 see the 8 Aust. Div. participating in decisive victories against our enemies so that we may soon return to our homes to enjoy a real peace on earth with goodwill to all men.

It was a message with which few of the men could disagree, although just to what degree those 'discomforts of alien land' might extend in the years to come, no one could say.

The new year saw promotions for a number of men, the 2/20th's Theo Lee, Herb Lamb and Jack Mudie among them (to corporal, staff sergeant and lieutenant respectively). Theo, who was in charge of advertising at a Sydney furniture store in civilian life, was joining a host of other NCOs who, like him and Herb, would go on to do sterling work for the battalion on the battlefields of Malaya and Singapore — men such as Garnett Judd, Roger Cornforth, Martin Chapman, George Gray and William Lothian. Jack, meanwhile, was trading his non-com's digs for the officers' mess and a commission alongside fellow lieutenants Frank Gaven, John Rowe, Frank Ramsbotham and others whose unenviable lot it was to carry the burden of leadership in action.

As January wore on, throughout the brigade the wait began for orders to move out. For the 2/20th, that order duly came early the following month, a couple of days after adjutant Captain Jim Lowe had noted with approval in the battalion's war diary: 'the lack of ... tension generally expected is very noticeable in all ranks.'

And so, on the night of 2–3 February, they began the long, hot train journey east to Sydney's Darling Harbour.

※ ※ ※

Over the ensuing months more men would join the 22nd Infantry Brigade, as reinforcements for the 2/20th Battalion and other units. Their departure from Sydney would follow a similar training schedule to that of the first wave and be dependent on the availability of shipping.

Henry Dietz was working on a sheep farm at Quandialla, near Young, when he enlisted on 3 April 1941, at the age of twenty-two. He would often drive the station owner, a woman, into town and it was there that he was interviewed by the military. Henry wasn't a country boy by birth, though. He was born in Botany, where his father had a leather tannery.

Henry's father was German and his mother was Swiss, and inevitably their surname caused some flak during his school years.

'I remember one of the teachers, Miss Malcolmson, asked me in class: "Dietz, where do your parents come from?"' he recalls. 'I said I didn't know, but the big bloke behind me shouted: "Go on, you're a bloody Hun — admit it."'

Henry's parents had migrated to Australia before World War I and were accustomed to the racist taunts that came their way. It was hard for their son, but soon enough, once in Malaya with the 2/20th, there'd be no doubts as to where his loyalty lay.

Arthur 'Snowy' Collins was only 7 stone 4 pounds and 5 feet 3 inches tall when he joined the Hunter Valley Lancers. Fortunately, size and physical strength were not all that was required to stay alive in those days, but you had to be tough, and Snowy had certainly come up the hard way. He'd grown up in Muswellbrook, west of Newcastle, along with his five brothers and two sisters. The Collinses were bushies and he'd always found it difficult keeping up with his dad and older brothers, who had a 5-tonne truck which they used for collecting wood. There were few decent jobs around when he left school at the age of fourteen, so he made a couple of bob chopping up trees in nearby woodland. No one took young Snowy too seriously, and even after he left home in his mid teens he had trouble convincing anybody that he was worth employing.

The army seemed to be the only option, but when he tried to join up at the age of nineteen, in late 1940, they told him to go back to school because they didn't believe his age. Baby-faced Snowy Collins was successful at the second attempt, and finally got to camp with the Lancers in April '41. Private Arthur Collins of the 2/20th Battalion was on his way, about to swap the dull provincialism of Newcastle and the Hunter Valley for the more exotic Orient.

John Cook was born in the Sydney beach suburb of Clovelly in February 1921 but grew up on his father's farm at Penrith, well west of the big smoke. After leaving Orchard Hills School, he got a job as a driver with Australian Glassworks. The eighth of ten children, he came from working-class stock and, like so many school leavers in those days, had only modest aspirations. Yet there was something special about John, and it shone through those baby-blue eyes. It was a spiritual strength that would set him apart from other men and would ensure his survival in the face of great adversity.

Private John Cook enlisted on 21 April 1941 and would soon join the rest of the reinforcements bound for Singapore.

Like George Daldry, Melbourne-born **Joe Byrne** was a fighter. Christened Harold Keith but known universally as Joe, he'd been working in blast furnaces before the war and trained as a blacksmith. Come 1940 he was living in Kogarah, in Sydney's south, and putting paravanes on merchant ships in Darling Harbour. The torpedo-shaped devices were designed to cut the moorings of submerged mines and the job was a protected industry. But Joe couldn't resist the lure of army life and the prospect of battle. 'I was Irish and I felt I was invincible,' he admits. 'I had a short fuse and I'd rather fight than eat.' Joe's determination to join up was initially frustrated, however. The enlistment officers informed his employer, and two policemen turned up to take him back to work. 'Don't come here again or we'll take you down to Long Bay prison,' they warned him.

Never one to accept defeat, he returned a few weeks later and said he was from the country, where there was no work. The date was 9 May 1941. Joe Byrne was twenty-one and would soon be on a converted troop ship bound for Singapore. He left behind his tearful family and a girlfriend by the name of Joyce. Unbeknown to her, Joe also left a ring behind, given to his brother for safekeeping.

Cas Cook was another volunteer who grew up on the land. He was born at Springwood, a pretty village in the lower Blue Mountains, but lived in nearby Penrith. John Eric Cook was nicknamed 'Cas' by his brother and it stuck — which was useful no doubt to many in the 2/20th's C Company, seeing as another Private John Cook from Penrith would be joining their ranks at the same time.

Born in November 1917, Cas was the son of Irish and English parents and had two brothers and a sister. Before his wartime service, he rarely ventured from his home near Penrith. Like so many working-class men of that time, his aspirations were modest: he held down a manual job, earned enough money to buy a few beers, and planned to settle down. Both his father and grandfather had been carpenters and his woodworking skills seemed to come naturally to him. Cas Cook, small of stature but resourceful enough to look after himself, saw his immediate future as a builder — until the war intervened.

When **Don Alchin** read the newspapers, it made him keener than ever to sign up. Don liked spoiling for a fight and could hold his own with the best of them. His dad had shown him how to survive back in the '30s, when Don and his older brother Merv were growing up in Stockinbingal and Temora, in the rural south-west of New South Wales. Alec Alchin was a horse dealer though he behaved more like a bush ranger. 'He didn't need a gun, he could fight like a bloody cat,' Don says of his father. 'Tough as goats he was, chasing brumbies up the mountains. But he taught us how to work. "Work and you'll always get by, no matter what you do," he'd say. And you know what? I've found that to be true. Dad lived till the age of ninety-seven and was always quick and lively.'

Don was just twelve years old when he got his first full-time job. There wasn't a high school in the area so there was no alternative but to find work. A lean and agile kid, he'd inherited his father's love of horses and so it was only natural he'd want to work with animals. Later Merv, who was working at a pub in Stockinbingal and training race horses in his spare time, found him a position as an apprentice jockey. Don was soon working for Jack Fuller in Cootamundra, where he spent two years before being suspended for allegedly 'pulling' a horse. 'I was only fifteen or sixteen at the time and the army looked like the best place for me, so I went to Sydney and tried to join up.'

His mum found out and demanded he come home, but it wasn't long before young Don had another go. This time he got an address in Redfern and headed straight for the Sydney Showground, where the military turned a blind eye to underage recruits. In Don's words: 'They'd take you with one leg there.'

Merv Alchin also signed up, and on the very same day — 10 June 1941. Just eighteen months older than Don, Merv wasn't prepared to be overshadowed by his kid brother and let him have all the fun. No way. Soon he and Don were being kitted out and bashed into shape before departing for Wallgrove, where they looked after horse transport. It suited them perfectly.

Don Fraser ended up with the 2/20th via a roundabout route that began in Melbourne. He'd been working as a telegraph clerk with AWA Beam Wireless when he signed up in September 1941 as a signalman with the 8th Division. The 21-year-old would leave Australia on 29 November, bound for Singapore, and enjoyed only a couple of months of freedom before the island capitulated. Like Jimmy Houston and Dudley Boughton, Don had the foresight to keep a secret diary. Amid his yearning for home and food and thoughts of his beloved mum, the young signaller's daily record of events at Naoetsu would include the immortal 'Dinner very tasty to my supersensitive palate, though I wouldn't give it to the dog at home.'

Mick McAuliffe was also among the last wave of reinforcements. Born in Lismore in October 1915, Mick grew up in the far north of the state, and spent much of his teenage years on the land. His father, Michael, owned a small dairy farm and most of his large family were put to work on it.

Mick had just turned twenty-six when he made his way down to Sydney to enlist on 21 October 1941. The war in the Far East was yet to be declared, but most Australians saw it as simply a matter of time before the Japanese launched an attack on the Malayan Peninsula. Sure enough, by the time he eventually stepped off the 45,000-tonne *Aquitania* and joined the 2/20th's B Company, Mick would almost be able to see the Japanese army knocking at the door of Singapore town.

❀ ❀ ❀

During 1941 these men and thousands like them set sail for war over a period of several months. Many left in style aboard the *Queen Mary*, the luxury Cunard liner that had been requisitioned as a troop ship. Others found themselves on less salubrious vessels, but any lack of creature comforts was forgotten in the excitement. They were embarking on the voyage of a lifetime, the first time most of them had been to sea, let alone abroad.

While some undoubtedly saw it as a boys' own adventure, the grim reality of what might lie ahead was beginning to emerge. A meeting of the government's Advisory War Council in early February 1941 reminded all Australians of the potential military threat to Australia. Acting Prime Minister Arthur Fadden and Labor's John Curtin issued 'grave warnings of imminent danger', the *Sydney Morning Herald* reported. 'The trend of the war was "to come increasingly close to us" and that responsibility was devolving on the people of Australia.' The outside world was truly closing in now.

CHAPTER 2

DESTINATION MALAYA

On Tuesday 4 February 1941, the RMS *Queen Mary* found herself anchored off Bradleys Head, on the north shore of Sydney Harbour. The 2/20th had been the last of the three battalions to be ferried across in groups from Darling Harbour and, after a night on board, the men were now preparing to set sail. The brigade's strength was complemented by a number of other units, including the 8th Division Signals, 2/10th Field Regiment, 2/4th Machine Gun Battalion, 2/9th Field Ambulance and 2/5th Field Hygiene Section. The last of these outfits would prove vital for staving off malaria-carrying mosquitoes in the tropical climes that awaited the infantrymen.

As a junior officer, Jack Mudie was lucky enough to be given a private berth on the *Queen Mary*. Those in the other ranks often had to make do with a hammock and a rather more basic standard of accommodation, however. The Cunard Line's twelve-deck, 1020-foot luxury steamship had a prewar capacity of 1957 passengers, but on this voyage she'd be carrying around three times that figure. Still, Bluey Firth, Kevin Timbs and others quartered below-decks would get to marvel at the splendour of the ship's lavish ballroom and opulent fittings — and what a world away it all was from anything the country pubs of Coonamble, Glen Innes and the like had to offer.

'It was a glorious day with hundreds of small craft bobbing about to farewell her,' Jack recalled of their departure. The liner, which was seen off by Governor-General Lord Gowrie and a huge crowd of well-wishers, weighed anchor at 1.30 pm and headed slowly towards open waters, with the men crammed onto every inch of the *Queen Mary*'s available deck space, searching the sea of faces for loved ones and friends. Appreciating the poignancy of the moment, no doubt they also searched the urban sprawl for familiar signs. Herb Lamb towards Waverley and home, due south of Bradleys Head; George Daldry and Jimmy Houston towards Darlinghurst, among the relatively uninterrupted inner-city skyline of the early '40s; and Theo Lee to nearby Cremorne, on Sydney's leafy north shore.

After steaming out of the harbour, they were joined by two other converted troop ships, the *Aquitania* and the *New Amsterdam*, the latter laden with troops from Theo's country of birth, New Zealand. The flotilla would sail on towards Melbourne and Adelaide and across the Great Australian Bight to Fremantle, where locally raised units would join those already on the *Aquitania* and *New Amsterdam*, before heading north.

Several other convoys were to follow in the ensuing months, notably that of 29 July, which carried the 8th Division's 27th Brigade and reinforcements for the 22nd. With cash in the men's pockets and the bar-canteen open during these voyages, it usually wasn't long before the diggers got down to some serious drinking and the inevitable game of two-up.

On board the *Johan Van Oldenbarnevelt* in late July, the party atmosphere became so lively that Major General Frederick 'Black Jack' Galleghan, commanding officer of the 2/30th Battalion, was forced to intervene. The officer, a near-legendary soldier who had served in World War I and was wounded twice on the Western Front, had a formidable presence and didn't tolerate dissent — as Henry Dietz discovered first-hand.

Lance-Corporal Dietz was ordered up to the top deck, to be told by Black Jack to keep his men under control. 'My, did he give us a lecture,' Henry remembers. '"This is wrong, that's wrong, things are getting out of hand — you've got to do something about it."'

Henry was having none of it. The Quandialla rouseabout wasn't averse to a few drinks and a game of two-up himself, and besides, he wasn't prepared to spoil the fun at this early stage of the voyage. Who knew what would happen to these blokes and how long they'd be away for, or even whether they'd ever get back in one piece? After all, they were going off to war — they had a right to let off steam, he reckoned.

On the way out of Black Jack's cabin, he passed another officer on the stairs. 'Here, you can have this,' Henry said, placing a hand up to his shoulder and ripping off his lance-corporal's insignia. 'Take the bloody stripe and keep it. I'm getting no extra pay, so what's the point,' he spluttered.

The officer urged him to reconsider, suggesting he might get a place at officers' school further down the track. 'No bloody way, mate,' Henry replied. 'My mates are here and I'll stay with my mates, thank you.' And with that, he stormed off into the night.

'They're not really your mates — you'll find out later,' the other man shouted after Henry as he disappeared down the stairs and headed back to C deck.

The small crowd that had gathered there was getting bigger by the minute. The usual cry of 'Come in spinner!' echoed across the water followed by whoops of delight from winners when the two pennies came up tails. A beer in one hand and a 10-bob note in the other, Henry planted his wager in the ring and waited for the spinner to toss the two coins in the air. More often than not he lost, and by the evening he'd done his entire 8 quid — 'And that was money in those days.'

Come lights out, he didn't even have enough cash to buy a packet of cigarettes. 'People who'd been so friendly to me earlier in the evening wouldn't so much as give me a fag. I was totally cleaned out. I found out about life the hard way,' he says, smiling philosophically. Henry wasn't alone in taking a dive in the win-or-lose world of servicemen's two-up, by any means. On his ship, just as on the *Queen Mary* six months before, there were dozens of similar tales of misfortune.

The morning after departure, on 5 February, the warm temperature and sunny skies of Sydney had been replaced by scudding clouds and a chill wind. Soon the heavy seas were claiming their first victims, as the landlubbers of the 22nd Infantry Brigade, mostly country boys who had never sailed before, suffered their first bout of seasickness. The heavy drinking of the night before hadn't helped to ease their queasy stomachs and now they were suffering.

To make matters worse, they didn't have much in the way of creature comforts. Some were sleeping below deck in hammocks, which were fine until they entered the Bight, but no good for soldiers without their sea legs who were getting their first taste of severe Southern Ocean weather. 'God almighty, it turned rough,' Don Alchin confirms, referring to the later journey on the *Johan Van Oldenbarnevelt*.

Despite the fact that it was almost impossible to stand straight, the men were still being drilled every day on deck, in an effort to maintain the high standards set at Ingleburn and Bathurst. For all the various units on board, regular drilling also took their mind off other matters — such as the danger of attack. Few talked about it openly, and the *Queen Mary* was said to be able to outrun any German U-boat, but there was always a nagging fear. To bolster their confidence on the voyage, the three troop ships, together with the *Mauretania*, which had joined them from Melbourne on 6 February, were accompanied by several smaller escort vessels while RAAF Hudson bombers flew low overhead.

By July and August, at which point Japan had just carried out an unopposed invasion of French Indochina, these concerns became increasingly realistic. 'We were frightened about submarines,' Don Alchin admits, 'and really worried about what might happen if we were torpedoed.' With the ocean liners converted to allow for maximum passenger capacity, the ratio of troops to lifeboat seats didn't bear thinking about. The threat was worse still for volunteers like Mick McAuliffe and Melbourne signaller Don Fraser, both of whom left Australia at the tail end of 1941. For Mick, the memory of his bucolic existence in far north New South Wales would soon begin to fade as the journey progressed. While outwardly optimistic, he privately wondered whether he would ever again see the deep blue light of an Australian sky or feel the crashing surf on his back. It was not a prospect anyone would openly discuss.

The diggers were also fed large doses of propaganda about the enemy, especially the Japanese, via both newsreel presentations and organised lectures from senior officers. Despite the fact that Emperor Hirohito's country was not yet at war with the Allies, the Japanese were nevertheless portrayed as the devil incarnate. Don Alchin again: 'Basically the government fed us a load of bullshit. First we were told the Japs had no guns and would be pelting us with rice balls and all that rubbish. Then we were told they weren't mechanised and that we'd knock the tail off them in a fight. And we believed everything Prime Minister "Pig Iron Bob" [Menzies] told us. By Jesus, did we get a surprise.'

George Daldry wasn't too concerned. As someone who could look after himself, the Darlinghurst teenager was enjoying the prospect of a fight. Although he didn't look for trouble, he always half expected it — and when someone had a go he would not be slow to retaliate. As he puts it: 'I used to have a saying: "I want to see some blood."' On land or sea George wouldn't change his ways for anyone, and since joining up, his army experiences had only fanned his pugilistic tendencies. 'Men are basically weak,' he adds by way of explanation. 'You can give a bloke a hit on the nose and more often than not he won't do anything. They'll beg for mercy.'

It was a philosophy that had worked well enough for him over the years, but would it have the same effect in war? None of the men were even sure who exactly they'd be fighting, although it would not be long before strong hints about their likely destination would emerge.

Jack Mudie recalled how a couple of boxes marked *ELBOW FORCE* fell open while they were being loaded onto the *Queen Mary* during the two-day stopover at Fremantle. Inside were booklets on Malaya. 'They contained a little bit about the people and some language tips, so we knew immediately where we were going.'

After taking on provisions, they headed north-west into the Indian Ocean, on course — as most had originally suspected — for the Middle East. But as the Western Australian coast disappeared from view late on 12 February, the 22nd Brigade's destination was confirmed. Four days later, at some point south of Sumatra, the *Queen Mary* sailed away from the main flotilla. The famed flagship of the Cunard Line steamed through the centre of the convoy and did a lap of honour around the fleet before turning north to join the British destroyer HMS *Durban*, which was to escort her on the rest of her voyage. While it might have been a little premature for any sign of victory, the *Queen Mary* and her crew of fighting men were certainly imbued with the will to win — wherever they were being sent.

The mother ship sounded her horn and the other three liners replied in unison. Along each deck, soldiers and sailors waved and shouted farewell cheers across the ocean. The volunteers from New South Wales were on their own, and now they knew for certain where they were headed.

※ ※ ※

Singapore was the principal disembarkation point for all Allied forces shipped in to defend the Malay Peninsula in the event of an invasion. The colonial outpost had represented and defended British interests in the Far East for so many years and, it was fully hoped, would continue to do so. Not for nothing had novelist J.G. Farrell once alluded to the British Empire's vice-like hold on its distant colony as 'the Singapore grip', for it clearly had no intention of letting go now.

The prospect of invasion was hardly a serious consideration for most of the locals, however. The people of Singapore, and in particular the expatriate Brits who were in control, considered their oriental power base virtually impregnable with its big guns and heavy military presence. Life went on much as before — the typical routine including golf and tennis, a tiffin curry lunch, afternoon tea at Raffles, cocktail parties, ballroom dances and a rubber of bridge after dinner — traditions that were too deeply engrained in Singaporean society to be abandoned simply because a war was taking place on the other side of the world. The daily rhythm would remain unfettered until brought down by the Japanese sword as it cut a swathe through the Far East.

After all, it had been like this for more than a century, as the prized British possession became the centre of the world's rubber industry and the commercial hub of the East, not to mention a port of immense strategic significance in the region. Ever since Sir Stamford Raffles established a fort and trading post there in 1819, Singapore had prospered beyond the wildest dreams of its colonial masters back in London. Raffles himself, who came from poor English stock, could never have imagined how the small marshy island at the bottom of the Malay Peninsula would grow and flourish in such a comparatively short time, nor how his surname would one day be synonymous with opulence and privilege. It was to the Raffles Hotel's Long Bar that civil servants and the officer class would repair for a peg of Scotch, and their mem-sahibs for a Singapore Sling. The bar was purportedly where Singapore's last surviving wild tiger was shot, in 1902, though reports of the incident may well have been clouded by inebriation, given the potency of the hotel's infamous cocktail.

Like so many members of the local ruling class, Sir Shenton Thomas, Governor of Singapore, tolerated the armed forces but believed that too many defence personnel on such a small island might project the wrong image. An overly strong military deployment, he reasoned, would only encourage hostilities with the Japanese, who he never believed posed a serious threat to his island home. And even if they did, then the mother country would rush to his aid under the so-called 'Main Fleet to Singapore' policy — whereby the Royal Navy was to steam at full speed to the Indian Ocean via the Suez Canal to protect the island.

It was into this pampered and highly class-conscious society that nearly 6000 members of the Australian Imperial Force began to arrive from the start of 1941. On 18 February, the *Queen Mary* sailed into the recently built Singapore Naval Base at Sembawang, in the sheltered north of the island, where the men were greeted by crowds of children. The diggers were clearly enjoying their role as would-be heroes and threw coins over the side of the ship for the kids to catch. What surprised them was the number of Japanese civilians who were also there, trying desperately to blend into the crowd while attempting to calculate the total strength of the troops on board. It was no secret that many Japanese who worked in Singapore in ostensibly legitimate occupations were really spies, passing on important intelligence to Tokyo.

If Singapore's elite were in denial, the volunteers in the newly arrived 8th Division certainly weren't. They'd come to do a job and were given little time to explore the delights of this equatorial Eden, even if they'd wished to. Within hours of their docking at Sembawang, in fact, the main groups of all three infantry battalions were heading over the Causeway to Johore Bahru and then on by train up the peninsula's west coast, towards Kuala Lumpur. The 2/18th and 2/20th travelled to Port Dickson, about 75 kilometres south of KL, while the 2/19th's temporary home was at Seremban, just inland from Dickson. Over the next six months, the battalions would rotate between these two sites; Colonel Jeater's unit, for example, moving out again at the end of March for Seremban.

☞ ☞ ☞

So far, military life had certainly lived up to expectations for the men of the 2/20th, and nobody was complaining on that front. But the heat and humidity were something else entirely. Training continued unabated at Port Dickson during February and March, although afternoon siestas were very much the order of the day for officers and other ranks alike, as everyone attempted to acclimatise to life on the Equator. Tropical diseases had been a regular topic of lectures given to the men, both during the voyage and back at Bathurst, but information was no prevention for the unpleasant skin rash with which a number of them were afflicted during their early months in Malaya. As if leading by example, 44-year-old William Jeater had a particularly severe case of the Singapore itch, requiring at least two periods of hospitalisation.

As the weeks turned into months the Australians would gradually become acclimatised to the heat, the jungle training and the route marches. It was unfortunate, though, that their uniform didn't match the conditions. The brown shirt and trousers might have provided effective camouflage in Bardia and Tobruk, where the 6th Australian Division had recently performed heroically, but it was hardly suitable for jungle warfare. Their heavy boots were a nightmare in the mud and the steel helmet they were expected to wear sounded like a dinner gong when it struck a twig or branch.

The food wasn't much better either. The locals used to describe the most common dish served up as 'yak' — not the beast of burden, but an unpalatable mixture of rice and prunes. Thanks to a letter home that somehow evaded the 2/20th's official censor, a concerned mother even took up her son's case with her local MP. As recounted by Don Wall in *Singapore and Beyond*, when news of parliament's involvement eventually got back to Malaya, an officer walked into B Company's mess hall and demanded to know if anybody had a complaint. Private Jack Kitchener, an Aborigine from Naremburn in Sydney, stunned all those present by standing up and replying, 'Yes, sir — this tucker's not fit for a blackfella!'

There were guffaws all round but it made no difference to the standard of fare. The men had to accept that they were in the army now and several thousand miles away from Mum's home cooking. Little did they realise then that they'd have given anything for a large serving of rice and prunes a few years hence.

As much as these factors were very real problems, the period until August that year still amounted to halcyon days for the members of the 22nd Australian Infantry Brigade. For a start, even if the Governor of Singapore was nervous about the size of the force that had arrived on his shores, the diggers enjoyed a warm and supportive relationship with the locals and were made to feel very welcome. The *Straits Times* reported favourably on every public demonstration put on by the visiting troops — be it an Anzac Day ceremony, with Major Andrew Robertson leading the 2/20th Battalion together with 8th Division signallers like Harry Julian, through Kuala Lumpur, or a parade in Port Dickson to mark the first anniversary of the formation of the 22nd Australian Infantry Brigade, on 2 July.

Plus, the men weren't short of a quid. With beer at 10 cents a bottle, and 3 cents for a packet of cigarettes, even lowly privates Daldry, Firth, Houston and Richardson had plenty of money left over from their army pay of 30 shillings a week, paid to them in Straits dollars. That figure would increase somewhat for the non-commissioned officers, of course. Herb Lamb, Theo Lee and (soon enough) Kevin Timbs had plenty of spare cash to pay for the postage of letters home and enjoy a big night out while on leave in the Port Dickson area. On rare occasions, they'd even get to go to Singapore itself.

In stark contrast to the sedate and relatively colourless confines of Sydney — and London, where the war had already taken a huge economic and human toll — life in Singapore was one long party. With its non-stop entertainment and cheap booze, the diggers had no trouble finding some fun when granted three-day leave in town, or while out in Seremban for that matter; the hard part was trying to stay out of trouble and avoid appearing on the lengthy 'punishments' list once back at base. Squad leaders like Lamb, Lee and Timbs would have their work cut out for them keeping their boys in line, but as Henry Dietz would later concur, the men were entitled to blow off some steam. They were all volunteers, after all, and they'd do the right thing when it counted. A more serious transgression occurred inside camp walls at Port Dickson, though, on the evening of 24 June, when the princely sum of 994 Straits dollars was stolen from the 2/20th Battalion's orderly room.

Around Seremban, an increasing number of popular nightspots were deemed out of bounds to all AIF personnel as the months went by, partly perhaps due to things growing too rowdy there for the tastes of both the management and military authorities. The names of many of these establishments, however — the Kobe

Hotel, the Mikado — would suggest that the reason was altogether more sinister. Likewise, Captain Jim Lowe's routine orders for 27 May, posted as usual on noticeboards throughout the battalion, specifically barred the men from visiting a Mr Konjiro Jono, 'Japanese Dentist', of Birch Road, Seremban.

Singapore leave was a more regular occurrence for the likes of Jack Mudie, and for Harry Woods from late March onwards, once the Narrabri-born bank teller had been promoted to lieutenant. Many officers were invited out to dinner and dances around town. Some even wangled an invite to the Governor's palatial residence on Orchard Road, where Sir Shenton and Lady Thomas would hold court in the ground-floor reception area during cocktails, which were invariably followed by a sumptuous banquet. Among the upper echelon of the brigade's leaders, Brigadier Taylor and his battalion commanders, Lieutenant Colonels Ferguson, Varley and Jeater, were all welcomed into the grand homes and estates of Singapore and southern Malaya.

Similarly, diversions from the serious business of preparing for war were welcomed inside the bases at Port Dickson and Seremban, if only in the interests of troop morale. Inter-battalion sports contests included cricket, soccer, rugby union, hockey and athletics, and announcements naming the 2/20th's teams often took pride of place on the adjutant's daily routine orders, along with rather more pertinent details regarding battalion training, town picquet duties, promotions, punishments and disciplinary hearings. A hotly contested Brigade Sports Meeting was held on Wednesday 14 May, featuring a full range of track and field events, and was won overall by the 2/19th Battalion.

In peacetime, Jack Mudie had been used to taking on classrooms full of unruly kids, and this experience no doubt proved useful when coaching potential hockey and football players. Jack would also represent the battalion on the field, at cricket and hockey, while Kevin Timbs — the Glen Innes drover no stranger to having to fight for possession with his eleven siblings — played some rugby union. The names of NCOs like Roger Cornforth, Dale Williams, Martin Chapman, Bill Lothian, George Gray and Keith Ainsworth, and Privates Wally Lewis and Keith Burling, all appeared regularly on the lists of players. Just like Mudie and Timbs, they'd also be included on the C Force nominal roll.

And lest it be thought that brawn triumphed completely over brain, the resident wits and jokers of the 2/20th had a field day of their own. First up was the Battalion Concert Party's *All in Fun Revue* of 19 April, which featured among other sketches 'The Great Big Faker', starring J.V. Mudie as one Adolf Hitler and Warrant Officer Cornforth in the role of Hermann Goering. Such revues and entertainment nights were always a great success, and something of a tradition among military units overseas, but it was with the written word that the creative side of the battalion really shone.

On 28 May 1941, the 2/20th published its journal, *Thumbs Up*, intended for a readership of proud families and friends back in Australia, anxious to put a face to these people and places they'd read so much about in their loved ones' letters. Thanks to the considerable talents of nominal editor Francis 'Joe' Wilson, a private in HQ Company, the folks back home were in for a treat.

Contributions came in from all across the battalion, including the ubiquitous Jack Mudie, with Theo Lee one of a handful of men on the publishing committee. Amid a wealth of in-jokes and innuendo, the unit came alive over the forty pages of reportage, verse and pictorial: merciless digs at the incomprehensible accents of the numerous Scottish-born NCOs, for instance (Sergeant-Major Lothian being a favourite target); references to 'P&O corporals', whole platoons getting lost on endless treks through the jungle, sick parades (E Company taking delight in having just 20 per cent of its strength available for duty); an ode to Tiger beer (credited to 'MacSozzle'); and jibes at officers that just stop short of military impropriety ... And just in case any New South Wales MPs were reading, a menu was reproduced, reputedly from the *Queen Mary* voyage, with the first course for each day's main meal being ... yak.

Colonel Jeater, who had been evacuated to hospital at Malacca on 19 April, and so missed the fun of the concert revue, added a sombre note to proceedings in his introduction to the journal, as did passages from battalion chaplain Padre Sexton and the 2/20th's intelligence officer. But there was no mistaking the spirit and unity alive and kicking among the volunteers from New South Wales.

By mid June, Joe Wilson and his team had a sequel under way that actually surpassed the original. This time the publication took the form of a weekly newsletter, its title, *Second Two Nought*, an obvious pun on the name of the battalion, and was aimed at a readership within the unit. Snippets of news from home appeared, along with updates on Australian troops' progress in Crete, Syria and the Western Desert. As before, no individual's reputation was spared: if someone was the source of even minor amusement in the unit, well then, the diggers deserved to have a good laugh at his expense.

Among the officers, Lieutenant Ramsbotham's reputation as a ladies man continued to be the subject of some ribbing, and if the battalion CO felt he was due a modicum of sympathy after being hospitalised again earlier in the month, he was mistaken. Under the wink-wink 'We're all itching to know' header, an anonymous columnist referred to a recent officers' ball and asked: 'Why didn't the Colonel dance — was he afraid it might be too rash?' Further down the chain of command, Jack Mudie and others in C Company were credited with sick parade 'honours' during the week, specifically 'a slashing win over E of 36 to 3'. While over in D Company, Herb Lamb was said to be suffering a bad case of that old drinkers' affliction 'Yaws'. 'What the hell's Yaws?' asked fellow sergeant John Hutchinson … who then, inevitably, had to shout Herbie a beer.

In places predictable, and always happy to go for easy laughs and debunk any hint of cultural elitism, *Thumbs Up* and *Second Two Nought* were never going to challenge *Punch* magazine in the sophistication stakes. But the Aussies would need to hang on to that same irreverent, larrikin sense of humour more than ever in the near future.

※ ※ ※

August 1941 was all about change for the 22nd Infantry Brigade and within the wider realm of the 8th Australian Division. During the first ten days of the month, with reinforcements and the 27th Brigade just days away from arrival, Lieutenant Colonels Jeater and Maxwell were posted to brigade-level commands, replaced as COs of the 2/20th and 2/19th battalions by Charles Assheton and Charles Anderson, respectively. Major Andrew Robertson would have been a more than acceptable candidate to many of the men in the 2/20th, having proven himself to be an effective and sympathetic leader during Jeater's periods of absence, but instead he continued in the role of second-in-command. Company commanders John Fairley and Charles Moses would also be transferred out of the battalion and on to divisional or brigade duties, their roles taken over by Captains Bill Carter (in C Company) and Roderick Richardson (in D).

Of rather less significance perhaps, with new junior leaders required to handle the influx of 'green' troops, Theo Lee marched out of the Officer Cadet Training Unit in Singapore on 23 August. Little more than a year before, Theo had shown up at Wallgrove a private; now he had his commission, as a qualified lieutenant.

Not that there was much opportunity to ponder the new appointments. After nearly six months of active service, during which the international situation had worsened considerably, the diggers were only too aware that they were engaged in a race against time. Large numbers of Japanese forces had entered French Indochina on 24 July, and already there were reports of military manoeuvres and amphibious training sessions in readiness, it was believed, for a seaborne assault on the Malay Peninsula. While the British military's school of thought was that any attack against Singapore would be made from the seaward side — hence the direction of the guns, facing the sea — they had to be prepared for an invasion overland from the north. And for most of the 22nd Infantry Brigade, that meant taking defensive measures along Malaya's east coast. Specifically, the strategically sensitive town of Mersing, a South China Sea port some 100 kilometres north of Johore Bahru.

The main body of the 2/20th Battalion began moving out from Port Dickson late on 28 August and reached Mersing mid-morning the next day. Ahead of them was a massive and laborious exercise, with hundreds of men drafted in to fell timber, shovel sand, build stockades and erect hundreds of kilometres of barbed-wire fencing around the small town. Equally, the Mersing River would hinder any advance by land from the north, so anti-tank and anti-personnel minefields had to be laid both at its estuary and alongside the north–south road that ran parallel to the coast between Mersing and Endau, about 35 kilometres further on. If the men of the 2/20th had to contain the enemy advance — that is, in the likelihood that the two Indian brigades way to their north at Kota Bharu and Kuantan would be unable to do so — this would be the most likely point of contact. Failing that, their fellow battalion in the 22nd Brigade, the 2/19th, held the all-important airfield at Kluang, midway between Gemas and Singapore on the main road running through the centre of the Malay Peninsula.

The 2/18th, meanwhile, moved in behind Mersing, carrying out much-needed anti-malarial work on the swamplands around Palm Grove. Beforehand, Dudley Boughton and Eric Richardson's battalion had a brief spell at Jemaluang, the site of an important crossroads to the south. Colonel Varley's boys would return to the Jemaluang area in the months to come and fight there with great honour.

From late September onwards, the reinforcements began arriving at their allotted companies from the AIF's general base depot. Having had a period to acclimatise after disembarking on 15 August, the Alchin brothers, Henry Dietz and others joined the unit to find a distinctly Australian influence on the main camp at Mersing, many of the thoroughfares having been re-christened with Sydney street names. It provided an air of familiarity to an otherwise foreign terrain.

Joe Byrne and Snowy Collins immediately headed north for Endau, where Lieutenant Jack Mudie and others in C Company were based. 'We were an isolated company,' Joe explains, 'the battalion itself was based at Mersing.' Jack, an old hand by this time, elaborates further: 'We expected the Japs to get to Mersing, so I was ordered to head north with my company of 120 men to the next river, at Endau, and wait for them.'

Joe and Snowy — like John Cook, Henry Dietz, Cas Cook and other newcomers in C — would find their new camp temporarily moved into Battalion HQ's area while the 2/5th Field Hygiene Section carried out its work.

Don Alchin was sent to the main group at Mersing, where A and B companies were deployed: Major Ron Merrett's A Company, just north of the river and out west through the Mayang rubber plantation; and B, under Captain Ewart, from the west of the Mersing bridge downriver to the coast. It was here that the men did most of their jungle training and dug trenches. At night Don and his mates in B Company slept under canvas, but by day the tropical heat started to get the better of them. 'Doing jungle training all the time, some of the blokes started developing malaria, and most of us suffered from the dohbi itch,' he remembers. Tinea Cruris, to give the dohbi itch its proper medical name, is a fungal infection that gets under the skin. It thrives when the human body is moist and chafed and would drive the diggers crazy.

D Company's George Daldry found himself dumped in the scrub for twenty-eight days, as part of the rigid training program. 'The jungle was so thick that you couldn't see anywhere. If you didn't have a compass you'd get completely lost.' George's company, Herb Lamb, Kevin Timbs and Jimmy Houston included, was deployed to the south-west of Mersing. Bluey Firth would become a corporal as from 1 November; his outfit, HQ Company, had set up close to the main camp.

What troubled other 2/20th originals like Lance-Sergeant Timbs (recently promoted from corporal) was the absence of air support in Malaya. The British had a decidedly motley collection of aircraft, including two squadrons of Vickers Vildebeeste biplanes, known disparagingly by those who had to pilot them as 'flying coffins'. Back when he had first arrived at Port Dickson, they hadn't exactly inspired confidence in the Allies' ability to protect Singapore or mainland Malaya from aerial attack, and they certainly didn't now. 'We were all pretty knowledgeable about what was going on and how prepared the British and Australian forces were to defend themselves,' Kevin admits. 'But we were also worried.'

Not a man to keep his opinions to himself, earlier in the year Timbs had taken his concerns right to the top. It was one of those all-too-rare occasions in military life when fate looks favourably on the humble soldier.

Soon after landing in Singapore, he came face to face with Prime Minister Robert Menzies, who was on his way to London and had thought to drop in on his men. 'Seeing Menzies, a few of us decided to put him on the spot and voice our concerns,' Kevin continues. 'One of our group asked bluntly, "When are we going to get air support?"

'Menzies replied, "Haven't you got it already?"

'"No," I chipped in. "The only bloody things we've got are three Rooster Buffalos and an old biplane!"'

Taken aback by the temerity of the questioning, but conscious of the need to project a confident facade, the PM assured him: 'Oh, that'll all be fixed by the time you see action. There'll be thousands of planes …'

Kevin had grown up in the Australian tradition of never trusting politicians, and he reckoned Menzies' pledge was wildly optimistic. He wasn't wrong.

Optimistic too might have been the thinking regarding a prisoner-of-war camp the men were ordered to build behind their lines. When the commander of Australia's 8th Division, Major General Gordon Bennett, visited Mersing on 30 September, he left his men in no doubt that the POW camp would be essential for holding all the Japanese who tried to infiltrate their positions. Of course, such a scenario was still academic at this stage, but it suggested that the top brass were beginning to show signs of concern, having previously given little serious consideration to an assault from the north.

It might also have explained why Air Marshal Sir Robert Brooke-Popham, Commander-in-Chief, British Far East Command, deigned it appropriate to drop in on the lads at Mersing during the same visit. 'Jolly good show' was the general tenor of his remarks, congratulating them on the standard of their work, and in particular the design of the barbed-wire fencing. Sir Robert might have felt the same when the 2/20th soccer team faced off against an RAF XI earlier in September, or when the AIF took on the British Army at rugby union on 20 November. But the general urgency of the Allies' predicament was evident in a pre-Christmas announcement to the 22nd Australian Infantry Brigade on 28 November: 'Xmas day will be treated as a Sunday, and no leave will be granted.'

More reinforcements emerged during October and November, by which time the 2/19th had moved on from Kluang to Jemaluang, some 30 kilometres south of Mersing. Come the start of December, across all the battalions' lines, both men and defences were well dug in, and the general standard of health seemed greatly improved. The 2/20th were ready for action, and given what they'd heard, it would not be long before it happened. Further reports of troop concentrations in French Indochina, just a few days' sailing time from Malaya, only added to the tension.

※ ※ ※

In the diplomatic world, it was known that pressure was being placed on Thailand to allow Japanese forces to use its facilities. It was the clearest indication yet that the Japanese were planning an assault on Malaya and Singapore from the north.

This did not bode well for Lieutenant General Arthur Percival, General Officer Commanding, Malaya, and the man who had the overall responsibility for defending Britain's interests in Singapore and the Malay Peninsula. Another Great War veteran, and widely respected by both officers and men, he knew in his heart that the Allied forces under his command were ill prepared for the battle ahead. There were almost 37,000 Indian troops on the peninsula, backed up by 20,000 British and just over 15,000 Australians, together with about 19,000 locally enlisted men. Most had little in the way of proper training, and the further north you went the worse they got. If the Japanese made their way south over the Thai border or came ashore at Kota Bharu, in the far north-east of Malaya, they would find little resistance. It meant the 2/20th would play a crucial role if the Allies were to keep the enemy out of striking distance of Singapore.

Jack Mudie was certainly prepared. Happy Jack thought it prudent to organise a few locals to light a bonfire three kilometres or so up the road from Endau village when they saw the Japanese coming. 'We acted as a forward observation post. The idea was to let the rest of the battalion know when we saw the enemy and observe what sort of equipment they'd got. Once we'd sized them up, we'd inflict whatever punishment we could and then retire.' In theory it was sound military strategy. The next few weeks would demonstrate whether it would work in practice.

Henry Dietz also found himself on the Endau River with C Company. There was a British gunboat there to add support if necessary and much of the river was mined. 'When the Japs came down the coast, we were supposed to explode the mines and blow the enemy to smithereens.' If only he'd known what would happen to the mines when the time came to detonate them.

While the lack of air cover had already been raised by Kevin Timbs with the Australian Prime Minister himself, there was also concern about naval strength. Singapore and the rest of the Malay Peninsula had little in the way of heavy naval back-up until 2 December, when Britain's most recently built battleship, HMS *Prince of Wales*, steamed into Keppel Harbour, along with HMS *Repulse*, an ageing battle cruiser, and four destroyers.

The arrival of the fleet was a symbol of British resolve to defend its far eastern outpost and a signal to Japan that the Allies meant business if attacked. Unfortunately for Empire interests, the *Prince of Wales* and its sister ships should have been accompanied by the aircraft carrier HMS *Indomitable*, but it was under repair in the United States after being damaged when it struck a reef. The *Indomitable* was carrying some forty-five aircraft with which to defend the small naval task force despatched to Singapore. Without the carrier, the pride of the Royal Navy, the *Prince of Wales* and the rest of the flotilla were all hopelessly vulnerable to attack by enemy planes.

Four days later, on 6 December, a convoy of Japanese transport vessels accompanied by cruisers and destroyers was spotted by a

Royal Australian Air Force pilot in the Gulf of Thailand. It did not require the mind of a military strategist to realise where they were heading.

That same day, at precisely 4.30 pm, Allied troops received the warning order 'Raffles', which was the first serious sign of imminent invasion. A shiver of excitement was felt down many spines that afternoon as troops moved into position in expectation of an attack. It was the moment they had been waiting so long for — yet, frustratingly, nothing happened. The Japanese were biding their time, coordinating their military operations so as to strike successively in a wave of sea and air attacks across the Pacific, from Malaya in the west to Hawaii in the east.

Shortly before dawn on 8 December, word came through that the Japanese army had landed at Kota Bharu, just south-east of the border with Thailand. Soon much of Asia and the South Pacific would report similar advances, culminating in the catastrophe at Pearl Harbor. Japan would be at war with the United States, Australia and the remainder of the British Empire.

Like the rest of the Allied forces, the men of the 22nd Australian Infantry Brigade had their role to play in the horror and the madness that would follow. If there was unease among those soldiers in the early hours of that Monday morning, it didn't show. Deep down they may have sensed fear and trepidation, but they had been trained to perform their task to the best of their ability and they were determined to conduct themselves with honour.

CHAPTER 3

BATTLE STATIONS

They say war brings out the best and worst in men, and there were many examples of both in the weeks and months ahead. There was heroism, fear, bad judgement and bloodlust on both sides as the Japanese fought their way down the Malay Peninsula and the Allies tried desperately to repel them.

Early intelligence indicated that the invaders had three divisions at their immediate disposal. The 5th Division had already landed at Singora, over the border in southern Thailand, and others had come ashore further east at nearby Patani. Parts of the Japanese 18th Division were even more brazen, they being the force who'd landed in Malaya itself, at Kota Bharu. Suddenly, the Allied units stationed in the north were facing a three-pronged attack.

Hundreds of men on both sides died in the seaborne and aerial assaults on Kota Bharu, which fell to the Japanese on 9 December. Officers and men of the RAAF's No. 1 Squadron were based at the airfield there and thus constituted a prime target for enemy fighters. It wasn't long before all military personnel in the area, including British and Indian forces, were forced into a humiliating retreat. A similar story played out in the north-west, where key points such as Jitra, Penang and Kroh were quick to succumb to the divisions that had landed at Singora and Patani.

With Percival and other chiefs still not ruling out the possibility of separate landings at Mersing–Endau or even a full-scale assault on Singapore, no thought was given to redeploying the units based in Johore. And so, with complete supremacy of the air, some 200 tanks (the British, by contrast, had none) and the same crack front-line troops that had pulverised the Chinese, Imperial Japan's 25th Army was looking invincible.

Two days before the Allies' withdrawal, on 10 December, Japanese planes had been sighted in the sky over Mersing, whose civilian population had been evacuated and Japanese sympathisers arrested. There were many, including the 2/20th's battalion barber, who were thought to be fifth columnists, and it soon became clear that some of the Malayan locals could not be trusted. Important information about Allied numbers, positions and troop movements was apparently being passed on to the Japanese as they made their way down the east coast. In some instances, signs were found on rooftops conveniently directing enemy aircraft to gun positions. Up in the Betong–Kroh sector of north-western Malaya, villagers had even guided Japanese patrols through the rainforest tracks to expose the Allies' forward positions.

Australia's top brass in Malaya reasoned that once the Japanese reached Kuantan, about halfway down the peninsula's east coast, they would move towards Endau by land and sea, rather than the more strongly defended Mersing, a little further south, where most of the 22nd Australian Infantry Brigade was based. As a result Colonel James Thyer, a senior staff officer with the 8th Division, recommended that Endau be strengthened.

Back over 'impregnable' Singapore, the Japanese air force had been dropping its bombs on the city with ruthless efficiency since the start of hostilities, the city being well within range of the bombers departing from their base in Saigon. But during the first sortie they'd inexplicably ignored the *Prince of Wales* and the *Repulse*, both of which were anchored in the naval dockyard. The battleship opened fire with its big guns as the enemy flew high overhead, although it didn't hang around for a return engagement. This was the island's first taste of war and the Royal Navy's first clash with its new enemy.

The British fleet sailed out of Sembawang a few hours later to join the battle further north. The strategy was to attack Japanese troop ships as they prepared to unload more men at Kota Bharu, but without aerial support the *Prince of Wales* and the accompanying vessels were sitting ducks. Later that day, Japanese spotter planes relayed the exact position of the flotilla to their headquarters and preparation was made to strike.

Senior officers aboard the British vessels knew they were in potential trouble and decided to head back to Singapore for protection. But they were many steaming hours away and by daybreak the next morning, 10 December, the Japs stood by to go in for the kill. Within a few hours both the *Prince of Wales* and the *Repulse* were sunk and more than 1000 sailors drowned. Those lucky enough to survive were picked up by another ship, HMS *Electra*, and limped back to base.

It was one of the darkest days of the war. Like the aircraft carrier that was meant to protect them, the British fleet sent to guard over its far eastern dominion thought it was invincible. In London, Prime Minister Winston Churchill told parliament: 'In my whole experience I do not remember any naval blow so heavy or so painful.'

The news soon filtered back to the men of the 2/20th Battalion, AIF. Kevin Timbs and his mates would have taken no delight in the Royal Navy's misfortunes, but there was little effort to conceal their sentiments: 'I told you so.'

※ ※ ※

By early in the new year, soldiers from the Japanese 55 and 56 regiments, a second force within their 18th Division, had reached Kuantan after landing at Kota Bharu on 28 December. Their immediate plan was to separate at this point, with 56 Regiment heading west to follow the first wave of 18th Division troops towards Kuala Lumpur, while 55 Regiment would press on south to Endau. In the longer term, the aim was that the freshly landed 56 Regiment would meet up with their comrades on the west coast and the combined divisions could then cut a swathe through lower Malaya until they reached Johore Bahru. Once the southern tip of the peninsula was theirs, Allied troops trapped on the east coast of Malaya would have nowhere to go.

British and Australian military chiefs were aware of the danger of their men being forced into beating a hasty retreat if the Japanese pincer plan became a reality, and it was vital for the Australians to hold their position. It said much for the defences set up by the 22nd Brigade that the full might of Japan's 25th Army considered them such a threat. Following Colonel Thyer's instructions, Endau had indeed been strengthened, and its defences and troop placement altered once it became clear they would be facing attack on land rather than from the sea.

On 10 January, with the Japanese making mighty gains down the west coast — Kuala Lumpur and the Aussies' old stomping ground of Port Dickson would surrender to enemy hands in quick succession — the Allied defence effort was divided into two groups, or 'forces'. The 27th Brigade would contribute to the strength of Westforce, out in Gemas and Segamat, while the 2/20th Battalion and the other units in the 22nd Brigade helped make up Eastforce.

Three days before this, Major Andrew Robertson had been put in command of the detached group known as Endau Force. Captain Carter's men were now joined by the 2/19th's D Company and an anti-aircraft platoon from the 2/18th Battalion to provide the first line of defence. Among these new arrivals was Lieutenant John Varley, another volunteer from Inverell and the son of the 2/18th's CO.

Another new face was a British customs officer named Captain Cope, whose boat, the *Sri Pekan*, added to the small flotilla of patrol vessels available to the Australians. With the enemy troops just days away, it was believed, and Jack Mudie's contacts a few kilometres ahead primed to start a signal fire once the main enemy force had been sighted, Cope's brief was to carry out a reconnaissance mission to the north. The objective was to establish the progress of the enemy and, if necessary, take punitive action against any members of the native population believed to be helping the Japanese. Merv Alchin and another private from C Company, Keith 'Donny' Donaldson, were selected to accompany the middle-aged Englishman, about whom very little was known. Beginning on 9 January, it was a mission loaded with risk — and one that ultimately would go down in battalion folklore.

Down south at Mersing, the Australians' somewhat paltry firepower was improved by the arrival of 2-inch mortars and anti-tank grenades. Lieutenant Frank Gaven, who had overseen much of the beach defensive measures carried out by A Company prior to Japan's invasion, didn't mince words when it came to these new additions, however. As he'd later write in *Singapore and Beyond*: 'There were insufficient weapons, insufficient ammunition, insufficient written instructions and insufficient time to train a sufficient number of personnel …'

While the Australian troops based on the east coast had been on alert for a month now, they had yet to experience any action. But the wait was almost over for members of Major Robertson's new force.

'It all started at Endau, so far as I was concerned,' explains Henry Dietz. 'It was a little town by the river and I remember seeing a few Jap planes fly over on reconnaissance missions. Well, one of our Tiger Moths was also in the area and we tried to wave at him to go back. He was like a sparrow with two big hawks looking down on him. They got him first go and he crash-landed into a clump of trees on the other side of the house we'd been staying. Of course, we all ran out in the confusion — me in my yellow sarong.'

Army uniforms had been discarded in the tropical heat and a sarong made more sense. Quite what Major General Gordon Bennett would have made of it is anybody's guess, but in the far corners of eastern Malaya you wore whatever you felt comfortable in.

By the time Henry and his mates reached the downed Tiger Moth, it was too late to save the pilot. He was dead — just like they would be if they didn't hide in the undergrowth, one of the blokes warned them, as the two Jap aircraft turned back to take another sweep along the river. Fortunately, the pilots didn't see them and left the 2/20th advance guard to their own devices.

Japanese and Australian troops in the Eastforce sector first came into contact on 14 January, when enemy soldiers dressed in black peasant dress were spotted on bicycles near the beach at Pontian, 20 kilometres north of Endau. The diggers, one of the newly arrived 2/19th platoons, ambushed them in the open, leaving many dead and injured. The Japanese retaliated later the same day, forcing the outnumbered Australians to retreat south to a mangrove swamp on the outskirts of Endau. The platoon was led by John Varley, who risked his life to swim the village's wide, fast-flowing waterway in search of a vessel in which to rescue his men. Struggling against a fierce current and rising waters caused by heavy rain, the 21-year-old officer secured a boat and brought his boys to safety the next day. It was a remarkable act of bravery, which rightly earned him the Military Cross.

Meanwhile, Jack Mudie and other men from C Company were readying themselves for action on the south bank of the Endau River, to the north-west of the village. Jack was at his forward observation post, waiting as always for that telltale sign of smoke further north. A member of his platoon finally saw it, billowing away in the distance early that morning. 'Right, they're coming!' he shouted. Jack would have to wait a few days before putting his plan into action, but when he did, it would be his finest hour.

By 15 January, C Company at Endau, like the rest of the battalion at Mersing, were coming under increasingly intense attack from Japanese aircraft. Across the brigade, anti-aircraft crews were offered prizes of 50 Straits dollars for downing single-seater planes and 100 for double-seaters, so there was no doubting the gunners' motivation, nor their accuracy. The problem lay in the ineffectiveness of their weapons against the enemy's bullets.

※ ※ ※

Merv Alchin would have used stronger language to describe his predicament on 15 January. Things had certainly not turned out as planned for the fresh-faced Temora farmboy and Donny Donaldson since they'd departed for Nanasi and Pekan, six days before.

From Mersing up to Kuantan, this had become a lawless stretch of coast, and it was known that some Malays had been robbing local Chinese merchants of their rice to pass on to the invading troops. As if the risks weren't enough, their leader, the British officer Captain Cope, had decided that their destination would in fact be Kuantan, a good 60 kilometres further than the official limit of the mission. There, Cope took it upon himself to arrest several perceived transgressors and lock them up in the town's police cells, with the intention of bringing them back down south. By now they were a long way from home base and a prime target for enemy snipers. The trio were rattling along in a ramshackle ute, which alerted everyone to their presence. Young Merv was up for the thrill, but weren't they pushing their luck?

Earlier, to make matters worse, they'd spotted what were believed to be the bootprints of Japanese soldiers on the beach at Pekan — which meant there were almost certainly enemy troops positioned between them and Endau. Cope had made provision for a quick escape if necessary, however. He'd requisitioned a boat that was tied up in the river; if it came to it, they would make for the craft and disappear downstream and out to sea.

Donaldson was from Drummoyne in Sydney and, at thirty-six years of age, considerably older than his fellow Aussie. Like Merv, he had expressed his concerns to Cope, but the officer insisted they should stay in the area as long as possible. For two days they avoided any direct contact with the Japanese, but soon the peace was shattered.

Eating at a local Chinese restaurant one evening, they were warned of an enemy soldier approaching. Cope and his men ran for the river, only to find their escape boat wasn't there. With the Japs in hot pursuit, the three of them jumped into the water, hoping to drift away in the strong current, but it was impossible to swim, with their weaponry weighing them down. Shots were fired in their direction, most likely just to get their attention — the fugitives weren't going anywhere.

'I was so cranky with myself — I'd been caught so easy,' Merv admitted later.

As they scrambled up the river bank, their captors produced a pair of handcuffs and locked the British officer's wrists behind his back. What happened next sent a chill down their spine. Removing the key from the lock, the Japanese soldier calmly tossed it into the water.

Merv and Donny looked on nervously. Throwing away the key could mean only one thing: the Japs had no intention of releasing them. They were as good as dead. Okay, both the diggers had their wrists bound with rope, but that was only because their hands were too big for the cuffs.

Logic told them that the longer they remained silent, the greater the chance they had of staying alive. Their captors wanted to know about troop numbers and particulars regarding defences. The two Aussies and the Englishman professed their ignorance, insisting that they had only recently joined their unit at Endau and had no knowledge of what was going on further south at Mersing. Despite the main interrogator intimidating them by sliding his sword across their necks, the men refused to co-operate.

It was the torture they feared most. The Japs were hardly likely to give up on a chance to find out about the Allies' strength and positions down the road. And Cope, who had confided to Merv that he was really a British intelligence officer, knew it all. How would they stand up to torture? Would they crack, or would they be summarily executed and left to rot on the road or riverside? Images of Japan's atrocities in China and countless other details provided during the army's training lectures filled Merv's mind.

The prisoners were soon moved on to Pekan before starting on the long journey south with the reserve unit that had taken them prisoner. By now their manacled and tightly bound wrists were swollen and painful. Merv Alchin had remembered the old schoolboy trick of keeping his hands one on top of the other and his wrists as far apart as possible when they were tied, thereby improving his chances of being able to free himself if the opportunity arose. It was a move that would ultimately save his life.

※ ※ ※

Back on Endau Force's front, the air attacks had become merciless by 17 January. With their positions obviously well known to the enemy by now, plans were in place to withdraw Major Robertson's hard-worked men upriver to Bukit Langkap. But not before Jack Mudie and his C Company platoon had had their say.

From their position to the south of the Endau River, they knew that the 56 Regiment was fast approaching now. The plan was for Jack's boys to hide on the far side of their river bank and fire mortars at the enemy troops as they gathered on the north side of the Endau. With jungle to their west and swamp and ocean to the east, the Japanese would be trapped.

'When the time came, there were about 700 Japs across the river,' Jack recalls. 'We could see them shouting and gesticulating. I couldn't understand their language, but the meaning was pretty clear: those at the front on the river bank were telling those at the back that there was a problem and they couldn't get across. Anyhow, they all ended up packed into this area not much bigger than a football pitch, and when I thought the time was ripe I gave the order: "Fire!"

'I instructed one of my blokes to fire a mortar at the front of the group and the other at the back, so they couldn't get away. Every time we fired, you heard the *bumph, bumph* sound of the mortar hitting its target on the other side. We must have been firing forty mortars a minute. The destruction was indescribable. I don't think any of the six or seven hundred escaped either death or injury. I had the pleasure of wiping out the whole of that first advance of Japanese.'

It was hard to believe that a man who, before the war, had been a respectable member of the community, teaching little children by day and wooing his wife-to-be by night, was capable of such slaughter. Yet within a year and a half, he had been transformed into a killing machine and he was now enjoying every minute of it. That's what war did to you. It was either them or you, and Jack had too much to live for to end his days on the banks of a Malayan river.

Further down the waterway, Henry Dietz was getting ready to blow the mines that had been placed in the estuary. 'As the Japs approached, we were supposed to explode the mines. But when the moment came, nothing happened …' It appeared that they'd been there so long that water had seeped into the firing mechanism and it had gone rusty. For Henry, the war started with a deafening silence, rather than what should have been a series of ear-shattering explosions.

Joe Byrne was with several other men when a Japanese mortar exploded among them. While the rest of his party died in the blast, he was fortunate to escape serious injury. Temporarily stunned, he regained consciousness to find that he'd lost most of his clothes and his back was hurting. More alarmingly, he could only see out of one eye.

He looked far worse than he was when help arrived. 'There was blood all over my face,' he says. 'But you know what it's like when you nick yourself shaving — you bleed like a stuffed pig and when you wipe it away there's nothing there.' Truth was, Joe was more worried about his loss of sight.

The enemy were getting closer to C Company's positions by the minute. Snowy Collins could even see them heading his way now. 'There were five of us guarding the road into Endau,' he explains. Then the Japs opened fire. Snowy and his mates thought it wise not to hang around — 'We just ran like hell,' he confides. It was either that or be overrun, which would have meant being taken prisoner or killed; little Snowy opted for retreat.

In what had already become a familiar tactic, the Japanese spread out, in the hope of getting behind the Australians' lines to trap their quarry. In the mayhem, it was every man for himself. Snowy Collins remembers seeing the company cook running for his life and being bombed. It was not a pretty sight. 'All we found afterwards was his arms and legs.'

The brave men of Endau Force made it out that night, save for a few stragglers. One of the last platoons to withdraw, Jack Mudie's group hitched a ride on the launch *Penegar*, which was soon motoring south under the cover of darkness through the long, slow arcs of the Sungei Endau.

❦ ❦ ❦

With Eastforce's front line effectively abandoned, the rest of the 22nd Australian Infantry Brigade soon began to feel the full brunt of the Japanese military onslaught.

The 2/19th Battalion, the majority of which had yet to engage the enemy, were unexpectedly redeployed from their defensive positions at Jemaluang and sent on to Bakri, near the west-coast port of Muar. On 18–19 January, now under the command of Westforce commander Gordon Bennett, the battalion performed a vital support role for the Victorians of the 2/29th Battalion, and the 45th Indian Brigade, allowing both to withdraw to safety, only to then become encircled themselves by the Japanese. A series of brutal fire fights ensued as the 2/19th attempted to break out, with the diggers suffering a staggering number of dead and wounded.

Up until 18 January, the 2/18th Battalion had likewise been away from the thick of the action. Much to the dismay of its members, though, the unit was now ordered to pull back from its support position at Mersing and take over from the 2/19th at the Jemaluang crossroads. The time would come soon enough for Arthur Varley's men.

For the 2/20th, time was rapidly running out as plans were under way to withdraw from their long-held fortifications on the east coast. Mersing was soon receiving intense enemy fire on the ground, as well as renewed attack from the air. The Aussies wouldn't be walking away without a fight, however, and A and B companies were right in the thick of it, just north of the town and around the Mersing bridge.

Lieutenant Ramsbotham's platoon from A Company carried out a highly successful ambush on 21 January. Having suffered heavy casualties in the ambush, the Japanese counter-attacked only to fall in the path of some devastatingly accurate artillery fire from the Australian gunners. But still the enemy kept coming — and were soon in B Company's area, around the bridge.

Don Alchin had a close escape when a bullet went through his boot but somehow missed his foot. He was prepared to stand his ground but the close shave brought him up with a jolt. 'If anybody tells you they weren't frightened, they're a bloody liar, and I wasn't looking forward to being knocked off,' he states firmly. 'We knew they were coming, because the intelligence blokes had told us — and by Christ, we soon found out they had plenty of gear.'

In the subsequent fire fight, half-a-dozen Aussies were killed. 'It certainly took the bloody shine off things. We were outnumbered and they had us beat before we started. Our officers reckoned we'd somehow cut them off, but it was the other way round. They got behind us and cut us off and belted the living daylights out of us. One night we lost a whole battalion.'

Despite the number of casualties, the men of the 2/20th continued fighting. 'We were shit scared but we were determined to get out alive, simply because we all wanted to get home one day,' Don adds. 'That's what kept us going. So I thought, Bugger this — I'm going to have a go.'

Francis 'Joe' Wilson obviously felt the same way when he assumed leadership of a group in 11 Platoon, and almost single-handedly cleared the enemy away from the section post. The 39-year-old private from Orange had already proved to be quite an asset as the battalion's literary editor, librarian and entertainment secretary; now his bravery in battle would see him awarded the Distinguished Conduct Medal.

But war was a lottery for those who fought. You could escape death by the skin of your teeth or be mortally wounded by stray fire. Or, like Don's brother Merv, you could fall into enemy hands.

George Daldry was also caught by the Japanese in Malaya — but it seems they almost felt sorry for him. 'It was during a bombing or mortar raid and I just walked into a patrol of Japs,' he recounts. Slight and boyish-looking, despite the pugilistic tendencies, he realised he didn't fit the conventional picture of the tall and muscular digger; 'To be honest, I don't think I was a very impressive-looking soldier,' he confides. The image worked to his advantage. 'The Japs fed me well and looked after me.'

Then, during a surprise raid on their camp, he unexpectedly found himself unguarded. Improbable as it might sound, George

Daldry simply got up and left. 'I just walked out and didn't know where I was going, but eventually ran into a group of our blokes who seemed to know where they were heading. So I teamed up with them.' Amazingly, he was free — but how long would his good fortune last?

※ ※ ※

By now, just behind the Japanese lines, the prisoners had been joined by three men from the 2/19th Battalion. The new arrivals had been cut off from their own side and betrayed by the Malays. Exhausted, hungry and thirsty, Cope and the five Australians found themselves bound hand and foot and tethered to a palm-tree trunk by night, while even by day their wrists remained firmly tied, cutting off the circulation to their hands.

Merv had almost been able to read the progress of the battles up ahead, at Endau and then Mersing, by judging the reactions of their captors. Many of the Japanese saw them as convenient whipping boys whenever their own men fell victim to Allied gunfire. Alchin and his companions were certainly aware of C Company's successful mortar attack on 17 January, for example, and the cheeky ambush carried out by A Company four days later.

To add to the suffering, they were made to carry heavy packs as, together with their guards, they made their way along the next leg of the journey to Mersing. On the roadside, dead bodies provided an occasional reminder of what happened to Allied troops who did not co-operate. A shiver of fear went down their backs as the diggers passed one soldier who had been disembowelled. Regardless of concerns for his own wellbeing, all the while Merv would find himself searching what was left of the faces of the corpses, wondering if his younger brother was among them.

And all the while, kicked and slapped about the head and body, the prisoners would regularly undergo further questioning by Japanese officers. Again, Merv, Donny and the Englishman would insist they didn't know anything. The interrogations and the bashings were becoming a daily theme, and the three of them wondered how much longer they could cope. There seemed to be no stopping the Japanese as they made their way inexorably south by foot or bicycle, slowly inching their way closer to Singapore.

But for a miracle, Merv Alchin knew it was only a matter of time before his fate would be sealed, either by summary execution or as a prisoner of war. He was determined that neither should happen, and in late January, soon after the 22nd Brigade had finally withdrawn from Mersing, he seized the opportunity to break free.

His chance came as he lay tied up in a hut one afternoon. At last the old schoolboy rope trick seemed to have worked. Waking up to find that one of his hands had slipped out of the rope, Merv pulled his wrists apart, his hands and fingers numb and swollen from loss of circulation. There was only one guard and he was sound asleep under a mosquito net. Merv's brain was working overtime as he planned his flight for freedom. He motioned to the others, who were weak from dysentery and clearly didn't have the will or the energy to join him. 'You go,' they said.

In a rare interview during the mid-eighties Merv recalled his dramatic escape. 'I suppose it must have been about 2 pm and one of the Jap guards went away to scrounge a bit of food. And this other fella, he was under a mosquito net and he was sound asleep. If there was going to be a move, this was it.

'I got my hand out and there was an old hook that the natives had been using over in the corner of this hut. It was steel with a handle on it,' he added.

Slowly bringing his hands from behind his back, he reached for the hook, slipped the guard's mosquito net back and thrust the weapon into his right temple. 'He was on his side and I drove it in fairly well, but I never finished him off because he pushed me to get out of the way.'

Merv grabbed a rifle but he was too weak to use it. The guard pushed past him screaming for help. 'By this time there were Japs coming and I knew it was too late. It wasn't any good thinking about trying to untie the others, they were just about done. I just took off through the long jungle grass … falling over and running.'

Somehow he missed the bullets being fired at him and the Japs didn't come after him because they knew the area was heavily mined.

'It must have been an area where our troops had set up and I went off the track out in the mangroves up to my neck in this wallow and that's probably what saved me.'

Savouring the joy of liberty for the first time in two weeks, Merv Alchin inhaled the tropical air and relaxed for a moment, though he couldn't remain there for long. Rising to his feet, he slid into the dark waters of the Mersing and made his way across to the other side. There was no sign of his battalion or any other Aussie forces.

I'll just have to walk and catch them up, he thought. But what would he be walking into exactly?

※ ※ ※

The initial prognosis was not encouraging for Private Harold 'Joe' Byrne. Having been cleaned up and bandaged back in Endau, he'd been sent to a casualty clearing station at Kluang before arriving by hospital train at Johore Bahru, for specialist optical attention.

A doctor who came from Joe's native Melbourne explained that while his left eye was good, he might end up blind in the other. 'There's something in there which, if we try to touch and the operation goes wrong, you'll lose your sight for good,' he told the 22-year-old. 'But if we leave it like it is, you'll be blind within the next three months anyway.'

It didn't take Joe Byrne long to reach a decision. Turning to the medic he quipped: 'You're from St Kilda and I'm from St Kilda — so you've got to give it a go, haven't you?'

Joe was wheeled down to the operating theatre the next morning and woke from the anaesthetic to be told that the surgery had been a complete success. 'I'm pleased to tell you, young fella, that everything's come out good,' the doctor assured him.

Joe looked up at him with his one unbandaged eye and replied, 'You see, all us southerners have got to stick together and have a go.'

Within a few days it wouldn't be just southerners who'd have to support each other but the entire 8th Division of the Australian Army. The situation had gone from bad to worse for the Allied cause in southern Malaya. Despite a brief moment of optimism following the 2/30th's inspired contribution to the Battle of Gemas on 14–15 January, the Westforce sector had never looked like being able to withstand the onslaught from the various Japanese divisions bearing down on it. The utter decimation of Lieutenant Colonel Anderson's 2/19th following the Muar battle was proof of that — a fighting strength of just 271 was reported when the unit regrouped late in the month.

For Eastforce, it was the enemy's air superiority that told the tale, as Japanese divebombers were able to keep up a devastating offensive from the sky. By dawn on 24 January, the Mersing bridge was blown, and two nights later the 2/20th began to pull out towards Jemaluang, which offered the only secure route down to Singapore.

But even in retreat the Australians made their presence felt across enemy lines. On 26–27 January 1942, the diggers of the 2/18th Battalion finally got a moment to show what they were capable of. Varley's men, together with more stunning accuracy from the 2/10th Field Regiment gunners, accounted for an estimated 1000 Japanese troops in their ambush at the Nithsdale Estate. This action, just off the Mersing–Jemaluang road, allowed the 2/20th an unhindered passage south.

There was an air of increasing desperation in military communiqués, even midway through the month. A cable dated 19 January, from General Archibald Wavell (Commander-in-Chief, ABDA Command, based in Batavia) to General Percival, raised the sensitive topic of complete withdrawal. 'You must think out the problem of how to withdraw from the mainland should withdrawal become necessary and how to prolong resistance on the Island,' he wrote. 'Let me have your plans as soon as possible. Your preparations must, of course, be kept entirely secret.'

Some defence chiefs nursed slim hopes that the Japanese advance down the Malay Peninsula would be halted in southern Johore, but such views proved to be wildly optimistic. When Batu Pahat, a small town about 100 kilometres north-west of Johore Bahru, fell to the invading forces, it was only a matter of time before the top brass had to give serious consideration to fleeing the mainland. The mood was summed up in a message from Percival to General Wavell on 27 January:

> A very critical situation has developed. The enemy has cut off and overrun the majority of the forces on the west coast … Unless we can stop him it will be difficult to get our own columns on other roads back in time, especially as they are both being pressed. In any case it looks as if we should not be able to hold Johore for more than another three or four days. We are going to be a bit thin on the island unless we can get the remaining troops back.

It was a gloomy prospect, but one that had to be addressed immediately if there was any hope of salvaging the situation. With Mersing and much of Malaya now in the hands of the Japanese, there was only one option.

Soon the battalions of the 22nd and 27th infantry brigades and sundry field companies, all of whom had fought so valiantly to stem the Japanese onslaught, were heading for the Causeway linking Singapore to the mainland. Many would make it, others would have to find their own way back across the Johore Strait. And some would die or be captured in the process.

After ordering the total evacuation of Johore Bahru, Major General Henry Gordon Bennett took one final look at what now had become a ghost town and pondered the deathly silence. 'There was not the usual crowd of chattering Malays and busy Chinese,' he'd later write. 'The streets were deserted. It was a funeral march. I have never felt so sad and upset. Words fail me. This defeat should not have been … There seems no justification for it. I always thought we would hold Johore. Its loss was never contemplated.'

The Australian battalions were among the last to step across the Causeway before it was blown up. But just before the depth charges were touched off around 8 am that morning, Jimmy Houston heard something that tugged at his heart strings and momentarily transported him to his boyhood days in Glasgow. It was the swirl of bagpipes echoing across the waterway. The Argylls, whose numbers had been so depleted in the battles of the past few months, still found the strength to mark the sadness of the occasion by playing 'A Hundred Pipers' and 'Hielan Laddie' as they made their way to the safe haven that was Singapore. Safe for now, but for the 2/20th the real fight was only just beginning.

CHAPTER 4

UNPREPARED AND UNDER FIRE

On 31 January, the 2/20th Battalion made its way across the 1.5-kilometre-long Causeway with a feeling of relief, but also an underlying sense of foreboding. Aware that it had taken less than two months for the Japanese to achieve the unthinkable and kick the Allies' arses out of mainland Malaya, the diggers privately wondered how long it would be before the enemy repeated the exercise in so-called 'impregnable' Singapore.

For his part, Joe Byrne was shocked by the lack of military preparedness when he stepped onto the island at Woodlands. His right eye bandaged, he surveyed a military and civilian population who behaved as though they were living on another planet. 'Most of the British garrison troops had never been across the Causeway and experienced the jungle conditions,' he remembers. 'They'd only read about it in books. A lot of them had their families with them and were living in a fool's paradise.'

While it must have seemed like another world to the Australians who'd spent the last few months on combat duty, at least Singapore offered the veterans of the 22nd Brigade a temporary sanctuary. The beleaguered 2/19th Battalion were still in shock as they recovered from the Battle of Muar. Charles Anderson had just been awarded the Victoria Cross for his courageous leadership, but part of the latter had involved him having to make the heartbreaking decision to leave his 150 seriously wounded behind at Parit Sulong. There, as all had feared, they were subsequently massacred by the Japanese. The popular Cape Town-born soldier would shortly require a stay in hospital, and the strain and general fatigue was likewise beginning to show for a number of other Australian officers on the front line.

The men of the 2/20th had also lost a lot of good mates during the campaign and, like the 2/18th, they were bitterly disappointed at the decisions to withdraw from Mersing and then Jemaluang, locations they knew intimately, where they'd constructed defences that even the Imperial Japanese Army had been keen to avoid taking on directly. Amid this anguish, though, there was cause for celebration, especially for a certain B Company man from Temora, New South Wales, named Don: NX31444 Private Mervyn Hugh Alchin had been reported alive and well. Not just that, but he'd made his way back here, to Singapore …

'But how the hell did you do it, Merv?' Don asked him, after hearing the crazy tale up to when his elder brother had made it over the Mersing. 'How the hell did you get all the way *here*?'

In short, once he was south of the river, Merv had walked. He'd walked, scrounging food from friendly villagers along the way, dodging Jap patrols, until stumbling across two British sailors who'd managed to scramble ashore after their ship was sunk. Both could hardly walk because of their badly injured feet, which Merv was able to treat with his limited medical knowledge. Soon they were up and walking again. One of the sailors decided to make his own way back by land, but Merv and the other British serviceman thought it would be safer to go by sea.

Somehow they managed to persuade a Chinese fisherman to take them south. Donning Chinese coolie hats to avoid being spotted by Japanese pilots who swooped down to check on marine traffic, within a few days they were within sight of Singapore and safety, just as Allied soldiers were preparing to blow up the Causeway.

The two brothers were overjoyed. Like Don, Merv Alchin

couldn't really believe he'd made it, that he'd escaped from enemy hands and evaded capture. This would be one to tell Dad, they agreed; Alec Alchin, horse dealer-cum-bushranger from south-west New South Wales, had indeed brought his boys up tough. But what about his mate Donny, and the four others Merv had left behind? Should he have stayed to help them, or at least have encouraged them to join him in his dash for freedom? There were no easy answers, but the memory of their faces would haunt him for the rest of his life.

Right now, though, Merv found himself confronted by an equally disturbing reality. He'd just seen part of the Japanese juggernaut that was rolling their way, he told Don and others around them — so where were the Allies' defences on Singapore Island?

As the Australians were learning, until very recently the British military had given no real thought to the possibility that the Japanese might overrun the island. First there was the historical precedent, which saw Singapore completely unprepared for attack by land. The heavy artillery defences, installed between 1934 and '41, had been placed there in an arc from the south-west round to the east, under the assumption that any invasion would come from the sea, of course. And as for any permanent fortifications on the northern half of the island, opposite the mainland, they were practically non-existent.

But, most amazingly, it wasn't until midway through January 1942 that the order had even been issued to begin preparing field defences. Lieutenant General Arthur Percival, General Officer Commanding, Malaya, had always felt that such a move would send the wrong message to the locals and sap morale. Churchill had been furious upon learning of the gravity of the situation and, via Wavell, his commander-in-chief, urged the entire male population to carry out defence work:

> The most rigorous compulsion is to be used, up to the limit where picks and shovels are available. Not only must the defence of Singapore Island be maintained by every

means, but the whole island must be fought for until every single unit and every single strong point has been separately destroyed. Finally, the city of Singapore must be converted into a citadel and defended to the death. No surrender can be contemplated.

After years of colonial paper shuffling and military lethargy, Singapore had at last been goaded into action, but it was too little too late. A memo from Brigadier Ivan Simson, chief engineer of Malaya Command and the man responsible for civil defence, said that although as much as possible had been done to construct shelters, only a small percentage of the real requirements for such a large population were met: 'owing to all this work not having begun or even seriously considered until half-way through the campaign'.

The result was, in the immortal words of Winston Churchill, 'the hideous spectacle of this almost naked island'.

※ ※ ※

Some 85,000 servicemen had now assembled on the island. In all there were forty-five battalions including six Australian and thirteen British, as well as three machine-gun battalions — two from the UK and the 2/4th from Australia.

While the numbers sounded impressive enough, many of the troops were untrained. The level of casualties on the peninsula had been high, and three of the Australian battalions now comprised little more than raw recruits who had recently arrived by ship. Not only were most of these newcomers unqualified in small-arms shooting, but some had never handled a rifle or even seen a machine gun. As for bayonet fighting, forget it. The new batch of volunteers from home could not be blamed for their lack of preparedness — after all, there simply hadn't been the time to train them adequately in Australia, let alone allow for the required months of acclimatisation in Malaya — but it was a frustrating situation for the originals in the 22nd and 27th brigades nevertheless.

Together these Allied battalions had to defend an island 42 kilometres long and 23 kilometres wide. Much of the land was flat and low-lying, densely covered with rubber and other plantations, with only a handful of hills offering a decent vantage point over an area of some 560 square kilometres. Added to which, a civilian population of around 1 million Singaporeans and refugees from the peninsula were either spread across the isolated villages and farmlands or crammed into the more built-up living areas. It was a defender's nightmare.

And the soldiers were on their own — there was little in the way of air or naval support. Most of the shipping had been bombed and, apart from the RAF's 232 Squadron, the air force had sought shelter in neighbouring Sumatra. The infantry still had artillery support, of course, but that would be subject to a clash of egos among the relevant senior officers over their various personal agendas. The defence of Singapore was shaping up to be one of the war's greatest debacles.

Those in charge now had to decide where to deploy their men. General Percival could not be certain of where the Japanese would attack. What he did know was that the Australians who'd distinguished themselves in Johore would have to play a key role in keeping the Japanese at bay in the final onslaught. The question was where exactly to position them.

In the end he had the decision taken for him, further up in the chain of command. Wavell concluded that the most likely stretch of coastline to be attacked was the north-east and ordered the British 18th Division to be placed there. The combat-weary Australians, it seemed, were being encouraged to take a backseat during the main action.

The newly arrived 53, 54 and 55 British brigades duly took up position in the so-called Northern Area, which stretched from just east of the Causeway to within a few kilometres of Changi, on the far eastern tip of the island, and included the now dismantled naval base overlooking Johore Strait. The 28th Indian Brigade was also placed in this sector, just west of the base at Sembawang.

In the Southern Area, the 1st and 2nd Malaya brigades and the Straits Settlements Volunteer Force were deployed to cover a coastal zone comprising (from west to east) Pasir Panjang, Keppel Harbour, Singapore city, the RAF base at Kallang, and Changi. The centre of the island, where the local water reservoirs were situated, was designated the Reserve Area and would be largely unmanned.

This left close to the entire western half of the island to be protected by the Australians, together with a token Indian brigade (the 44th). Their strategically important sector included what was left of the Causeway, much of the north–south main road and railway line into the city, a clutch of crossroad villages, Tengah Airfield, a smaller fighter airstrip in the island's north-west corner, and the entire coastline surrounding these features. It was a massive responsibility.

To add to the problems in this Western Area, much of the terrain was impenetrable — 'a scraggy waste of stunted rubber tangled undergrowth', as Major Oakes from the 2/26th Battalion later put it. The mangrove swamps and fast-flowing streams made walking and transportation extremely difficult. And from the north of their sector down as far as Tengah, the Kranji River and its tributaries effectively divided the 22nd and 27th Australian brigades, making it almost impossible to switch forces between east and west.

Having provided a highly effective rearguard during the Allies' final retreat from southern Johore, the three 27th Brigade battalions under Duncan Maxwell set up their camps in the east of the Western Area, from the Causeway out to the Kranji. Should the Japanese follow up any main attack in the north-east of the island with an assault on Woodlands, Black Jack Galleghan's Tamworth-raised 2/30th would be there to greet them, along with Arthur 'Sapper' Boyes' 2/26th from Queensland, and the Victorians of the 2/29th under Samuel Pond.

South-west of these positions, Brigadier Taylor had established his 22nd Brigade headquarters just outside Ama Keng. The village sat midway along the sealed Lim Chu Kang Road, which ran vertically up from the RAF base at Tengah through rubber plantations to the sector's northernmost point. With the 44th Indian Brigade deployed way to the south, below Jurong, the heavily reinforced 2/19th Battalion was placed on the coast due west of Tengah. B and C companies were selected as its forward troops, located on the headland formed by the Murai and Berih rivers.

North of Anderson's men, the 2/18th held the ground west of Ama Keng, comprising the Karang River and a section of coastline known as the Putril Narrows. C and A companies were well forward here, the distance across the Johore Strait as little as 500 metres in places. It was a frightening prospect for Sydney boys Eric Richardson and Dudley Boughton.

Immediately above them, northwards from the Sarimbun River and fanning out east to the banks of the Kranji, was the sector allocated to Colonel Assheton's 2/20th Battalion.

Lieutenant Frank Gaven, A Company's second-in-command, was dumbfounded when he viewed the terrain that awaited them. 'I have never felt such a feeling of desperation in all my life,' he'd admit in *Singapore and Beyond*. 'I then realised that forward defence in this situation was an impossible task.' But defences positioned well forward were exactly what Percival and his staff over in Singapore city required — only one battalion in the whole 8th Division was permitted to hang back from the front line, so denying the Australians anything approaching substantial reserves. It was madness.

Down in the ranks, they were likewise far from happy with what they saw. Joe Byrne was stunned by the lack of fortification along the coastline. 'There was no barbed wire, *nothing*, until we got there,' he states. 'So we had to run something up pretty quick.'

Joe's mates in C Company had made it back from their spell at Bukit Langkap and then Robertson's Wharf relatively intact, but they were having problems finding a healthy commanding officer. With Bill Carter hospitalised, Captain Cecil Gibbings had recently taken over the role; by the end of the first week of February, he too would be confined to a sick bed. As of late January, Jack Mudie of Naremburn, New South Wales, suddenly answered to the role of company 2-i-c.

He, like Theo Lee, Henry Dietz and the others, found himself in an area extending from the Sarimbun north to a point level with the mouth of the Malayu River, over on Johore, and east through the Namazie Estate to the battalion's HQ, on the sealed road. Theo's platoon was positioned in the south of this sector, on a ridge close to the local planter's house; Jack's 13 Platoon set up its posts some way further north and began to dig in furiously. Behind Jack, at a crossroads about a kilometre west of the main road, were Henry and Snowy, both members of Lieutenant Roy Homer's 15 Platoon.

Two other C Company platoons were placed in this crucial sector, one set forward to the east of Mudie's position, the other reinforcing the ground around Homer's men. With the wide Malayu offering the enemy ideal launching facilities across the strait — but mostly hidden from their view — Merv, Joe, Snowy and the two Cooks, John and Cas, would certainly have their work cut out.

Further up Lim Chu Kang Road, the men in Rod Richardson's D Company were hoping to have their workload shared, with a Chinese guerrilla group known as Dalforce. These troops were led by the commander of the Federated Malay States Volunteer Force, whose surname was Dally, hence the name of the unit. Unfortunately, their eventual arrival would cause serious consternation among the ranks. Most of the Chinese were dressed in native gear and wore a white headband, and thus closely resembled enemy troops that the Australians had spotted around Mersing a few months earlier. While there was no doubting Dalforce's loyalty to the Allied cause, trying to separate them from the enemy in semi-darkness would only add to the battalion's woes.

Until those volunteers arrived, Herb Lamb, Kevin Timbs, George Daldry and Jimmy Houston were left with a defence sector covering the RAF fighter strip, set within the ubiquitous rubber trees, and a 3-kilometre-plus arc of coastline where the Johore Strait widened and curved round to head east. North of them was the gaping mouth of the Skudai River; to the north-east, the imposing vista of Japanese-occupied Johore Bahru.

With so much to look at, Captain Richardson set about creating an observation post on the roof of the plantation bungalow, just off from the end of the airstrip road. Immediately in front of the bungalow, Harry Woods, the banker from Inverell, was tasked with setting up positions for his 18 Platoon, offering a relatively uninterrupted view into the Malayu and Skudai estuaries.

East of D Company, Major Ron Merrett's men did their best to patrol the inpenetrable ground on the left bank of the Kranji River. A Company had three platoons on the move here but, with the mangroves denying access, all that could be done in the way of forward defence was often to place men out in boats to act as sentries.

The thick vegetation was a far cry from the sparse plains of Coonamble that Corporal Bluey Firth had been accustomed to prior to enlisting a year and a half before. His outfit, the multi-tasking HQ Company, divided itself between positions surrounding Assheton's headquarters at the turnoff to Sarimbun and a substantial forward post at the top of Lim Chu Kang Road, between C and D's sectors. A pair of 75-millimetre anti-tank guns and a platoon from the 2/4th Machine-Gun Battalion supplied further encouragement for Sergeants Lamb and Timbs as they directed their sections to dig in nearby. Some 3 kilometres directly south-west, the 2/4th provided a similar service for Theo Lee and his men near the planter's house. The 2/18th and 2/19th battalions could likewise count on machine-gun and artillery support in their sectors.

As for Don Alchin and new-boy Mick McAuliffe, B Company was the 2/20th's dedicated reserve group and had encamped just off Neo Tiew Road, to the south-east of battalion headquarters. Their motorbike-riding CO, Archie Ewart, was also facing a dearth of available junior officers; his brief was to supply reinforcements for the front-line troops should the need arise. While Private McAuliffe struggled with the heat, humidity and frequent rain, Don knew full well how quickly that need was likely to arise. If the Japs attacked here on the north-west of the island, he and his mates wouldn't be hanging around behind the lines for long.

The boys of the 2/20th Battalion had certainly picked the shortest straw. In total, they would be responsible for 8000 metres of beach frontage — almost double the frontage that the whole 27th Brigade had been given on the eastern side of the Kranji. They knew it was a big ask: just 750 men to prevent untold thousands of Japanese from coming ashore.

Although publicly Percival agreed that the north-east was the most likely first point of invasion, privately he feared that the north-west was the real 'danger area' and felt the Aussies were far better suited for the job, should this turn out to be the case.

'I had specially selected it for the Australian Imperial Force … because I thought that, of the troops which had experience of fighting on the mainland, it was the freshest and most likely to give account of itself,' he explained later.

If the Japanese didn't land on the north-east corner and chose the north-west instead, Joe Byrne and his mates would almost certainly be in the front line.

Forced to construct field defences from scratch, speed was of the essence during that first week of February. And there was soon evidence that the enemy was on its way. Byrne remembers seeing convoys of trucks shuttling west along the coastline opposite his position in the C Company sector, on the other side of the Johore Strait. 'Right along the water's edge they went, about seventy or eighty bloody lorries and other heavy vehicles. It was obvious they were heading our way.' That sounded like a lot of military transport — so would the Japanese be launching their main offensive in the north-west after all?

General Gordon Bennett turned up on the morning of 2 February to watch the enemy for himself, and assured his men, 'We'll blow them all away tomorrow.' The diggers weren't convinced. Word had come down the line that, with command of their big-gun support having reverted to the Royal Artillery from the temporary brigade level enjoyed at Mersing, the Kranji area simply wasn't a priority for the Allied gunners. What would they be 'blowing them all away' with exactly? Aside from the needless communication problems this chain-of-command issue raised, the Commander of Royal Artillery had also deemed it practical to substitute the 22nd Brigade's regular artillery field regiment, the 2/10th, with the 2/15th — much to the consternation of the brigade's battalion COs.

The men from the 2/20th reasoned that the gap between their posts was so wide, they were in a highly vulnerable position anyway.

It was the waiting they found the hardest. Within a few days of arrival, the men had dug in — now they had to brace themselves for the inevitable attack.

On 6 February, as Japanese shelling on the north-eastern front intensified and reconnaissance planes circled ominously, brigade headquarters ordered C Company to send a night patrol across to the mainland. With his platoon having been posted away from the essential forward posts, Lieutenant Roy Homer was the only officer available; and because they had nothing better to do, Snowy Collins, Henry Dietz and two others in the platoon volunteered to go with him. Some of their mates thought they were foolhardy, reminding them of the old army advice that you never volunteered for anything. Perhaps Snowy and co thought it would break the monotony.

Whatever their motivation, there was no turning back as the men climbed into a canoe and paddled out into the Johore Strait. If they were caught, as Merv Alchin could tell them, they would at best be imprisoned, at worst executed as spies. The five men clambered ashore on the west of the strait and settled just beneath Japanese lines. 'They were so close you could hear them moving around giving orders,' says Snowy. 'We were up to our ears in mud in the mangrove swamps. Just as well the lieutenant knew where we were, because we didn't have a clue.'

The reconnaissance trip lasted twenty-four hours and almost ended in disaster on several occasions. 'We nearly ran into the Japs two or three times, and we were certainly lucky to get back,' Henry admits now.

Their brief was to establish the number of landing boats and gun emplacements the enemy had on the other side of the water. Surprisingly, they found only moderate boat concentrations and a lot of equipment that appeared to have been discarded. The gun posts were extensive, however. What really caught Private Ray Potts's attention was the massive kitchens: clearly the Japanese knew that an army marched on its stomach. As the cooks went about preparing thousands of meals for the invading force, the 22-year-old from Wahroonga was tempted to lob a grenade at them.

Despite the fact that they were mostly hidden in the mangroves as they went about their work, they were able to obtain a detailed picture of the Japanese invasion machine before making the perilous return voyage the next night. One of the problems they faced was avoiding the searchlights, which shone their beacons across the water every twenty seconds or so. To be caught in the beam would expose them to the Japanese and gunfire. Picking the right moment was crucial.

'Well, I can tell you it was nearly touch and go,' remembers Henry. 'There were Japanese and British gunboats in the area, and us trying to avoid being seen in our collapsible canoe. It was a real nightmare ... All of a sudden Lieutenant Homer said: "We've got to take the risk." So I gave the canoe a push, we jumped in, and away we paddled.'

On the Singapore side, there was increasing concern for the safety of the five men. The order was given for a second patrol to make the crossing — in fact, they were just drawing cards to see who would go when Homer's men returned. Everyone breathed a deep sigh of relief. It had been a successful mission, with useful intelligence gathered. However, with the Australian positions so spread out along the south of the strait, Japanese patrols had been able to do the very same thing under the cover of darkness.

These were anxious days for the men of the 2/20th, but there was also levity. Some soldiers were detailed to destroy any items that might be of value to the Japanese when they landed. Mindful of what had previously happened when the Japanese occupied Hong Kong, the Governor ordered that every bottle of alcohol be smashed. He also decided to incinerate the money stashed away in the State Treasury. Among the various currencies was a cool 5 million Straits dollars — then equivalent to £600,000 but now worth tens of millions of Australian dollars. One morning a small unit of men, including George Daldry and Don Alchin, were despatched to the commercial centre of Singapore with instructions to burn all the money held in the Treasury strongroom.

The order was to remove all the money from the vault, build a bonfire in the yard outside and set fire to it. It was not an easy mission. Never before had these men seen such a fortune, and now they were being asked to put a match to it. What happened next received little acknowledgement in the formal wartime records of Singapore's dying days, but it was hardly a surprise.

As the small group prepared to carry out the order to burn the money, wads of notes started disappearing into back pockets. And not just a few dollars; currency worth thousands was secreted about their person. Of course, what they were doing was strictly illegal, not to mention in clear contravention of army orders — but who cared? They could either put it on the bonfire or let it burn a hole in their pocket. Predictably most opted for the latter.

'There was millions, and the bonfire was as high as me,' George remembers. 'As the flames started licking the first few notes, we all started grabbing bundles. The wads were tied up with rubber bands, so it was easy to snatch a few thousand.' One man used his armoured car to hide some of the money he'd stolen.

'There was no control,' Don confirms. 'You could take whatever you wanted, and we did. When we all got back to camp we started playing two-up for bets of $1000 a time. We were just rolling in dough, and because we had so much, it became like Monopoly money.'

Which brings us to the extraordinary tale of Larry Farmer, whose real name has been changed here to protect his family from embarrassment. Even today they refuse to admit to the accuracy of the story, which Don Alchin and others insist is true. 'Blokes said he buried two or three million dollars, although I had it on pretty good authority that it was nearer a million,' says Don.

Farmer, it appeared, had the foresight to keep his pile of cash to himself and not fritter it away on gambling. He also realised that it would be difficult to hide it from the Japanese in the event of what now looked like imminent invasion. There was only one alternative: dig a deep hole and bury it. One night, armed with a shovel and a torch, he found a quiet spot and began digging furiously. He didn't want anybody to stumble across the cash by accident. Next, he took a mental note of the exact location and filed it away for future reference.

What he couldn't have foreseen was how fate would prevent him from recovering his illicit fortune for some years. Larry Farmer's idea was to dig up the money as soon as possible, but the Japanese had other plans.

※ ※ ※

Back up north, hostilities were hotting up. Designed as a bluff by the Japanese, enemy troops north of the Causeway were visibly active during 7 February, as if in a state of high alert. That night, right on cue, the Imperial Guards Division launched an attack in the Northern Area after taking Pulau Ubin, an 8-kilometre-long island in the wide, seaward portion of the Johore Strait.

Meanwhile, over in the north-west of Singapore Island, the 22nd Brigade positions were still being pounded by enemy aircraft and shelling from across the water. Even Bennett's headquarters, some distance from the coastline, was hit, killing one man and sending documents flying. The following day, ten Hurricane fighters from the squadron based at Kallang intercepted a large force of Japanese divebombers in the skies above Sarimbun Beach and inflicted substantial damage. Men from the 2/20th and 2/18th battalions enjoyed the spectacle, but that would be the last anyone saw of the RAF in the Western Area.

The date was 8 February (see Singapore map on page 349) and the continual bombardment from artillery and mortar fire was clearly aimed at softening up the Aussies prior to an amphibious assault. Many Great War veterans likened it to the concentrated shelling they'd experienced at Pozières and elsewhere on the Western Front.

Surprisingly, casualties had so far been light, mainly thanks to the construction of slit trenches, which offered a degree of protection despite being prone to flooding. But the damage done to the brigade's communication lines was devastating. Already, 24-year-old Harry Julian from Lismore and fellow signallers like Don Fraser, another one of the recent arrivals, faced an impossible task. With the eyes of Malaya Command successfully diverted elsewhere by the Japanese feint in the north-east, a clear picture of developments here in the Western Area would be denied those outside the sector, let alone the units actually within it.

Come mid evening, in the very north of the 2/20th's sector, a group manning one of D Company's observation posts in front of the plantation bungalow could clearly hear Japanese seacraft approaching. Shots were fired as part of a prearranged signal to alert other men in the area. Unfortunately, though, the searchlights that had caused Lieutenant Homer and his reconnaissance party such concern a few nights earlier were no longer working. With the only illumination coming from oil tanks ablaze on the banks of the Kranji, the Johore Strait was otherwise deadly black.

Just west of the observation post, the machine-gunners from the 2/4th platoon were forced to fire indiscriminately at the Japanese boats. More by luck than judgement, they succeeded in hitting their target, and to great effect. Within seconds of the initial fusillade, there was screaming from the first wave of men caught in the gunfire. Barges began to sink, and those who did manage to wade ashore were cut down at the water's edge. There seemed to be no end to the sickening sight. Wave after wave of enemy soldiers were mown down as D Company troops added to the fire raining down on the would-be invaders. Before long the indistinct silhouettes of more landing craft could be seen diverting to the west, towards HQ Company's forward position, in response to the reception they'd received here.

By now the action was hotting up in C Company's sector also. Near Sarimbun Island, a large force swept by in front of Theo Lee's position, headed for the 2/18th's stretch of coastline. A kilometre or so north-east of Theo, Jack Mudie and his platoon were soon engaged in a grenade attack on enemy barges that had succeeded in doing the inevitable — namely, infiltrating between the Australians' widely spaced forward posts.

As Don Alchin and his mates had feared, B Company had indeed been called up for active reserve duties. Hours before, the company's 10 Platoon was shifted from the echelon area out to the coast, in an attempt to plug the large gap between C Company's sector and HQ's position. Now, with the enemy gradually finding and exploring the empty spaces, they too were in the thick of it.

Not everybody covered themselves in glory that night. Down in Homer's 15 Platoon, located at the crossroads about 1000 metres in from Mudie's beach positions, Henry Dietz saw how the tension simply became unbearable for one man. 'All of a sudden an officer said, "Don't do anything until I give you the order to do it." So we knew the Japs were coming,' the Botany-born rouseabout remembers. 'And I'm trying to pass this message down the line when I see this bloke of ours running away through the rubber plantation. He just cleared out and left us.'

The story of how one officer deserted his troops when they became separated near the Kranji certainly rankled with Jimmy Houston. 'About fifty of our lads who were surrounded by Japs were not strong enough to swim the river,' the Glaswegian dock worker would record in his diary. 'Well, this officer instead of helping them across the river dived in and swam for his life, leaving them all to look after themselves.'

So was it cowardice, panic, or just a basic survival instinct? Having been victimised throughout his youth for his German parentage, Private Dietz was prepared to give them the benefit of the doubt, even if Jimmy wasn't. 'Oh, you can't call it *cowardice*,' Henry insists. 'It's what happens to a bloke when he can't control himself in action. I suppose we were all nearly at cracking point. I don't care how good you are, there's nobody who could honestly tell you they weren't frightened then.'

Within two hours of the first assault attempt in the D Company sector, the situation had become tenuous for the 2/20th Battalion. All across the front, the Aussies had inflicted considerable losses on the Japanese initially, but the attackers just kept on coming. The HQ Company and 2/4th Machine-Gun positions now had to contend with a Japanese barge-based mortar attack — the enemy had the will and certainly the weapons for the job. A short way east, in the stretch covered by Harry Woods's men and the other two D Company platoons, bitter close-quarter fighting was taking place in the semi-lit darkness.

Like all the diggers, George Daldry would never forget the evening of 8 February. For him there was added significance — it was the last time he'd ever see his brother Charlie. Another D Company man, Charles Daldry had just returned from hospital that day and was rostered on for look-out duty down at the beach with his mate Spud Murphy. Knowing that Charlie was still suffering the effects of malaria, George felt sorry for him. 'I'll go down and do it for you,' he'd offered.

'No, I want to go down with Spud — he's my mate,' insisted Charlie.

For the younger Daldry, it would forever be a case of what-if. 'Unfortunately, the Japs landed shortly afterwards and he died a terrible death,' George explains now. 'We think he was bayoneted.'

Throughout this period of chaos and tragedy, Colonel Assheton's unenviable plight was to try to read the situation enveloping his area of command. With communication lines restricted, many of the messages to and from his officers in the field were taking an eternity to arrive. And by midnight, the 22nd and 27th brigades had lost contact with one another, so he held no hopes of seeing the division's reserve battalion, the 2/29th, arriving any time soon.

Knowing how susceptible his concentrations of troops were to being outflanked by the enemy, Assheton had no choice but to order them all to withdraw overnight and form a prearranged perimeter around his headquarters, at the T junction formed by the Lim Chu Kang and Sarimbun roads, just in from C Company's sector. From there, given what he'd learnt about the brigade-wide losses, the commanding officer of the 2/20th Battalion would have to organise a full retreat out to the edge of the Western Area.

First to arrive, at around 2 am, and set up position in the west of the perimeter was C Company, now led by Jack Mudie. Most of the remaining groups and platoons would get there over the next two hours. D Company, however, had not even received the instruction from Assheton.

With Dalforce troops having withdrawn before midnight, Captain Richardson had already pulled his men back behind the fighter airstrip anyway, some 2 kilometres inland; but there they'd stay until dawn, subjected to the full fury of the principal landing force from Japan's 5th Division. It was a nerve-racking night for the boys in D Company. Two platoons from Ewart's B Company were sent north in the early hours of 9 February, to cover the airstrip road turnoff and attempt to link up with Rod Richardson's troops — that was all Assheton could do for them.

With the Japanese 18th Division having delivered a pounding to the Australian battalions down the coast in its push eastwards for Tengah Airfield, the colonel fully expected to find some resistance on the road south. But that was the only route out for the growing number of wounded in his regimental aid post: down Lim Chu Kang Road to Tengah, and then east towards Bukit Panjang, on the island's main north–south road. As for the men who were able to walk, they would simply have to make their way on foot through the untamed jungle and upper reaches of the Kranji's main tributaries.

With dawn breaking, Archie Ewart motored south on his bike to ensure that the 2/18th still held the road into Ama Keng, but returned with a bullet wound to the neck for his troubles. An A Company platoon led by Roger Cornforth was swiftly despatched to clear the area.

Meanwhile the wounded had been crammed into all available trucks, which were assembled along Neo Tiew Road, in the original B echelon area east of battalion headquarters. The convoy left around dawn, but were ambushed just a short way down the main road. Only the troops riding in trucks at the rear of the convoy survived the ensuing massacre. Mostly able-bodied men from displaced sections within HQ and B companies, they too would be forced into the jungle, ever wary of encountering more of the enemy.

From 9.15 that morning, the 2/20th and the men from Dalforce, the 2/4th and other supporting units all began to move out from the battalion perimeter for the relative safety of Bulim, east of Tengah Airfield on the Choa Chu Kang Road. They headed off in groups, which rapidly became subgroups whenever the enemy, hot on their heels, moved in for the kill. Men carried their wounded mates, even though they themselves had been hit. There was just as much courage shown during the desperate retreat as there'd been on the beaches the night before.

Charles Assheton likewise acted with great honour and genuine concern for his unit. Having instructed Merrett's A Company to provide cover for the withdrawal, the colonel had then made for Roger Cornforth's 7 Platoon positions, north of Ama Keng, to consider what could be done about the enemy units threatening his departing troops from ridges to the south. At 11.30 am, he was just leading an attack on a group from one such unit when he was hit by a full blast of automatic rifle fire. Born in Kalgoorlie, Western Australia, but a resident of Glen Innes, Charles Frederick Assheton was aged just forty when he died.

※ ※ ※

Only the Kranji and a sustained response from the Australians interfered with the Japanese army's swift progress through the west of Singapore Island. Across the 22nd Brigade front, things had played out pretty consistently for all three of the battalions: success in repelling initial landing attempts, followed by enforced withdrawal to avoid groups becoming outflanked, and finally full-scale retreat as more enemy troops were able to pour onto the beaches unchallenged. The 2/18th had appeared to buckle early, but its carrier platoon still inflicted huge damage later on around Tengah Airfield, wiping out almost an entire company of Japanese. In the 2/19th's sector, Major Andrew Robertson (CO in Anderson's absence) had attempted to evacuate his seriously wounded. Like the 2/20th's attempted breakout, the convoy was instantly ambushed and destroyed, Jap divebombers being the main culprits this time along with various land-based arsenal. *The Grim Glory* would be a more than apt title for the 2/19th Battalion's postwar official history.

The Kranji would make the going tough for the diggers also, its swamps and often impenetrable jungle making the week-long training sessions in the scrub around Port Dickson seem like an adventure holiday. Amid the mayhem that ensued as the 2/20th survivors endeavoured to trek to Bulim and regroup, there were countless reports of further atrocities and lucky escapes.

John Cook, the twenty-year-old former Australian Glassworks driver from Penrith, certainly had luck with him that day. But his close mate Roger Mort, a friend since childhood, had only minutes to live as they lay side by side in a field, sheltering from enemy machine-gun fire. The two C Company men, together with Henry Dietz and Cas Cook (another Penrith local), had just recced a river bank and could see Japanese troops massing across the way. They thought their position was well concealed, but John and Roger were not as well hidden as they thought.

In the volley of gunfire that rattled out across the river, Roger Mort was hit in the back. Unaware of the severity of his wounds, his first concern was for John. 'You okay?' he queried.

'Yeah,' replied John, before noticing the blood pouring from the top of his mate's body. Part of his back had been blown away.

Roger Charles Mort was one of the 2/20th originals, having enlisted in July '40. He died soon after this skirmish, and John never really got over it. There was no counselling for the traumatised and no time to weep. The only option was to continue the fight.

Up until quite recently, Mick McAuliffe had been a dairy farmer out at Tregeagle, in northern New South Wales. Now, frightened and exhausted, he made his way east towards Bukit Timah with other members of B Company. Once there, perhaps he'd be able to digest the scale of the Japanese advance, but right now his head was filled with images of men falling all about him. 'Two of the blokes who came over with me on the *Aquitania* got killed but I was lucky. They missed me,' Mick remembers. 'Before we knew what was happening, the Japs had surrounded us. It was uncanny. They were behind us and opened fire. It was like all hell had broken loose — you didn't know whether it was coming from east or west. But somehow I survived it.'

As for D Company, stranded overnight behind the small airstrip in the north of the battalion's sector, they'd finally made it home to the perimeter at around 10 o'clock that morning. But rather than a message from Colonel Assheton, it was the sound of enemy tanks approaching from the beach that had got them on the move.

'They'd spray us with everything,' remembers Herb Lamb. 'As

well as bombs and machine-gun fire, they also used to throw grenades down onto us. One fell right between me and my mate Alan Edwards, but amazingly it didn't go off.' Both men decided to go their separate ways and eventually Herb thought he heard an armoured personnel carrier nearby. He ran in the direction of the engine noise but was foiled by a pig's wallow. Wading through the mud, he then slipped and fell into the mire. 'I was a real mess, but it was handy camouflage!'

Maybe it was Herb's lucky day. Earlier a Japanese machine-gunner had opened up and hit his rifle. 'The fore-end of my bayonet was shot clean off my gun,' he marvels. 'They had beautiful weapons — automatics, you see. We had to make do with old Boer War-style Lee Enfields.

'Anyway, I made my own way back and came across this bloke who was badly shot. I got my field dressing out and shoved it down on his main artery, but I couldn't stop the flow. I just had to leave him.

'So there I was, unarmed, with my rifle shot to pieces and me dead beat, when this ute comes along. It turned out to be driven by a bloke from Dubbo called Charlie Beazley, who I knew very well. I used to play crib with his father and I'd gone out with his sister.'

Talk about a small world. Fate or Dame Fortune were clearly working in his favour that day. After being given a lift by Charlie Beazley, Herb cleaned himself up and tried to get back to his battalion.

As is the way in war, there were many examples of men who survived against the odds. Merv Alchin's escape at Mersing had already put him in that category. But there were also cases of people being declared dead when they were still alive.

Officially Kevin Timbs had been killed by a bomb that hit a house he'd been sheltering in. Or at least that was the story his family was given. But in one of those extraordinary coincidences thrown up by war, it transpired that there were two Kevin Timbs. One was a lance-sergeant in the 2/20th Infantry Battalion, the other a signaller. Neither man had met until that fateful day in Singapore when they both found themselves under fire.

'The Japs were peppering the hell out of us and I heard this other Kevin say he was getting under the house. I knew it was foolhardy and shouted out, "If a bomb or shell hits the building, you're gone."' Whether engineer Kevin didn't hear him or simply ignored the advice is difficult to say, but seconds later it happened. 'Bugger me, he did get under the house and a shell hit him, and he was gone,' recalls lucky Kevin.

With both men sharing the same names, it was inevitable they would be confused. Sure enough, a few months later word got back to Kevin's family in Australia that he had been killed. The messenger was none other than Major Charles Moses, the peacetime ABC boss and former D Company commander who went on to a staff job with the 8th Division. 'I got on well with him because he was always getting me to organise the football, so we were quite friendly,' Kevin explains. 'My brother had heard me mention Charlie Moses, so he contacted him on his return to Australia.'

Moses had heard about a Sergeant Timbs getting bombed in the fight for Singapore and so told Kevin's sibling: 'Ah, Kevin Timbs. He was a very good soldier, but sadly he was killed in action.' The news stunned the family, out in Glen Innes. Patrick and Kate Timbs went into mourning for their lost son.

※ ※ ※

Within forty-eight hours of the first enemy troops setting foot on Singapore, the Allies knew they were in serious trouble. On 9 February, the Japanese had landed in the south-west of the island, in the Indians' sector, and were soon pushing inland. Up in the north that evening — and despite the fact that his machine-gunners had successfully foiled an assault by the Imperial Guards — with Tengah about to fall into the enemy's grasp, Brigadier Maxwell felt compelled to withdraw his units also. He'd even disobeyed Bennett's order in doing so.

And by 10 February, after more bitter fighting north and south of Bulim, involving the 2/29th, remnants of Major Merrett's A Company and the 2/18th's carriers again, the Australians had lost the so-called Kranji–Jurong line. A third of the island was now in Japanese hands. The diggers in the 2/20th had barely caught their breath, in other words, before they were being moved on again, south-eastwards to the new brigade area at Racecourse Village.

With the situation becoming increasingly desperate, General Wavell reminded his men that they still greatly outnumbered the Japs who had crossed the Johore Straits, and therefore should be in a stronger position to repel their advance. 'We must defeat them,' he exhorted. 'It will be disgraceful if we yield our boasted fortress of Singapore to inferior enemy forces.' Warming to this theme, Wavell urged fellow officers to give no thought to sparing their troops or the civilian population — or themselves, for that matter: 'There must be no question or thought of surrender ... I look to you and your men to fight to the end to prove that the fighting spirit that won our Empire still exists to enable us to defend it.' That same day Wavell flew back to Java.

The British commander-in-chief's comments did not sit comfortably with some of the Australians, who reckoned the Poms had woken up to the dangers a little too late. What had they been doing for the past year or more? Sitting on their backsides shuffling paper and dancing the night away in the fleshpots of Singapore, most likely. At the same time, among many of the diggers there was a growing sense of dissatisfaction regarding their own leader, Major General Gordon Bennett. As events would soon play out, the Melbourne-born soldier would do little to endear himself to these doubters in the ranks.

By now water on the island was running short. Supplies from the mainland had been deliberately cut and the only way to make a cup of tea was to beg, steal or borrow the water from homes or buildings that kept some in reserve. The boys in the 2/20th found themselves roughly midway between Tengah and Singapore, as the crow flies, due south of the Causeway. Appreciating the return to civilisation, George Daldry and his mates filled their billy from a place near the Racecourse Village post office. 'We used to take it in turns to go down there and fill up a kettle of whatever we could find to make a cuppa.' One particular trip left him with an indelible experience, however.

'To get to the tank you had to pass this unit of Indian anti-aircraft gunners, and most days you'd have a joke with them,' he recalls. 'This particular day I'd asked what was happening. They smiled back and chatted as though they didn't have a care in the world.'

It took George less than two minutes to pour his water and begin to make the return journey. Just as he turned off the tap, there was a massive explosion. The Indians had taken a direct hit. 'There were about ten of them and they were all dead. So badly were they burnt, they looked like charcoal. And what sticks out in my mind was their teeth: they'd had these incredibly white teeth, and somehow the blast hadn't coloured the teeth at all.'

Like the various Indian units, the 22nd Australian Brigade had suffered heavy losses over the past few days, but the worst was yet to come. Late afternoon on 10 February, perhaps in response to Wavell's demands, they were ordered to fight back in an effort to retake the Kranji–Jurong line.

Coordinating with attacks to be carried out by the 44th Indian Brigade, in the south, and the 2/30th Battalion to the north, two hastily assembled forces were tasked with a contribution in Brigadier Taylor's sector. X Battalion was formed from composite companies within the three 22nd Brigade units but, oddly, was commanded by a virtual stranger, Lieutenant Colonel Arthur Boyes (previously CO of the 2/26th). Leading the 2/20th contingent was Captain Rod Richardson, assisted by platoon leaders Jack Mudie, Harry Woods, John Rowe and Jim Brookes. The force partnering X Battalion was Merrett Force, consisting of the relatively intact A Company of the 2/20th and a similar-sized group from the 2/19th.

While Boyes's mixed unit was to push through north-west to a trig point on the Jurong Road level with Bukit Timah, as a first objective, the plan was for Ron Merrett's men to provide support on both flanks. It was a highly dangerous venture, but its ill conception and sloppy preparation turned it into a virtual suicide mission. To begin with, the X Battalion diggers' weaponry was woeful: as little as half-a-dozen rounds per man, some armed with only garden tools. Just as worryingly, Bennett's orders had been based on flimsy military intelligence bordering on plain hearsay. The claim was that the Indian brigade were up ahead and had the enemy on the run; there were Jap tanks parked to the east of the Jurong Road trig point, on the high ground at Bukit Timah, but they weren't going anywhere, apparently.

Moving forward nervously through the pitch-black night, Richardson's men noticed a worrying number of dead Indian troops on their uninterrupted march to the trig point. Only the swishing and squeaking of the rubber plants around them broke the silence. Arriving at the site at around 10 pm, together with the other companies, they set about establishing a perimeter camp around the large fuel dump that had been denied the Japanese.

Henry Dietz was there with X Battalion. Unlike when he and Snowy set out on Homer's recce, though, this wasn't a mission he volunteered for. He'd been given the impression that the tide had turned in the Allies' favour; Henry wasn't so sure. Preparing to snatch a few hours of much-needed sleep, he loosened his belt but kept his faithful Tommy gun by his side. 'I had a couple of .50 rounds and three or four .25 rounds on it, and they were pretty heavy,' he says of his paltry stash of ammo. 'Anyway, I'd just got settled down when everything went up. There were factories on fire all around us and night suddenly turned into day.'

It was 3 am precisely on 11 February, and the night had indeed turned quite suddenly into day. The tanks of fuel had just exploded.

Before Henry could even register this, the full might of the Japanese 18th Division had launched a bloody assault on the camp, bayoneting many of the Australians as they slept and using small-arms fire and grenades on the rest. Such was the element of surprise — there had been no time for the half-dozing sentries to issue a warning — that X Battalion was simply overwhelmed. Casualties screamed with pain while those fortunate enough to remain unscathed during the first few minutes of the attack engaged in vicious hand-to-hand fighting in order to defend themselves. It was a slaughter. Some 200 diggers had set up camp there a few hours before; by daybreak most were dead or seriously injured. The Japanese had simply been waiting for their supply lines to catch up to their forward positions, hence the seemingly abandoned tanks.

Over the next hour or two, Merrett Force would be similarly rebuffed. The Allies' first attempt to strike back had ended in unmitigated failure.

Unlike the doomed X Battalion, however, a good portion of Ron Merrett's men did at least make it back to base. But not Roy Homer. The 25-year-old platoon leader from North Bondi died from wounds sustained while attempting to withdraw to brigade lines, at Reformatory Road. From now until the cessation of hostilities, like the majority of diggers in the tortured 22nd Brigade, Henry Dietz, Snowy Collins and others in 15 Platoon would be supernumerary troops: available for immediate detailing anywhere across the brigade sector, to help plug a gap or beef up the numbers, with no thought for section, platoon, company, even battalion, continuity or loyalty. Jimmy Houston, Bluey Firth, Dudley Boughton, Eric Richardson — all the originals who'd made lasting friendships with their comrades since the middle of 1940 could now find themselves fighting beside total strangers.

Lieutenant Harry Woods was among friends, but the Japanese weren't far away. Another X Battalion member to get away in one piece, Harry made for the comparative safety of Reformatory Road. He and his platoon hadn't gone far, though, before they walked into a large party of enemy troops — who immediately opened fire. Harry was shot in the shoulder and thigh. 'Both bullets missed the bones, fortunately,' he said, 'so I could still walk reasonably well. But I lost quite a lot of blood.'

The 24-year-old managed to hitch a ride back to Allied lines with a British despatch rider. On the way they were strafed by machine-gun fire from a Japanese fighter plane, but their luck held out and the Australian officer was safely delivered into the hands of a British medical orderly. Handed an ice-cold bottle of Tiger Beer, Harry slaked his thirst while being questioned, after which he was sent on to Alexandra Military Hospital by ambulance. Like Jack Mudie, Henry and the other survivors of the Jurong Road debacle, Lieutenant Woods had already avoided death several times over the last three days. But for Harry, his guardian angel's work was far from over.

Even before the disintegration of X Battalion, a new Y Battalion was being formed to help consolidate the 22nd Brigade's position. Having recently returned to the 2/20th after Anderson's recovery, Major Robertson was able to collect together just ninety men from his original unit — Captain Bill Carter and Theo Lee among them; Y Battalion had nevertheless moved off and taken up positions overnight astride the Holland Road–Ulu Pandan Road junction. Next day, 11 February, Captain Jim Chisholm arrived with a company of 2/18th men to help bolster the battalion perimeter. A New South Wales grazier who, like Robertson, was well respected by the Aussies, Chisholm also found himself leading parties of Indian and British soldiers.

Furious fighting extended across the entire front. The Japanese were determined to secure control of Singapore by the end of 11 February so that the victory would coincide with the anniversary of the first Emperor's accession to the throne. That very morning, General Tomoyuki Yamashita, commander of the Japanese forces in Malaya, sent aircraft to drop boxes over the island containing a note addressed to the High Command of the British Army. It read in part:

> My sincere respect is due to your army which, true to the traditional spirit of Great Britain, is bravely defending Singapore which now stands isolated and unaided. Many fierce and gallant fights have been fought by your gallant men and officers, to the honour of British warriorship. But the developments of the general war situation has already sealed the fate of Singapore, and the continuation of futile resistance would only serve to inflict direct harm and injuries to thousands of non-combatants living in the city, throwing them into further miseries and horrors of war, but also would not add anything to the honour of your army … Give up this meaningless and desperate resistance and promptly order the entire front to cease hostilities.

Yamashita, soon to be nicknamed 'the Tiger of Malaya', made it clear that the alternative was the annihilation of Singapore.

With Wavell's orders to fight to the death still ringing in his ears, General Percival passed on the Japanese demand to the commander of Far East forces, pointing out that there was no point in responding to Yamashita's note, as any reply would of course 'be negative'. But Percival knew that there was some truth in what the Japanese commander had said. Singapore's water supply was extremely low, fuel was running short and there was only enough food to last the military for another two weeks. More immediately, Percival was also worried about the onward march of the Japanese Guards division, whose tanks had landed in the northern sector of the island the previous day, near the Causeway, and were making their way across the centre of the island.

Worry and stress were very much getting the better of Brigadier Harold Taylor at this point. In dire need of sleep, and painfully aware that the lives of his remaining troops might depend on him being able to keep a clear head, he was forced to hand over his command to Arthur Varley, the 2/18th's CO, during the night of 11–12 February.

As the Japanese began to amass on Y Battalion's front, Brigadier Varley instructed Frank Gaven's forty-strong 'Composite Company' to join Robertson on his right flank. Like Gaven, Jack Mudie and John Rowe had quickly dusted themselves down after the sickening events of the previous night, and here they were now, back for more. Also adding to the strength of Composite Company (which, despite its predominance of 2/20th men, was officially a 2/18th section) was another true hero from the Endau fighting, Lieutenant John Varley, MC, of the 2/19th.

The Allies fought courageously to maintain their line, but under continuous bombardment, General Percival had no alternative but to pull back yet again. And still the Imperial Army kept coming.

By 12 February, about half the island was in enemy hands and Percival was forced to acknowledge that it was 'only a matter of days' before the Japanese would be in the city itself. The following day, the Japanese commander moved his headquarters to the Ford

Motor Company plant, situated just north of Racecourse Village off Bukit Timah Road — provocatively close to the city itself. Meanwhile, the Governor and his wife, Sir Shenton Thomas and Lady Thomas, abandoned their official residence in favour of the Singapore Club. Percival remained in his bunker at nearby Fort Canning, with its unrivalled views over much of the island and from where he could monitor the Japanese advance. At daybreak on 14 February, what was left of the 8th Australian Division were manning a sector that stretched to just above the Buena Vista Road junction on Holland Road — some 3 kilometres back from the perimeter established by Y Battalion three days before. More importantly, though, the enemy had successfully forced back the Indian and Malaya brigades south of their sector.

In the growing desperation, there were signs of anarchy. Some reports spoke of a residue of Australian and other troops defying authority. A number of them had been seeking to secure their escape by boat.

Three days after Harry Woods was wounded, he was caught up in one of the greatest atrocities in the history of World War II: the slaughter of innocent civilians, doctors and patients at the Alexandra Military Hospital, in the very south of the island. On the morning of 14 February, as Lieutenant Woods lay in bed recovering from his injuries in an upstairs ward, renegade Japanese troops arrived at the front entrance. They'd been chasing a detachment of Indian troops along the Ayer Raja Road when the Indians fell back into the hospital, still firing. Sensing a disaster in the making, an officer on duty ran to the reception area with a white flag. Unmoved by the offer of surrender, the soldiers bayoneted the officer and charged inside. Doctors and nurses were ordered to raise their hands and move down the corridor. One by one they were also stabbed with bayonets. Medics who pleaded for their lives pointed to the Red Cross on their uniforms, but it made no difference. Even a patient lying on an operating table received no mercy.

Every patient who was capable of walking was being ordered outside, where they were tied together and systematically slain. Harry Woods, unable to walk at this stage, could hear the cries and the commotion from his upstairs ward, but the Japs hadn't yet made it up to his floor. Another soldier in the ward went downstairs to investigate. Horrified by what he saw, the sergeant lunged at one of the Japanese bayonets as he too was ordered outside, only to be executed minutes later.

Many civilian staff who survived the initial carnage were later made to stand in a small bungalow overnight. The next morning they were all forced outside and stabbed to death.

A failing memory diminished the scale of the terror that Harry Woods recalled subsequently of that fateful day. The blood, the family photographs and the rosary beads that were scattered across the hospital grounds were a blur. But of one fact he was certain: it was a miracle he survived.

※ ※ ※

Later that day, to the south of the Australians' new sector, the Japanese 18th Division consolidated its position in the Alexandra area, where much of the Allies' ammunition was stored. Meanwhile, their 5th Division carried on tearing away at the British brigades, to the right of the 8th Australian Division positions, while the Imperial Guards applied pressure on the Indian and Malayan units defending the eastern approaches to the city.

As the enemy continued its advance towards Singapore town, Major General Gordon Bennett and other senior officers knew the end was nigh. The bombing campaign was now targeting highly populated residential areas. It wasn't just soldiers who were the casualties anymore, but countless civilians also. Mothers with babies in their arms staggered through clouds of dust and smoke. Others clawed at the debris with their bare hands to rescue family members who were trapped and dying under fallen masonry. In peacetime, diggers like Private Cas Cook and Signalman Harry Julian had trained in the building industry; now they were part of the destruction, as houses, shops and churches — any edifice that might offer the enemy cover — became just another target for removal.

Bennett himself wrote of the devastation in his book *Why Singapore Fell*:

> There were holes in the road, churned up rubble lying in great clods all around, tangled masses of telephone, telegraphy and electric cables strewn across the street, here and there smashed cars, trucks, electric trams and buses that once carried loads of passengers to and from their peaceful daily toil. Bombs were falling in a nearby street. On reaching the spot one saw that the side of a building had fallen on an air raid shelter. A group of Chinese, Malays, Europeans and Australian soldiers were already at work shovelling and dragging the debris away. Soon there emerged from the shelter a Chinese boy, scratched and bleeding, who immediately turned to help in the rescue work. He said, 'My sister is under there.' The rescuers dug furiously among the fallen masonry. At last the top of the shelter was uncovered. Beneath was a crushed mass of old men, women, young and old, and young children, some still living — the rest dead. This was going on hour after hour, day after day, the same stolidity and steadfastness among the civilians was evident in every quarter of the city.

Percival had already observed that 'there must come a stage when in the interests of the troops and the civil population further bloodshed will serve no purpose'. The implication of this message to General Wavell was clear, but the Supreme Commander of Allied Forces in the Far East was having none of it. After reminding Percival that any damage done to the Japanese now could benefit the Allies elsewhere, he summed up the situation in fewer than a dozen words: 'Fully appreciate your situation, but continued action essential.'

The 22nd Brigade had been under constant fire now for the best part of a week, and under the most hostile conditions. Many men had existed on only a few hours' sleep a night and minimal rations.

So it was quite a surprise to them when they learnt that there was food and drink aplenty to be found at Tanglin Barracks, on Holland Road, which led into Orchard Road. Indeed, the contents of the barracks stores included luxury foods, fine wines — which had somehow escaped the Governor's destruction order — and all manner of military clothing. But such was the intensity of the enemy bombardment that the temptation of a little unofficial looting had to be ignored. A pity. Shortly it would all be in the hands of the Japanese, but the Aussies weren't prepared to hang around.

The enemy was only a day away from winning one of the greatest prizes of World War II. Once Singapore fell, Sumatra and Java to the south would follow, and from there, it was only a hop, skip and a jump to Darwin and a foothold on northern Australia.

With Japan having naval dominance in the Bay of Bengal and the Indian Ocean, Australia's oil supplies in the Middle East would also be threatened — and a country without oil could survive for only so long. While Singapore was only one piece in the jigsaw, it was central to the big picture. Without it, the entire Far East, Australasia and the South Pacific were in peril.

Events were rapidly coming to a head. A communication from the Governor to the Colonial Office in London read: 'There are now one million people within radius of three miles. Water supplies very badly damaged and unlikely to last more than 24 hours. Many dead lying in the streets and burial impossible. We are faced with total deprivation of water, which must result in pestilence.'

The view was further reinforced in a message from Percival to Wavell, but he still wouldn't budge.

'Your gallant stand is serving a purpose and must be continued to the limit of endurance,' he wrote back.

Come the afternoon of 14 February, with Japanese troops only 5 kilometres from the southern shoreline of Singapore city, thoughts of evacuation were inevitable. Surprisingly, perhaps, there were still many small vessels moored in Keppel Harbour, enough to evacuate about 3000 people. Places were allotted to essential staff and to civilians with specialist knowledge. There was space enough for

100 members of the Australian Imperial Force, as well as nurses and technicians who were no longer required.

A group of senior officers and certain VIPs selected by the Governor were preparing to embark on the *Osprey*, a launch that was supposed to hold ten people (it eventually left with thirty-eight). A small number of soldiers, Australians among them, who were also intent on making their escape, threatened to shoot unless they were allowed on board. Indeed, several rifle shots were heard as the *Osprey* sailed away without them. It was not the army's finest hour.

In London, Prime Minister Churchill was aware that surrender was probably only hours away and made his views known in a message to Wavell: 'You are of course sole judge of the moment when no further result can be gained at Singapore and should instruct Percival accordingly.' It was the clearest hint yet that the powers that be had conceded defeat. Only a ceasefire between the warring parties would halt the wholesale slaughter of thousands of soldiers and innocent civilians.

※ ※ ※

On the morning of Sunday 15 February, a joint military deputation made its way along the Bukit Timah Road to the front line of Japan's 5th Division to pass on the Allies' intentions. A meeting was arranged between Generals Percival and Yamashita in the Ford factory, where it was agreed that hostilities should formally cease at 8.30 pm local time. A white flag was hoisted atop the broadcasting centre in Caldecott Hill, and at precisely 5.15 pm, Percival and his staff arrived at the car plant to sign the surrender documents.

It had taken the Japanese just seventy days to complete their advance down the Malay Peninsula and at a cost of around 10,000 men. In comparison with the Allies, who suffered nearly 140,000 casualties, the enemy had got off lightly. Those British and Australians troops who survived to tell the tale marvelled at the superiority of the Japs, who'd conquered a Singapore fighting force of some 85,000 with just three divisions. How did they do it?

While the Japanese enjoyed naval and air superiority and had highly experienced front-line troops, there were some who believed it was one of the biggest con-tricks of the war. The Japs were running short of supplies and were in no position to contemplate a long and costly siege of the island. It wasn't only the armchair generals who were to subsequently conclude that if the British and Australian military leaders had not lost their nerve, they might have contained and eventually repelled the enemy.

Among the ranks, there was talk of the top brass letting them down, particularly the British. Joe Byrne, who had just discharged himself from hospital to find his unit, was effectively on the run when told the war was over. 'I thought, Oh Christ, don't tell me they've given it away that easily. That means we've all been sold into slavery … We were not impressed.'

Kevin Timbs, by now an acting sergeant, admits his men were extremely hostile to the idea of surrender. 'We reckoned that if we'd stayed at the perimeter we could have held them back,' he insists. 'So we weren't happy when told to lay down our arms.'

Others shared his misgivings. 'If we'd had our way, the Japanese would never have got past us,' said Jack Mudie. 'But the order came from the British, so we put all our arms and equipment in a heap and prepared for the long march to Changi.'

Relations between the Australians and many of the British officers had become tense in the final days of the fighting. Henry Dietz, tired and filthy after weeks of combat, happened upon an English officer in a clean uniform with his buttons brightly polished, demanding to know the current position of the enemy. 'They never offered us anything, not even a cup of tea,' Henry adds.

Don Alchin was more fatalistic about what was happening around him and realised there was no way out. 'There were thousands of people living on a small island and they were being strafed and bombed night and day,' he notes. 'There were mass burials and little in the way of food and water. We had our backs to the wall and there was no way out.'

But there was a way out for some. Early the next morning, Henry Gordon Bennett got away with two other officers, including Major

Charles Moses, and managed to sail to Sumatra. Bennett's escape from Singapore was to prove one of the most controversial episodes of the campaign. When he arrived back safely in Melbourne on 2 March, he was surprised by the hostile reception. At least one army chief told him his escape was 'ill advised', although this was not a view shared by Prime Minister John Curtin, who paid tribute to his gallantry. As for Moses, the Lancashire-born broadcaster returned to Sydney, where he would continue to serve as general manager of the ABC until his retirement in 1965.

Among those left behind, there were mixed emotions about Bennett's hasty departure. Some of the men in the 2/20th weren't too impressed. Over the next three years they would have plenty of time to dwell on it.

CHAPTER 5

PRISONERS OF THE JAPANESE

An acrid haze hung over Singapore on the morning of 16 February. The smoke from burning buildings and oil storage tanks cloaked the entire island, blackening the skin and clogging the lungs of anyone who ventured out into the eerily silent dawn.

By now the Australians were discarding their arms, tossing knives and guns into makeshift stacks, as instructed by their junior officers and section leaders. A number of the diggers were concerned they'd have nothing with which to defend themselves, and so began secreting some of the smaller weapons about their person. Despite the surprisingly sympathetic treatment he'd received as a prisoner up at Mersing, George Daldry decided to hold on to his trusty .45 revolver. Jimmy Houston, never one to miss the main chance, saw someone drop a pistol on the heap and grabbed it. The weapon might come in useful, he reasoned, if it came down to every man for himself.

After all, for well over a month now, these men had got used to waking with a start from a brief, fitful sleep, the first reaction always being to reach for the security of their weapon. It was a hard habit to break. Merv Alchin and George aside, no one really had any idea what to expect, and everyone feared the worst.

Initially, though, the Japanese seemed friendly enough, as groups of them began appearing in the 2/20th's sector.

❃ ❃ ❃

The most pressing challenge facing the victors was how to contain more than 50,000 British and Australian troops and where to put them. The answer was Changi, out on the eastern tip of the island. With the village's civilian jail already allocated for the many Dutch and British expats left in Singapore, the nearby British garrison offered barracks and bungalows aplenty and no shortage of wide-open spaces in its many parade grounds. Selarang Barracks, in the south of the sprawling complex, would be home for the 14,972 men of Australia's 8th Division for an indefinite period.

Late on 17 February, after another unsettling night in their defensive positions around Holland Road, the Aussies assembled at Tanglin, near the Botanic Gardens, and set off on the march halfway across the island to begin their new life in captivity. After what Mick McAuliffe would describe as 'a big walk' — well over 30 kilometres, in fact, along the winding country roads — they'd eventually arrive at Changi well after midnight.

Soon to be the subject of much speculation back home in Glen Innes, Kevin Timbs now found himself receiving some undue attention here also. A mate who had a brother in the Australian military police reckoned the Japs had already shot six men and the MP had heard Kevin's name mentioned. 'Don't make yourself noticeable,' he was advised. 'Because if you do, they'll shoot you too.' What was it about? Not normally the shy, retiring type, Kevin decided to fall back to the rear of the column and lie low all the same.

Another man not known for backing away from confrontation was George Daldry. Just before his squad was given the order to form up, however, he'd come face to face with a group of fearsome Tokyo Guards and instantly began to have second thoughts about the gun he was carrying inside his shirt. 'They were a gruesome-looking bunch and pretty rugged-looking,' he remembers. He knew that if they found him with a firearm, he'd probably be shot. 'I had to lose them and the revolver, so I walked calmly to a piece of grass while their attention was distracted, and dropped the gun surreptitiously to the ground. I was lucky to get away with it, because they would have shown no mercy.'

While George began the long march with a sense of relief, Sergeant Timbs made a point of keeping his head down and avoiding eye contact with any of the Japanese escorting the prisoners. Back at the end of the line, several men were sick or injured and having trouble keeping up. With unsubstantiated reports already doing the rounds that anyone falling too far behind was being despatched with a single shot to the head, it was yet another concern for an anxious mind.

After close to five weeks of battle, Kevin was getting used to scenes of carnage, but every now and then he would be sickened by what he saw. It wasn't the scale of the bloodshed that shocked him that February morning, but the squelching sound emanating from beneath his boot. 'I just felt something soft under my foot, and glancing down I realised I'd stepped on a human hand. I looked across the road, and there was the wreckage of a blown-up truck, with the body of the driver lying on the ground. His hand was missing.'

Snowy Collins was nursing a festered toenail, which was causing him great discomfort. But the diminutive bushie from Muswellbrook didn't dare stop. 'I was dying to sit down and take my boot off, but I knew if I did they'd probably shoot me,' he explains.

On arrival at Selarang, at 2.30 the following morning, the men of the 2/20th were given a mug of tea each with a slug of rum and directed to a block on the south-west corner, one of seven such barrack buildings around the main parade ground. There, they were divided up into their original companies and assigned quarters accordingly, on the top two levels; the ground floor would serve as the battalion's mess area for now. The other units in the 22nd Brigade and those in the 27th occupied the remaining blocks in what would come to be the official AIF internment camp during Japan's thrust through South-East Asia.

Among the ranks, first impressions weren't too positive. 'We felt it was terrible at the time,' says Mick McAuliffe, before adding: 'But three-and-a-half years later we'd have thought it was great.'

In fact, Selarang Barracks had a certain suburban respectability. Set within an area of great natural beauty, offering breathtaking views of the South China Sea and north across the Johore Strait to Pulau Ubin, in many ways the various camps on the Changi peninsula were more than any prisoner of war could have hoped for. Even the rations over the first few days seemed half edible. Each POW was allowed .11032 pounds of meat, and the same amount of flour; just over a pound of rice, a quarter-pound of vegetables, .033 pounds of milk, close to half a pound of sugar, and small amounts of tea, salt and cooking oil.

And the local village offered plenty of opportunities to top up that allowance, for those who had the wherewithal. George Daldry might have forfeited his revolver, but he had hung on to the stash of Straits dollars he'd pocketed outside the Treasury building. 'It certainly came in useful in Changi, where you could buy stuff off the natives,' he admits.

Once the battalion's canteen was opened midway through March, however, the promise of good food failed to live up to expectations. Soon men were being given a tasteless rice ball and maybe a stinking piece of fish to eat — a diet that would become all too common as their incarceration continued. Apart from the food, Selarang's other drawback was the overcrowding. Each of the main blocks housed about 800 men, who were packed in like sardines. Some slept on bare concrete, others on the grass outside. Hygiene was poor and dysentery was rife. Given the meagre diet and their weakened state after months on the front line, most soldiers had little resistance to disease and many died.

Aside from the very real suffering brought on by these deprivations, the men were bored, dispirited — seething even. Throughout the 8th Division, commanders were sensitive to this, troop morale being paramount in the military. Lieutenant Colonel Robertson, the 2/20th's new CO, and his fellow senior officers certainly didn't hang about when it came to organising their new battalion headquarters or finding ways to keep the men occupied.

By 19 February, the day after the unit arrived, an educational scheme was announced, with the intention of training the men in a variety of peacetime occupations, and patrolling of the unit's area was immediately under way. Over the next few days, both an entertainment committee (headed by Theo Lee) and a battalion agricultural party were established; and within weeks, the massive field bakery was up and running, sports tournaments were organised, and wiring and ablutions facilities both nearing completion. It was typically army, typically Aussie 'can do' — and it was remarkable. But this wasn't Port Dickson.

Perhaps the brass were trying just a little too hard in their efforts to keep the boys motivated. The Allied military, after all, had been left with sole command of the troops while the Japanese busied themselves with the logistics of occupying the island, and it was easy for the confused, displaced diggers to see their officers as captors.

Jimmy Houston's diary shines a clear light on a number of developments during the 2/20th's years in captivity. Already bitter about the conduct of certain junior officers on the battlefield, he didn't hold back whenever he perceived that his superiors were taking advantage of their position.

> When we were at Changi the Japanese sent thousands of pairs of boots to us, new and old. But the fools we have in charge of us wouldn't issue anything out to the privates. Though they didn't forget to help themselves. The officers had the pick of everything. When the Japs sent us our kitbags they were put away at the top floor and a guard put over them. The following day all the officers had new shorts and socks on. They ratted the men's kitbags. Still, one shouldn't expect anything better of them.

Perhaps it was just the frustrations of a free-spirited man who'd volunteered to defend king and country and then seen that country's military representatives sell him out. Like Kevin Timbs, Joe Byrne and many others, Jimmy was mad at the world. Mad as hell.

※ ※ ※

In spite of some dissension in the ranks, Selarang soon became a well-ordered institution. With AIF officers responsible for discipline, their units continued to function as fully efficient military machines. The Australians, who seemed to be more adaptable to the somewhat basic living conditions than their British counterparts, even constructed a rudimentary plumbing system. Within a few months they'd managed to install hand-operated showers. Facing an acute need for fresh food, the men cultivated about 20 hectares of land on which to grow fruit and vegetables for themselves. There was also a small poultry farm, which would produce a staggering 40,000 eggs in the three years until June 1945.

Because, despite the casualties over the past months and the new situation they found themselves in, the 2/20th Infantry Battalion was still that — a battalion, a *unit*. New names might have now filled the posts of adjutant, quartermaster and brigade major after the deaths of all three at Kranji, but an infantry unit had a life of its own and went on regardless.

In that spirit, battalion strength was still measured religiously with every hospitalisation or whenever another straggler returned from the outside world, having been caught wandering the island by the occupying forces. While a semi-recovered Harry Woods's return to the unit on 2 March was no surprise, the arrivals of Hayden Webster and Len Serong were quite unexpected.

Webster — Don Alchin's company sergeant-major in B Company — had last been seen leaving with the convoy of wounded at dawn on 9 February. A regular star on the cricket pitch for the battalion, the 37-year-old from West Wyalong had somehow made it back from the ambush on Lim Chu Kang Road despite suffering a nasty wound to the hand. As for Serong, he'd been on the beach with Theo Lee's men, stopped to tie a boot-lace during the first withdrawal, then looked up … and he was alone. A hugely talented soccer player from Annandale in Sydney (he even earned a place on a Malayan state team), young Len had decided to simply stay put in the area until picked up by the Japanese — all of seven weeks later.

Similarly, transgressors in the ranks continued to be punished with days or weeks in detention, while, on the other side of the coin, recent promotions were confirmed. Among the officers, Bill Carter and Frank Gaven both officially stepped up a rank, like Robertson, in confirmation of earlier appointments. War, peace or captivity, the battalion lived on.

As with the other barracks serving as camps at Changi, Selarang was thus transformed into a military co-operative where each man worked for the common good. And this didn't only apply to food and physical comfort. Thanks to education officers Jack Mudie and Albert Yates, there were opportunities to nourish the mind, with a wide range of classes run by those who had a specialist knowledge of skills, languages and countless other subjects. Students could learn French, geography, mathematics, law, shorthand, engineering and even medicine. And under Theo Lee's stewardship, there was plenty of entertainment in the evening from musicians, singers and would-be actors, who staged variety shows and concerts, as well as a high standard of plays.

Those who preferred a little intellectual stimulation gathered to discuss politics or contemporary history. Others created their own world, pretending to hold their meetings in a pub or some kind of imaginary environment that reminded them of home. 'So much was bizarre, fearful and uncomfortable by necessity that for intellectual escape — the only variety that was available in Changi — the prisoner strove to attain the virtues of everyday living,' journalist David Griffin would write in *Meanjin* magazine, nine years after the war. 'Each man created for himself a microcosm into which he could crawl: flowers, hobbies, poultry, painting, writing, what you will. And the most contented prisoner was he who could build the most perfect microcosm and disappear most effectively within it.'

Perfect microcosms would seem to be in keeping with a more cerebral diary writer like Dudley Boughton, but even Private Jimmy Houston wasn't immune. The following extract was written a few months into his stay:

> Sunday. Got up early. Had a shower and shave. Went to Mass and Holy Communion. Had breakfast at 9.15 a.m. No parade so the day is our own. Believe me, it's a beautiful day, just an idle one for doing a bit of washing. I had a few games of bridge, then went over to see the cricket match between the 20th and 2/10th Field Ambulance. The game was very dull but I had a good book. I returned to the cot and read 'til tea time. This being the first Sunday of May reminds me that it's Mother's Day. It's a beautiful night, one of those nights that one dreams about but very seldom see. It's beyond me to describe nights like these.

The feeling of lazy days merging into one is quite apparent in Jimmy's words, yet even by this point, the Japanese had made their first steps towards significant change for the Aussie POWs. Having previously imposed no control over the prisoners within the Changi area — it was only the Allied officers who restricted their movements, otherwise the men were free to roam over the whole of the 25-square-kilometre complex — barbed-wire boundaries surrounded Selarang, India and the other barracks from the second week of March.

Even before then, the Japanese had recognised the potential of POWs as slave labour. Working parties were formed within three weeks of the Australians' arrival and sent out west from Selarang on a daily basis to unload ships, clear debris and perform countless other tasks. Over the coming months, however, a number of alternative camps in and around the city would become available for the workers — including Great World, Lornie Road, Adam Road, Adam Park, Sime Road and River Valley. From the Japanese point of view, the change of location brought the workers closer to the labour sites and therefore increased productivity. For the Australians, the result of the relocations was twofold: on one hand, battalion unity was undone as hundreds of men could be away from Selarang at any one time; on the other, the diggers were delighted — it gave them a degree of freedom and the opportunity to purloin food and valuables along the way.

The first party to move out for an extended period left Changi on 21 March, when Major Carter led a group of around 280 to the Great World Amusement Centre on Singapore city's waterfront. Merv Alchin, and Don temporarily, were put to work on the wharves, where naval and cargo vessels were busy replenishing the Japanese war machine. Like the rest of the 2/20th, the brothers from Temora were keen to get out of camp and away from the restrictions imposed by their officers. An added incentive was that men on working parties received an extra 110 grams of meat, plus, if you were lucky you could scrounge some scraps from the Chinese, who were extraordinarily sympathetic to the POWs' plight. For many of the men, the real bonus was purely fiscal. Before long, with demand back at Changi severely outweighing supply, those fortunate enough to be assigned on work details at Great World and elsewhere would be doing a roaring trade in black-market goods.

The next significant departure of men from the battalion took place on 18 April, when Captain Frank Gaven and seventeen others from the 2/20th contributed to a mixed-unit de-mining party. First stop on the four-month trip was Mersing and Endau. Aside from the poignancy of being back there, it was a dangerous job for all concerned. While the sodden firing mechanisms had malfunctioned for Henry Dietz and a number of others back in January, an accidental detonation during Gaven's trip accounted for three Australians and a dozen locals. More chilling moments came with the discovery of corpses dating back to the hostilities. Of these, three bodies appeared to provide the final chapter in Merv Alchin's adventure story: they were found with their arms bound, buried in a hole close to the northern end of what remained of the Mersing bridge. These were almost certainly Captain Cope and the two diggers from the 2/19th who'd joined the party north of Endau. As Merv had anticipated, there was no way the Japs intended to keep them alive.

Lieutenant Colonel Robertson led the next big party out of the barracks, on 5 May. Along with 200 members of the 2/20th were men from the 2/18th and 2/19th battalions and 8th Division Signals; this was the nucleus of what would ultimately become C Force, bound for Japan, by the end of the year. Robertson's party was based at Lornie Road at first, north of the city, their accommodation consisting of a group of houses that had formerly served as quarters for RAF personnel. Not only was the camp more than agreeable to the men after Selarang's cramped conditions, but the nearby Chinese cemetery proved to be a perfect venue for black-market activities.

The men got down to clearing roads, shifting rubble and erecting fencing. At first there was little effort to keep them inside the camp boundary. Whenever they were off duty, the diggers would wander off to nearby villages and purchase food and beverages for themselves, including bottles of that serviceman's favourite — Tiger Beer. Jimmy Houston, who had a lifetime love for the bottle, recounts a typical day off at Lornie Road:

> The Japanese arrived at 10.30 a.m. and got straight to business. Shortly after eleven o'clock, counting was completed and the parade was dismissed. I went back to bed and slept 'til lunch was ready. In the afternoon I called for the 'guvnor' as the tonsils were dry. He was playing two up so I had a few bets and won a few dollars. Then we left and had our beano six bottles of Tiger each. I was in a cheery mood when I got back to the canteen.

Eventually the Japanese got wise to the lax routine after a few of the Aussies were caught outside the fence. Jimmy was just going over the wire himself when a muster parade was called.

> It appears that the Japs saw a few of our boys in the cemetery, went after them and caught two. All men not

working were marched down to the battalion to witness a public thrashing of the two men. It wasn't a very pleasant sight to see two of our own mates getting smashed across the face with a leather belt and getting the skin lifted from their shins through the application of the boot.
It left a very nasty taste in our mouths.

Later there were veiled threats of execution if any more men were caught outside. But after what they'd heard from the Alchins and others down at Great World about Jap guards decapitating Malayans suspected of theft (and leaving the heads on show for all to see), Robertson's men thought it wise to take the threats seriously. Suddenly the off-duty wanderings ceased and the supply of beer dried up.

By the end of July, they were ordered to move a short way west to the Adam Road camp, whose attap palm huts were quite a letdown after Lornie Road. Far from disappointing, though, was Jack Mudie's battalion concert party. To create an outdoor venue in which to perform, they cleared an area and built an amphitheatre, and even lighting facilities were erected. Jack and his fellow entertainers put on a great show for the men. One of the main performers was Private Wally Lewis, from Parramatta, whose musical talents would likewise be much appreciated at Naoetsu in the years to come.

The makeshift stage became so popular that working groups from other units, including the British, would use the amphitheatre to present their own shows. The Leicesters formed a jazz band, producing a set of instruments that were a marvel of ingenuity. The bass drum was made from an old fuel drum cut in half, with a length of canvas stretched across one end. A row of coconut shells added a little more percussion and half-a-dozen mouth organs did the rest. They called themselves 'Duke Beri Beri and His Boys', the name inspired by the disease that some of the POWs were beginning to develop as a result of vitamin deficiency.

Distractions from the realities of prison life were always welcome, but still the work went on. One group of men had already been sent on to Bukit Timah, just 10 kilometres to the west, which had been the scene of such fierce fighting in the closing days of the battle for Singapore. In true Shinto tradition, the Japanese wanted to build a shrine there in honour of their dead.

The massive job of felling trees in the area had been under way since April, but for John Cook and others, the task was to construct the monument itself, set within parkland beside MacRitchie Reservoir. 'The work at the shrine was very hard labour,' John recalls, 'such as mixing thousands of tons of concrete by hand to build a set of steps up the side of the hill. Each of these steps was about 25 feet long and about 2 to 3 feet wide. The rations were always in short supply, thus those words that were to be rued later on were uttered: "We can't be any worse off than we are here."' In all, the Australians would lay 121 of these steps, on the slope of what the Japanese had renamed Victory Hill.

Dudley Boughton, who was an accomplished carpenter, was also among those working on the Syonan Shinto Shrine and remembered it as 'a beautiful thing in glorious surroundings'. Plus, doing the work earned him a 5 cents a day bonus, which helped him buy cigarettes. A packet of twenty cost 20 cents. 'They were lousy to smoke and burnt your mouth — it was like smoking cabbage leaves,' he wrote in his diary. Javanese tobacco was a little better but smelt like hay; while English cigarettes, even some of the worst brands, were 'very good in contrast'. Dudley and his mates couldn't wait for their ration, which was handed out every ten days.

Amid the poor food and living conditions, occasionally there were glimpses of another, more civilised world. One day Boughton saw his first white woman in several months, accompanied by her husband and small child. They rode past on bicycles and wished the prisoners good afternoon. Who they were and where they came from was a mystery. Perhaps Scandinavians with a diplomatic passport, Dudley thought, before wondering how anyone could carry on an ordered family life in such a bleak and hostile environment.

Allied POWs were permitted to build a memorial to their own dead at this time, in the form of a simple cross, located behind the

Japanese shrine. For the Aussies, a further opportunity to honour their fallen comrades came in late August when Colonel Robertson led a burial party over to the north-west of the island. It was a chilling moment for all those present. Judging by the simple memorials to the enemy dead, Rod Richardson noted with pride, the 2/20th diggers had taken thousands of Japanese down with them in the D Company forward posts alone.

Such gestures of respect from their captors were much appreciated by the Australians, even if they were also surprised by them. It was all the more perplexing given that at this very time, across the island at Changi, things were beginning to get very nasty for prisoners of war under the Japanese.

※ ※ ※

Back at Selarang, the spirit of unity within the various Australian battalions and other units was gradually being eroded — which was exactly what senior officers had been concerned to avoid happening, of course. A combination of factors was responsible for this state of affairs, all of them outside the control of the prisoners left at Changi.

From their earliest days in captivity, news had leaked out of the Japanese intention to send working parties of POWs overseas. Sure enough, within ten days of Andrew Robertson's party leaving the barracks for Lornie Road in early May, some 3000 Australians under the nominal command of Brigadier Varley had been despatched to Mergui, in the south of Burma. While the Japs had simply told them they were being moved to a better locality with more food, what actually awaited them was years of backbreaking work, sickness and deprivation on the Burma–Thai Railway, Japan's bold venture to link its recently gained territories from Bangkok to Moulmein.

With the departure of this so-called A Force, the 22nd Brigade had lost two inspirational commanders in Arthur Varley and Charles Anderson; the 2/20th Battalion's contribution to A Force was relatively small, at sixty-eight men, but among these were a number of very popular characters — company COs Ronald Merrett and Arch Ewart, and other-rankers Joe Wilson and Hayden Webster. More recently, on 18 July, a similar-sized group had left the battalion with B Force, bound for Borneo.

Add to this siphoning off of personnel the long absences of the men on Singapore work parties, and each Australian unit was soon transformed into a series of fragmented groups. In the case of the 2/20th, for example, it's quite possible that the 200 members of the battalion in Robertson's mixed-unit party (not to mention the CO himself) were away from Selarang from early May until the start of September, when the Japanese shrine was completed — if they went back at all. By 20 May, when at the very least 300 personnel from their ranks were elsewhere, the 2/20th had been forced to abandon its block and bunk up instead with 27th Brigade units across the square.

Another consequence of the local work parties was the escalation in black-market trading as a wider range of items became available. It wasn't all bad, of course. Certainly, the men still looked out for their mates as before, as Harry Woods could testify. Frank Ramsbotham had made a point of looking out for his old classmates from the Liverpool officers' course, Harry and John Rowe, when he was on the prized Great World detail earlier in the year, while they were recovering from their wounds. Jimmy Houston, too, was on the receiving end of his friend Jack Redman's largesse — and would be in a position to repay the corporal from B Company further down the line. And there were many more examples of men sharing, giving away what they'd pilfered, if a mate needed it more. But still, the prevailing capitalist ethos among the majority, like the absence of much of the battalion, hardly help foster the idea that they were all in this together.

To beg, steal and borrow was now part of everyday life for most of the POWs. The arrival of the barbed wire back in March had fuelled the market for various stolen goods, food, medicine, clothing and anything else that was in short supply at Changi. In short: everything. Those who borrowed money were charged extortionate rates of interest, and everyday commodities soared in price. By

July 1943, a pound of cigarette tobacco would cost nearly $160, prompting the release of a camp order condemning the black market in goods and money. 'There can be no moral justification for charging such a harsh and unconscionable rate,' the order read, 'and those doing so are exploiting for their own profit the needs of their fellow prisoners due to sickness or misfortune.' Things weren't quite at that level in August '42, but then it was early days.

'Fair dinkum prison now,' Boughton would write scornfully in October. 'Some bastard has pinched my spoon and took my sugar the other day. Great fellows, some of the great AIF. I don't think it would be possible to get more scum in any body of men in the world than the AIF here, under these conditions. It's certainly every man for himself.' By his own admission, Dudley was upset at the lack of news from home when writing this, but the message was clear in his final sentence.

If there were shades of the market forces at play in the novel *King Rat* here, it was because the author James Clavell also spent time in Changi, having been captured along with other members of his Royal Artillery regiment. Clavell's fictional version of the camp may have been too extreme for some, but it pulled no punches. Like war, captivity also brought out the best and worst in men, and Changi was living proof of both.

And now things were getting worse. Until now, the prisoners had been left largely to their own devices by their captors, but the arrival of a dedicated team of Japanese prison officers late in August flagged a significant tightening of security. Four Allied prisoners had been recaptured after escaping from a camp at Bukit Timah and were currently being held in Singapore city. Two of them were Australians: Rod Breavington and Victor Gale, from the 2/19th Battalion. As a result of this breakout, the new prison commander, Major General Fukuye, requested that all the POWs at Selarang sign a statement swearing they would make no attempt to escape. Bar just three men, all the prisoners refused to sign it.

Fukuye responded by having the barracks' 17,000 prisoners (British POWs having arrived to replace those Australians who had already left Selarang) assemble on the central parade ground.

The date was 31 August, and for five days the men would sit it out in the heat with precious little water, and with sickness already rife among them. On 2 September, Fukuye tried using the execution of the escapees as a means to break the stalemate. The four men were executed by a party of Sikhs, with a group of senior Allied officers ordered to witness the shootings, but still the POWs refused to co-operate. Only when men began dying of dysentery — which, in the close confines they were all in, would have spread like wildfire — did their officers back down. With the pledge reworded so that Fukuye's request was formally acknowledged as an order, the men were instructed to sign the document.

The infamous Selarang Barracks Incident also fostered growing resentment towards the Sikh guards, who had crossed to the Japanese side and were now seen as traitors by the Allies. The Indians did nothing to improve relations by insisting that their captives salute them and show due respect. Those who failed to do so were beaten up.

While most troops tried to put on a brave face amid all the suffering, many were homesick and depressed. The *Syonan Press*, the locally produced Nippon propaganda sheet and one of the few links with the outside world, didn't help. The Japanese rag took great delight in reporting how American forces were having such a great time in Britain and Australia in Dudley Boughton's words: 'killing and raping women and generally making bastards of themselves'. As Dudley went on to note, such claims hardly put the men in a positive frame of mind.

Through a combination of word of mouth, Japanese propaganda, and a radio or two acquired at Great World, the Australians were kept surprisingly well informed of what was happening at home. It wasn't always encouraging, by any means — especially when it concerned the bombing of Darwin or Broome, shortly after they'd arrived at Changi — but it was better than not knowing at all. They even got to hear of the Japanese midget submarine attack in Sydney Harbour soon after it happened, on 31 May. The war's progress would be reported randomly and in snatches, depending on the source, and invariably in those early days the headline news would give little cause for comfort.

What they lacked was family contact and gossip from home that could tell them how their loved ones were doing. Dudley's diary entry for 1 October summed up the mood:

> Yet another month without news from home or anything at all to break the terrific strain both mentally and physically. Many conjectures as to the time we'll get out of this. Some bloody still hold to the belief that Christmas will see us out of this. Plenty for next year and the rest, anything up to 1947. For myself I can't see any chance of being free before 1944.

By the end of October the emotional pressure was taking its toll. 'Bloody near Christmas now. Am starting to get properly fed up with the terrific strains of being cooped up here with your mind at home all the time,' a clearly frustrated Dudley Boughton lamented. 'Can't possibly do anything about it, but wait and hope. Impossible to escape. Mosquitoes, if nothing else, would finish you off within a month.'

And if not the mozzies, then certainly Fukuye's team of prison guards. In the eight months since capitulation, morale had sunk to an all-time low. How would they cope with another year of this or worse?

The answer would lie in their ability to remain sane amid the madness. And strangely enough, it would take the brutal regimen of a slave camp like Naoetsu to restore the goodwill and esprit de corps that had marked the Australian units prior to capture. It was as if the diggers needed a clear-cut enemy again — what else were they doing in the army? Until then, they would attempt to gain comfort from the familiar, steadying their nerves and boosting their spirits by holding competitions or performing simple acts of kindness.

No Australian could ignore the first Tuesday in November: Melbourne Cup Day. And so on 3 November, the boys staged their own version in the prison camp. Instead of horses, they bet on frogs at 10 cents a wager. Prizes were $2, $1 and 50 cents, with all the profits being donated to the English children interned in Singapore. It was to be their Christmas treat.

An altogether different Christmas was in store for the men under Andrew Robertson's command, who had now moved on to the Adam Park camp. From the middle of November, the rumour mill had gone into overdrive regarding the Japs' plans for them. In the midst of this uncertainty, Cas Cook's twenty-fifth birthday came and went. For a man who'd rarely left the familiar surroundings of Penrith, New South Wales, before enlisting, his birthday wish for the next year didn't involve another trip into the unknown.

Towards the end of the month, with no details having been given regarding their destination, they knew from the weight of their new uniforms that it wouldn't be a tropical climate. Most of them guessed that they were heading for Japan, though. A few days before their departure, every man received a medical examination, which included a glass rod pushed up the rectum. This provided much mirth among the Aussies and their guards.

※ ※ ※

On 29 November 1942, 550 Australians under the command of Lieutenant Colonel Andrew Robertson of the 2/20th Battalion boarded the Japanese cargo and passenger ship *Kamakura Maru* at Sembawang. The 17,000-tonne vessel was the pride of the Japanese merchant fleet and before the war had sailed regularly between Tokyo and the United States. As well as the Australian contingent, there were about 1400 Dutch, American and British POWs and a number of Japanese civilians who were being repatriated from Western countries. The 2/20th Battalion made up a large portion of the Aussies, but those men from other units on board, such as the 2/18th and 2/19th, were becoming increasingly familiar faces after all the months together on the Singapore work details. While Don Alchin had old mates and new around him now, there was at least one important name that didn't make it onto Colonel Robertson's nominal roll. Fate had again decreed that he and Merv should go their separate ways. Don's elder brother would leave Singapore four months after him, bound for Thailand and the infamous railway. Merv would also be sent to Japan as slave labour after a spell on the Burma–Thai train track, but it would be nearly three years before they were reunited.

While approaching the vessel by barge, the first batch of men were struck by the ceremonial appearance of the Japanese soldiers on deck. Each had a white cotton sling over his shoulder, and in each sling was a small white square box. All of them stood to attention with their arms raised in salute. Later it was learnt that Japanese diplomats repatriated from Australia had been welcomed aboard the ship. It was also rumoured that the boxes contained the ashes of the Japanese sailors who had died in the midget submarine attack in Sydney Harbour in May.

The *Kamakura Maru*'s destination was Nagasaki, on the 'home island' of Kyushu, which entailed a potentially dangerous zig-zag crossing through the South and East China seas. Many Japanese vessels were later bombed or torpedoed as they made their way back to their home ports, carrying prisoners from the Philippines, Singapore and other Japanese-occupied territories. It is estimated that more than 10,000 POWs lost their lives in such circumstances, many of the ships sunk by British and US aircraft whose pilots were unaware of their human cargo. Fortunately for those on board the *Kamakura Maru*, in late 1942 the US Navy was still recovering from Pearl Harbor, while the British had enough on their hands in Europe, the Atlantic and the Middle East, thus allowing the POWs a safe voyage.

It usually took just over a week to sail from Singapore to Japan. Although the ship was overcrowded, most of the Aussies took over the aft end of B deck, stripped off and basked under the tropical sun. 'It was a luxury cruise ship before the war, but we didn't get too much luxury,' Mick McAuliffe recalled. 'We slept out in the open and it was a fairly pleasant trip until the weather deteriorated.'

Snowy Collins remembers it differently. 'It was very uncomfortable and we only got one meagre army meal a day — watery rice, I think it was. As for the toilet, that was a couple of poles sticking out over the side. You had to hang on for dear life.'

Hard as it was to believe, given the size of the boat, these were the only facilities available to the Australians. It seems everyone had a similar opinion when it came to the ship's dunny. 'If you wanted to go to the toilet you had to climb onto a plank over the side,' Henry Dietz agrees. 'If you fell off, it was too bad.' To John Cook, the best description came from a Yankee POW named Tex who, after climbing over the guard rail from the toilet, exclaimed, 'Well, I've ridden some of the wildest horses in Texas in my lifetime, but none of them come up to riding that there shithouse!'

Many of the POWs welcomed the enforced idleness of shipboard life, but the guards didn't share the relaxed mood. Some were decidedly nervous, including one guard who would lash out for no apparent reason. Men who did not bow low enough to passing NCOs also received a vicious forearm jab to the face.

Apart from random acts of violence and the precariously placed toilet facilities, the first part of the voyage proved fairly uneventful. It was only when they got further north and left the tropical temperatures behind them that the pattern changed.

By 4 December the weather had turned so bad that the men were forced to seek whatever shelter they could find from the bitingly cold winds and ocean spray. Confined to the outdoor deck as they were, there was little to keep them from the elements.

Harry Julian and his mates in Signals seemed to have the answer. They found some space in a large open area at the stern, but it soon filled up. 'We were all there crammed together, lying down and wondering what would happen to us. There must have been more than 500 of us, and at night we'd shelter under the roof, which stretched over the stern.'

Buffeted by heavy seas, the ship was tossed around and many of those on board became seasick. At first they'd welcomed the small twice-daily meals of rice and stew, such as it was, but by day five nobody had much of an appetite.

'We were packed in like sardines,' Jack Mudie remembers of the voyage, from its midpoint onwards. 'And every night we watched the Southern Cross behind us drop lower in the sky.' Familiar stars had always offered some comfort to Jack. If he could see the Southern Cross he felt at home. Perhaps Neno, his sweetheart from Queanbeyan, might be watching at the same time, he consoled himself: somewhere under a New South Wales night, far from the war and uncertainty of life as a POW.

No doubt a similar picture was filling Theo Lee's mind as he thought of Joy and the burst of stellar activity lit up by the harbour lights in Cremorne. These were the sorts of fantasies that kept men going as they lay on the windswept deck of the *Kamakura Maru*, blissfully unaware of the hellhole they were heading for.

Having grown up under the big skies of Lismore, Signalman Harry was no stranger to the magic of the Southern Cross either. But it was things on-deck that held his attention right now. 'One night I had to get out quick to go to the toilet and there were so many people in the way, they had to pass me over their heads,' he recalls. 'Eventually I came face to face with a Jap standing there with a machine gun, and there was an aeroplane strapped to the deck as well. I've no idea why it was there, because it couldn't have taken off. But I clearly remember it.'

Apparently nobody would be able to forget the gents' on this ship. Typically sharp, Joe Byrne's recollection adds a bit more detail: 'You'd have to go up some stairs and across the upper deck if you wanted to go to the toilet.' And, in line with Harry's recollection, that meant having to pass some guards who were in front of a fixed Bren gun (which had been appropriated from the British in Singapore). The weapon gave Joe and some of his mates the kernel of an idea.

It was obvious to the Aussies that the Allied troops on board the ship outnumbered the Japanese. Sure, below decks there were quite a few Japs accommodated in cabins, as well as the crew. But the guards, although heavily armed, appeared to be few in number. Overpower the guards and the *Kamakura Maru* could be theirs, surely. Once they were in control, they would turn east into the Pacific and steam towards the United States, maintaining radio silence all the way until they were close to friendly waters. It wasn't such a bad idea. Didn't fortune favour the brave? A couple of stoushers like George Daldry and Herb Lamb would certainly have been game.

The idea was to storm the gun emplacement on the stern when the guards weren't looking and open fire when they retaliated. Kevin Timbs, whose knowledge of firearms was extensive, was just the man for the job. Or so his leaders reckoned. A colonel who was in on the plot told him: 'We're going to take this ship and you've been nominated to get that gun. There are two of our officers down on the next deck who reckon they can win control of the ship, if you can take the gun and knock out those guards.'

Suddenly 23-year-old Kevin Brendan Timbs from Glen Innes was going to be their saviour. Kevin took a deep breath, considered the request for all of two seconds, and replied, 'All right, I'll have a go at it.'

What a military triumph if it worked. It would be one of the greatest escapes of World War II. On the other hand, if it failed, they'd probably all end up on the sharp side of a sword ... Not that it was the thought of death or failure that finally got the better of Timbs. Rather, it was a question that none of them knew the answer to: was the bloody weapon loaded? The magazine was clipped to the top of the Bren gun, but it was impossible to see whether the clip was full or empty.

'If the machine gun didn't have any ammunition, I'd be a goner,' Kevin explains. 'I'd have only a few seconds to gain the advantage anyway, but if it wasn't loaded, the Japs would cut me down, and probably all those round me.'

That was the way that another of the senior officers saw it also, which finally put paid to the plot. Even if the plan had worked, they were probably being shadowed by Japanese submarines, which would have sunk or crippled the *Kamakura Maru* rather than allow it to get away.

There would be many hair-brained schemes like this in the months and years ahead, as idle minds hatched ever more complicated and potentially suicidal plots. Desperate times called for desperate measures and the men of the 2/20th would shortly learn what sheer desperation really meant. If they'd known what they were facing when they arrived in Japan, the plot to wrest control of the *Kamakura Maru* might have been viewed as a risk worth taking.

※ ※ ※

After nearly nine days at sea, the ship finally reached Nagasaki. It was late on 7 December and the weather was bitingly cold. By Singapore and even Sydney standards, it was freezing. The Aussies weren't used to such icy winds, and although some of them had been given heavy uniforms to wear, others were still in their tropical gear. This was early winter in the northern hemisphere — far lower temperatures were to come in the new year.

Of the 550 Australians who had set sail on the *Kamakura Maru*, 300 were now selected and separated from the others; their destination was to be a little-known town about halfway up the west coast of Japan called Naoetsu. Within units such as the 2/18th and 2/20th battalions and 8th Division Signals, it seems the cut-off point for inclusion in the group was decided purely on an alphabetical basis — anyone at the rank of private or signalman whose surname began with the letter A through to S stayed with Robertson and a large group of officers and NCOs. Those privates or signalmen whose surname fell between T and Z, together with all the 2/19th men, it appears, would be sent with another group of more senior personnel to work in a shipyard at Kobe.

After disembarking the following morning, the Naoetsu group assembled in the railway station and caught their first glimpse of Japanese society. As they walked up and down the long platform to improve their circulation, some of the men saw a group of women appear from a house on the other side of the railway line carrying three live chickens. The birds, which were presumably part of that evening's supper, were killed in a most inhumane manner. Instead of wringing their necks, the three women stamped the chickens to death, completing their mission with such gusto they burst out laughing. The Aussies didn't see the joke. Their teeth were still chattering, especially the men still in their tropical gear. Eventually someone took pity on these blokes and issued them with fur-collared greatcoats made from hessian.

During the afternoon, a row broke out between Colonel Robertson and a Japanese interpreter, a private named Kuriyama. 'Line up these men so that they can be counted,' the private ordered. Robertson, presumably wishing to assert his authority, declined. 'I don't take orders from privates. If there are any orders for me, get an officer to give them to me,' he barked. None of the Australians who witnessed the incident could have realised it at the time, but the exchange did not bode well for the commander of C Force.

A few hours later a train drew in and the 300 men climbed aboard and took their seats. The atmosphere was surprisingly cosy. Even the heating was on. There were seventy-two POWs per carriage and Japanese guards with fixed bayonets stood at either end to prevent escape.

Joe Byrne, the St Kilda-born blacksmith turned Sydney paravaner, was only twenty-two and had always felt invincible, but he was apprehensive when he stepped aboard the carriage. 'Now, I'm Irish and at my age you had a hell of a lot of confidence in yourself — most of it unfounded,' he admits. 'But we were going into the unknown. We didn't know what would happen to us, so it was an unnerving experience.'

After the train pulled out of Nagasaki, the window blinds were ordered down as the POWs headed north, passing through militarily sensitive areas. But the guards seemed friendly enough now, and even the food was tasty. That night, they crossed the strait over to the island of Honshu, grateful to be warm and away from the icy sea breeze for the first time in close to a fortnight.

The next morning they were allowed to raise the blinds for a while to take on supplies, so allowing the Australians to obtain their first long look at enemy terrain. Several of the men were surprised at how familiar some of the scenes looked. At first glance, Tokuyama seemed like Bathurst. And there were other stations — with names such as Hasirana and Nissi Wakuni — that could have been designed by the New South Wales state rail authority, they reckoned.

It was only the thatch-roofed houses set against the rice fields and the distant, snow-capped mountains that shattered the illusion. As well as the smiling Japanese faces that greeted them on the platform at every station.

Smiling Japanese faces? Quite inexplicably, the diggers were being welcomed with a degree of respect that none of them had anticipated.

John Cook was stunned by the reception as they pulled in to one platform. 'There stood a long line of Japanese women all dressed in white Red Cross uniforms and with the Red Cross insignia on their white caps. Each woman was standing with head bowed and hands clasped in front of her. When the train stopped, these women supplied each man with a small cardboard box containing a large rice ball, some dried fish and pickles. Most men will agree that this was the only civilised incident that happened to them during their three-year stay in Japan.'

Even the guards in the carriages became quite sociable, treating the men with a level of courtesy that had so far seemed foreign to the enemy forces. Dudley Boughton was impressed. 'The Jap guards on the train were very fine types and very friendly and decent to us, helping us any time they could,' he wrote. 'They could quite easily have been the reverse, as so often we've experienced. They even pleaded with us not to sleep on the floor and when we did they simply smiled and stepped over us.'

A particularly touching moment came at Kanazawa, when two Japanese officers saluted them on the platform as they drew in. Dudley was obviously deeply moved.

> I'll never forget that place. There were half-a-dozen old ladies who ran themselves to a standstill running up and down the platform with tea. Then the whistle went and they all lined up and bowed, the officers saluted and even the station porters stood to attention. One of the Japanese guards who spoke English explained that they felt sorry for us and this was their way of showing it.

They were towards the end of their journey now, from Nagasaki up to the central west coast of Japan. It would be more than two-and-a-half years before most of those who had arrived on the *Kamakura Maru* that December morning would leave Japan. Sixty would die. The rest would endure a level of suffering that would seem impossible to survive by today's standards.

These boys — all volunteers, mostly wide-eyed country kids — had left their homes and joined up for the Second AIF, eager to get out and see the big wide world. Though this was one journey they hadn't bargained for.

PART II

CHAPTER 6

WELCOME TO HELL

It took more than two full days for the POW train to snake its way through the hills and valleys of southern Japan via Hiroshima, Nagoya and finally Naoetsu, a small industrial town some 320 kilometres north-west of Tokyo. Today the final stage of the journey is much the same. Gazing out of the window, the men of the 2/20th and the other units that now comprised C Force would have passed through tiny villages surrounded by rice fields and wide-open plains until reaching the outskirts of the town that was to be their home until mid 1945.

The carriages weaved their way past the Shin-Etsu Chemical Company factory on the right and Nippon Stainless Steel's plant, on the same side but closer to the Sekigawa River. More than six decades later, both industrial complexes are still there, although the steel factory is now called Sumitomo Metals.

The two plants were major local employers during the war years and played an important role in the Japanese economy. The chemical factory produced silicon, as well as carbon electrodes for use in factory furnaces. Nippon Stainless relied on scrap metal for much of its production and made steel for the Japanese war machine. Both factories faced manpower shortages, however, because so many locals were away at war. This was why the Australians were needed — to keep the massive furnaces going in the two plants and perform all manner of other strenuous tasks.

The train pulled into Naoetsu station on the night of 10–11 December. Outside in the snow, there were trucks waiting to transport them to the first of their new homes, an old schoolhouse. Once there, to everyone's surprise, they found that the interior of this unremarkable-looking building had been converted into squad rooms. There were twenty-five men per room and each man had a bed space with seven blankets to protect him from the bitter winds that battered this coastal community every winter. Vladivostock was only 370 kilometres away, on the opposite side of the Sea of Japan.

Neatly laid out on the floor for each POW was a hessian work uniform, a pair of sandshoes, mess gear and a straw mat for sleeping on, measuring 2 feet by 6 feet — about 0.6 by 1.8 metres. There was no actual bed. While the rooms were basic, the Australians were too tired to worry about creature comforts by the time they got to sleep, just before daybreak.

They were woken by bugle at 6.30 am and had roll call an hour later. It was at this point that everyone was given a number to sew onto their jackets, starting with number 1 for Lieutenant Colonel Robertson and then through the officers, NCOs and other ranks, in a roughly alphabetical order. Breakfast followed at 8 am, but not before each man was asked to call out his number — in Japanese. There was inevitable confusion as the wrong sounds came out, prompting much amusement among the Aussies and irritation from the Japs, but at least the numbering system brought a sense of order to the camp.

From 1 through to 300, these prisoner numbers would identify the POWs in the eyes of the Japanese, much as the volunteers had been defined in army circles by their service numbers ever since enlistment. Following Robertson's top ranking came six captains, reflecting the various mix of units that made up C Force. Alex 'Sandy' Barrett and Jim Chisholm originated from the 2/18th Battalion, while Cecil Gibbings, Jack Hepburn and Albert Yates represented the 2/20th. It was Hepburn who had replaced Gibbings as C Company's commanding officer back in February, at Seramban, only for the Dorrigo solicitor to fall ill himself the very same day. Yates was a school teacher and another Glen Innes man, born and bred; he'd also turned his talents to fixing the wiring at Selarang soon after the battalion's arrival there. In between these two subgroups from the infantry battalions, at number 4, came Captain Robert Chown, the highest ranking of some forty signallers in C Force.

There were half-a-dozen lieutenants on the Naoetsu nominal roll. Of these, Jack Mudie, Theo Lee, Harry Woods and Roger Cornforth were all well known to the diggers in the 2/20th and most likely the other units also, due to the various composite groups assembled during the fighting for Singapore. But Alan Campbell's inclusion represented something of an oddity. While there were a few Queenslanders among the 300 men in C Force, Brisbane-born Campbell was one of only two members of the 2/26th Battalion here. He'd been training as a church minister before joining up; like Captain Sandy Barrett, the Australians' chief medical officer at Naoetsu, Campbell would find his prewar experience of some use over the next few years.

The 2/20th monopolised the POW numbers allocated to warrant officers, 14 through to 20. Of these, Scotsmen Bill Lothian and George Gray, and Martin Chapman, a Geordie, had all been the subject of much ribbing back in the pages of *Thumbs Up* and *Zero Two Nought*. Like fellow WOs Keith Ainsworth and Dale Williams, the three British-born diggers had excelled on the sports field for the battalion. They'd be needing a different set of skills now, though.

Prisoner-of-war number 21, Staff Sergeant Herbert Lamb from Waverley, led the first of the non-com categories. Among a host of sergeants, corporals and lance-corporals from the 2/20th Battalion were Kevin Timbs and Bluey Firth, at 36 and 46 respectively.

Numbers 71 to 300 were allocated to the foot sloggers, the privates and signalmen. Within the ranks of these 200-plus diggers, age and length of military service meant nothing — 39-year-old Jimmy Houston drawing 189 while another 22nd Brigade original, Harry Julian, hung number 212 on the front of his jacket — men were simply allotted numbers according to the position of their surname in the alphabetical order. Eric Richardson of the 2/18th was another one, way down the order as POW 287. It was the very same criterion that had determined whether they'd come here or not, of course.

Of the second-wave volunteers, the August '41 arrivals, Don Alchin wore number 73, Cas Cook 128 and Henry Dietz 144. As for Don Fraser and Mick McAuliffe, they'd hardly had time to memorise their Australian service numbers before being shipped off to war. Now, having been transported to another strange land, Don was POW 164, and Mick POW 251.

From 11 December onwards, the Australians' POW numbers determined where they ate, worked and slept — even when they slept, when it came to allocations for night shifts. All the work parties were created from the numerical system, which meant that everyone kept to the same group, worked in the same place and slept alongside each other in the same rooms for the duration of their stay. This then was Naoetsu, Camp 4-B. Or, to label it properly: Tokyo POW Camp, Branch 4, Naoetsu Niigata.

※ ※ ※

Naoetsu was one of the oldest cities in the region. There had been a commercial harbour there for more than 1000 years. It also had a reputation for producing the best rice in the country. Such historical and economic data was of little concern to the POWs, who were still coming to terms with the prospect of losing their freedom indefinitely.

In the first few days they did little more than smoke, eat and play cards in between medical inspections and filling in various forms. They could light a cigarette in the corridors of the former schoolhouse, but not in their rooms. Bizarrely, the men were also asked to pose for photographs, individually, during these early days, each man's POW number clearly visible on the square patches sewn onto the left breast pocket of his army jacket. Even the Jap tucker seemed tasty and plentiful, the POWs receiving two good meals a day, comprising rice and a bowl of thick soup with onions. Some of the men were given new pigskin boots to wear, and there were hot baths for those who wanted to clean up and thaw out. Cigarettes could be purchased, and tooth powder, not unlike Australia's famous Calverts brand, sold for the equivalent of 10 cents a tin.

Before their arrival at Naoetsu, the men had been assured that they were going to a holiday camp. While none of them had believed it then, the conditions in their new quarters were much more tolerable than they'd expected. As Dudley Boughton, POW number 80, admitted:

> To date it's like a holiday resort here, except for the cold and of course the confinement. But the views from the windows of the little boys and countless people going to work, as well as the surf on one side and snow on the other, are all novel and highly interesting to us.
>
> The meals are grand to what we are used to. In fact we've had more varieties of food here in one week than I have had altogether since February. The Japs are all really fine fellows, as are all the Japs here in appearance and treatment of us. They seem to be only too pleased to do anything for us which is quite the reverse to Singapore and especially the boat.

Just how badly Dudley had misread the situation was soon to be made graphically apparent. For the moment, the Japanese were keen to make life as agreeable as possible for their new charges — and it seemed to be having the desired effect. So far they had not been told about their work, and although the camp was cold and sparsely furnished, most of the men could put up with such discomforts. They even started to learn the language, to ease the boredom of prison routine. This false sense of security continued as the men in C Force became familiar with their surroundings and got to know the men who were to guard them. It did not take long before the facade was shattered.

The civilian guards would turn out to be the worst — 'the most vicious and sadistic of all the guards', in the words of POW 120,

Private John Cook. Some were ex-soldiers who had seen service in China in '37, and most were locals. To describe them as violent would be an understatement. Until recently they had been traders, shopkeepers and skilled craftsmen, family men who were well respected in their community. Now they were transformed into evil brutes whose sole intent was to impose suffering on their captives.

'Each was issued with a stick which they carried at all times,' John continued. 'They were probably told that the men were enemies of the Emperor and were to be treated as such.' The sticks became synonymous with these particular Japanese; Naoetsu's civilian guards were known as 'the Dog Wallopers', in reference to the long, thick wooden clubs they would use to bludgeon anybody who drew their wrath. During their years at Naoetsu, just about every man in the camp was smacked around the head by the dog wallopers. And not just a light crack, but several heavy blows to the face and skull.

The Dog Wallopers' nicknames read like the cast from some bizarre wartime comedy show. But there was nothing funny about the way they went about their duties. There was Yanagizawa (Gummy), Sekihara (Fish Face), Akiyama (Horse Head), Uishiki (Whisky), Obinata (Boofhead), Nakamiya (Baby Face) and Susuki (Hoppy). Others were variously referred to as Silent, Mental, Yellow Peril and Pluto.

Above the civilians were the serving soldiers who, apart from normal guard duty at the camp, would soon accompany parties to and from work. They included Sergeant Shibano (the Bull), Sergeant Aoki (the Faith Healer), Private Kuriyama (Snake Eyes), Private Katayama (the Cat) and Private Taguchi (the Germ).

The first hint of what these characters were capable of came on 18 December, a week into C Force's incarceration, when the men were first split up into work parties. Following reveille at 5.30 am, they were made to do fifteen minutes of physical training on the parade ground, which was covered in slush from the overnight snow showers. After about ten minutes of push-ups, an order came for 'all the weak men' to stand up. Those who remained on the ground were then dismissed, but anyone who'd dared to admit to their lack

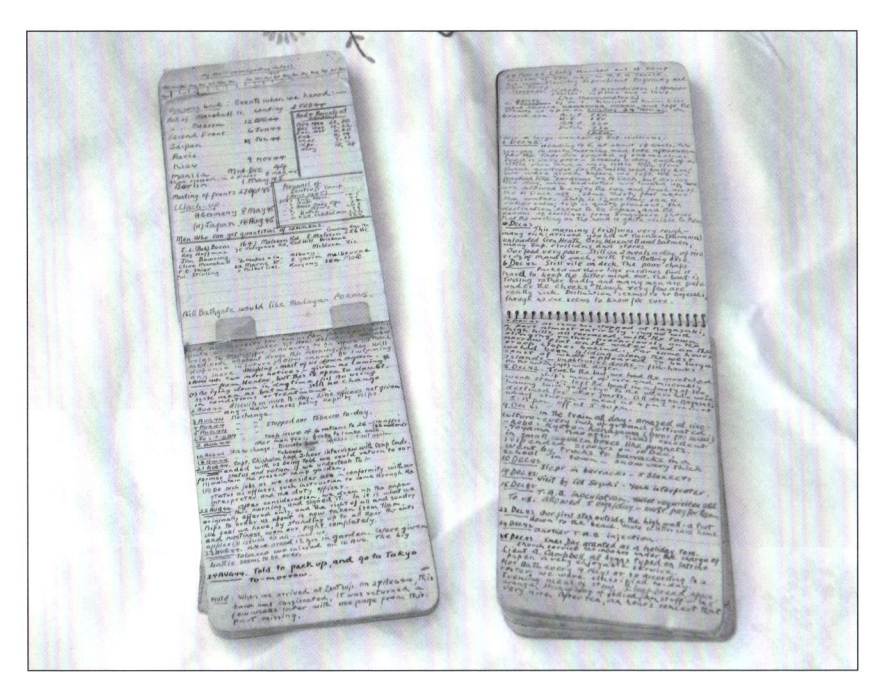

Tiny notebooks, little more than the size of a cigarette packet, which Jack Mudie used to write his diary of life in Camp 4-B.

Don Alchin (left) and brother Merv were separated for much of the war. Merv's heroic escape from the Japanese was to enter 2/20th Battalion folklore.

RIGHT: Private Dudley Boughton asked his best friend to keep his diary safe, shortly before he died in Naoetsu aged twenty-nine. Norman Reed kept his promise and handed over the moving account of life as a POW to Dudley's family after the war.

LEFT: Henry Dietz swapped a sheep farm in country NSW for the tumult of war in the space of a few months. He could never figure out his captors: 'I could no more go back to Naoetsu than fly,' he remarked in later years.

RIGHT: Glasgow-born Jimmy Houston was thirty-seven when he joined the 2/20th. Older and wiser than his young mates, his maturity enabled him to write one of the most detailed POW diaries of the war.

LEFT: Snowy Collins reckoned his hard childhood helped him to survive the war. 'Only the boys who'd already done it tough came through it well,' he claimed.

LEFT: Kevin Timbs. A mix-up over similar names led to him being reported dead. Later, he refused to accept an invitation to the opening ceremony of the Naoetsu peace park. 'I couldn't forgive them,' he said of his captors.

RIGHT: Mick McAuliffe grew up on a dairy farm in northern NSW. His loss of freedom as a POW hit him hard. 'Imprisonment was the worst thing. It wasn't so much the physical suffering but the mental torment,' he recalled.

LEFT: Captain Sandy Barrett asked a fellow officer to take a scribbled note to his wife Joan, in case he didn't make it. Barrett's medical experience saved many lives at Naoetsu, but the Australian military never saw fit to award him for his extraordinary efforts.

RIGHT: Louis Zamperini inspecting the damage after he crash-landed, following a raid on Nauru. Ever the survivor, he took 600 bullet holes in his aircraft.

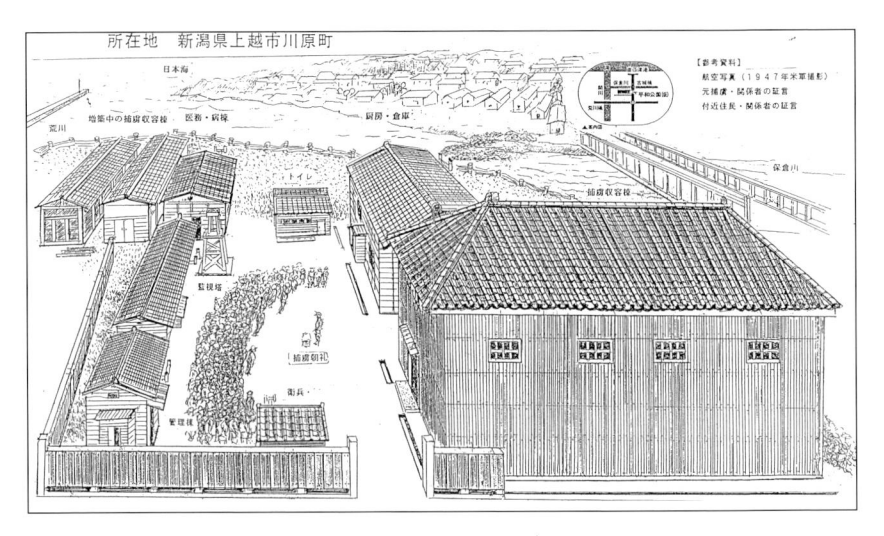

A sketch of the camp looking towards the main entrance. Inside to the right was the two-storey building where the men slept. To the left was a single-storey barracks occupied by the guards. At the far end of the walled compound stood the kitchen, which adjoined the latrine.

Copy of a sketch drawn by Private Colin Nicol of the row of terraced houses seen through his prison window.

Australian and American POWs and their guards pose during a camp concert towards the end of the war. Top left: Camp commandant Lieutenant Oota and Sergeant Aoki. Sitting left to right: Louis Zamperini, Private Kono, unknown, and Sergeant Shibano, also known as the Bull.

The camp parade on Christmas Day, 1944. Lieutenant Alan Campbell conducts the ceremony in front of his men and several Japanese guards. Standing in front left to right are Private Kono, a storeman, Sergeant Shibano, and Lieutenant Oota (far right). Theo Lee stands just behind Oota.

The remains of the cookhouse at Camp 4-B. It stood there until the 1980s.

Tokuon-Zan Kakushin-ji, the Buddhist temple where the local priest allowed the caskets of the dead men's ashes to be stored, after the Japanese guards threatened to throw them on the local rubbish dump.

Downtown Naoetsu as it is today.

The entrance to the Shin-Etsu Chemical Company, which produced silicon as well as carbon electrodes for use in factory furnaces during World War II. It was where three of the camp's most sadistic guards were based. More than six decades later, the plant is still operational.

A statue of a koala stands at the entrance to the Naoetsu peace park museum, which was founded with the help of the Australian–Japanese Friendship Society.

The Naoetsu peace park. The twin angels with eucalyptus and cherry blossom leaves in their hair were erected on the site of Camp 4-B as a gesture of friendship between Australia and Japan. The base is paved with bricks made from Australian clay.

of physical fitness was made to do another ten minutes of push-ups. As a result, they missed breakfast.

It was a salutary lesson: never complain or admit to weakness, otherwise you'll be treated even worse. Such was the measure of Japanese logic.

The first work parties moved off that day at 7 am, after the obligatory bow to the Emperor. One hundred and fifty men were sent to the Nippon Stainless Steel plant, where half of them were divided into squads to make up the factory's outdoor work party. The jobs for these unlucky men included breaking up the slag and scrap iron, loading it into skips and then transporting the skips to the foundry along a railway line. It was backbreaking work, in freezing wind and rain.

The other Stainless workers were employed in the foundry, where they were made to load the furnaces with the contents from the skips. The temperature might have been warmer but the conditions were equally exacting. Sweat poured from their bodies, which still had to be heavily clothed, to protect them from the scorching heat of the flames. To add to the problems of both the inside and outside working parties, they were under the constant supervision of the civilian guards, who weren't shy in delivering a bashing to anybody seen to be slackening off.

It was much the same story at the Shin-Etsu chemical factory, where three of the camp's most sadistic guards were based. The worst outside job there was having to carry large rocks to a designated area, before smashing them with sledgehammers. It was one of the most arduous forms of slave labour and, as at Stainless, there was no shelter from the fierce winter weather that usually lasted from December until March. Not only that, but it wasn't as if the POWs had any previous experience in the art of crushing quartz or the other minerals necessary for manufacturing carbide metal silicon. Sergeant John Puddephatt, of the 2/20th's C Company, was one of the very first victims of the guards' cruelty that day. His series of humiliating slaps across the face was delivered by Gummy, one of the civilians, who was forced to perch on a large rock so as to be able to reach up to the big man from Dover Heights in Sydney.

For the indoor work party at Shin-Etsu, the real endurance test was the carbon section, where the electrodes were manufactured. They were 3 metres long and the carbon dust that was needed to fill the moulds had to be shovelled in by hand. It was a filthy job, and it was impossible to stop the dust from entering almost every bodily orifice. After a few weeks in the carbon section, the men would be positively negroid in appearance. The dust that discoloured their skin was almost impossible to remove in the limited washing facilities available in camp, although occasionally the men got to have a communal bath at the end of their shift, in the drain close to the furnaces. One of the few advantages of working in the carbon section was the lack of supervision. The guards hated the dust as much as the men.

But there was one task harder, and that was furnace work. This involved shovelling a mixture of quartz and coke into the flames for ten hours a day. There were six furnaces — four producing carbide and two silicon — which could only operate efficiently at a white-hot 1204 degrees Celsius. To cope with the searing temperatures, the men had to wear heavy protective coats with hoods, and a pair of thick mittens. Dark goggles had to be worn and a towel wrapped around the face. No bare flesh could be exposed to the intense heat without the risk of burns and blisters.

Just wearing the protective clothing was exhausting enough. Lifting the quartz and coke into the furnace as well required superhuman strength. In recognition of the arduous nature of the job, each man was allowed to take a thirty-minute break after every half-hour of shovelling, at which point another worker would take over.

'As soon as we were relieved we would go to the rest room and consume great amounts of water to replace the liquids that we'd lost,' John Cook recalled of that first day. 'To illustrate just how severe this work was on the body, when the protective coats the prisoners were wearing dried out, there would be streaks of white salt visible on the back of them which had come from our sweat.' Dehydration was a serious problem and the loss of salt soon led to a condition that became known as 'the burning pisses'. John explained: 'Men would scream in agony as they tried to do a pee and only a couple of drops would come out.'

All of the jobs at the Shin-Etsu furnaces were physically demanding — mercilessly so — and the crushing of the quartz was no exception. Here, the rocks had to be unloaded from railway trucks beneath the furnaces. As always, the guards were quick to pick on any man who didn't appear to be pulling his weight.

Added to these various tasks at the factories, squads were sent out on coal duty to the harbour or by the riverside, to replenish the stocks of fuel needed to power the furnaces. Being right by the water, this work was another painful chore during the winter months, but at least it broke the monotony to some extent. Other than that, the only respite for the squads making up the Nippon Stainless and Shin-Etsu work parties would be the occasional shift to kitchen, sick-room or other camp-based duties.

In the first day or two, many of the guards were jumpy. Most of them had never seen a European face and were convinced that some of the prisoners would try to escape. This initial period of apprehension would pass quickly enough for the Japanese. Then they'd be walloping the POWs purely for the fun of it in most cases.

The 280-odd Australians marched back wearily to the camp that first day. Once there, they were made to form up on the parade ground and await the Japanese commander's address. 'Today at factory you all work very hard,' Lieutenant Shicata acknowledged, before barking: 'But tomorrow you must work harder!'

The Naoetsu boys couldn't believe what they were hearing.

※ ※ ※

Gradually the men became accustomed to the daily routine, even if the escalating violence shocked them to the core. Already the Aussies had learnt that it was best to take their punishment like a man, and that meant standing throughout the beating. Those who fell down would be kicked all over the head and body, sometimes by as many as three guards at the same time. Before long during that first week at work, anyone in the Shin-Etsu 'rock gang' who

Gummy and his colleagues felt wasn't putting their back into it would be summoned over and given a belting with the dog walloper. Likewise those in the outdoor work party at Stainless. In the furnace areas at both factories, the only difference was that the Japanese might have been slightly reluctant to administer a walloping there and then, due to the dangerous and unpleasant conditions so close to the foundries and, in Shin-Etsu's case, the much-loathed carbon section.

To George Daldry (POW 142), the carbon section was the worst job in the world. And he only spent a day there, filling in for someone who was sick. 'I was told if I didn't go there I'd be shot.' He didn't need any more persuading. 'You couldn't see more than a few feet in front of you because of all the dust. Fortunately the other bloke came good, because I wouldn't have survived another day.'

A trained blacksmith, Joe Byrne (prisoner number 98) had been welding paravanes a couple of years before this. Now he'd have the misfortune to be a Shin-Etsu furnace worker for most of his time at Naoetsu. Someone always got clobbered on the shift, he remembers. 'Not always the same person — although sometimes the guards would work on the same person each shift until he could take it no longer. They were a pretty vicious mob.'

Joe can still remember the dog-walloping stick in vivid detail. 'It was 3 feet 6 inches long and one-and-a-half inches wide,' he states without hesitation — about a metre in length, and 4 centimetres across. 'It was rounded hard wood and they used it like a baseball bat. They'd break arms, legs, ribs and anything else they could take a poke at. They just beat the hell out of you. You were always at the whim of the guards, which meant they could clobber you for no reason at all.' Those men in the rock-crushing party noted how the guards' clubs were the same size as the handles of the large sledgehammers used for smashing the rocks.

Powerless to defend themselves, all that could be done in this regard was for squad leaders to report the increasingly numerous incidents of guards abusing prisoners to Colonel Robertson, who would attempt to take the matter up with the camp commander.

Confined to camp, he and the other commissioned officers were not permitted to accompany the men out to the worksites; instead, Warrant Officers Lothian, Gray, Chapman, Ainsworth and others, as well as senior NCOs such as Herb Lamb, would lead the various work details.

Those who were on day shift would rise at 5.30 am, attend roll call, do their exercises, eat breakfast and brace themselves for the march to work. In winter the work parties had to dodge deep puddles of ice and slush as they made their way through the narrow streets, their feet and hands made numb by the sub-zero temperature. Once night shifts were introduced to allow for maximum capacity from the factories, these winter marches became a treacherous ordeal — one wrong step in the darkness could see a man tumbling on a bank of snow and sent crashing down to the lower ground beside the road.

It took around thirty minutes to reach Shin-Etsu, about half that to Stainless, and once inside they were given their instructions and warnings for the day. No talking to Japanese workers. No furtive glances at the women they saw. And don't forget to bow to the sun before singing the national anthem.

Come lunchtime, with the steel plant being so close to the converted schoolhouse, the men in the Stainless work party were marched back to camp for a hot meal. Those employed at the Shin-Etsu factory were less fortunate. By the time their food arrived on a two-wheeled cart pulled by a couple of the prisoners, the vegetable soup of boiled barley was usually cold.

After completing their ten-hour shift at the factory or plant and marching back to camp, there was no time for rest. Instead, they'd be made to line up on the parade ground and listen to the camp commander's words of wisdom. Before being dismissed, there would be random searches, just in case anyone had secreted stolen food or any other illegal item on their person.

If water supplies were low, a group of men would be ordered to take the water cart to a well a few kilometres outside the camp. Up to fifteen prisoners would be detailed for this job, which involved filling several wooden casks and pulling the cart (now much heavier, of course) back to camp. And all this after a full day's work in the furnaces or outside with the sledgehammer smashing up rocks.

Before being able to retire for the night, there was an 8 pm roll call. Every man had to stand to attention in front of his rolled-up sleeping mat, with his fingers stretched down his sides and his thumb in line with the seam of the trousers. This position had to be held without movement for the entire roll call. Any slight twitch of the hand, eyes or shoulders would be reported by the guards, who would patrol the squad rooms, and the whole procedure would have to start again.

This nightly event would vary in duration from fifteen minutes to a couple of hours, depending on the sadistic nature of the Japanese duty officer or orderly sergeant. A good roll call was when the orderly sergeant arrived and was told the number of men present, sick or on other duties. If everything added up, the sergeant would move on to the next room; eventually everyone would be dismissed, allowing the POWs a little free time before lights out. (In reality, most fell asleep long before then.)

A bad roll call was when the orderly decided to amuse himself at the men's expense. On these occasions each man had his gear inspected, and if anything was out of place, the whole squad would be required to stand to attention until well after the roll call. Sometimes the unlucky offender would be made to stand outside in the corridor for a few hours. Each time a member of the Japanese camp staff walked by, the prisoner would get a smack across the face.

The worst of all roll calls happened every second Tuesday on average. The orderly sergeant would be accompanied by one of the civilian guards, Susuki (Hoppy). As well as his normal duties, he was the part-time camp quartermaster whose job it was to carry out kit inspections. Susuki was renowned for his sadistic nature and the fortnightly kit inspection offered great potential for satisfying his violent streak. If anything was damaged or missing, the man responsible would be severely belted, while the others had to stand perfectly still and keep silent. Any man caught so much as moving a finger would be similarly bashed. Sometimes they'd have to stand motionless for two hours or more, depriving the POWs of much-needed sleep.

Come the next morning, when the torturous cycle started all over again, even getting out of the schoolhouse doors to the parade ground could be painful. Invariably the last few men would be belted across the head and face by whoever was on early morning guard duty. Usually that job fell to Private Kuriyama. Snake Eyes seized every opportunity to wield his dog walloper. The desire to be first out of the door created a bottleneck, much to the delight of Snake Eyes, who would descend on those at the back with vicious glee.

'You had only a few minutes to get up, make your bed and get out on the parade ground,' Snowy Collins explains — POW 129 to the Naoetsu guards. 'We were on the first floor and there was only one exit. There was just one stairway about 5 feet [1.5 metres] wide with a narrow door at the end, and 200 men were all trying to get through at the same time. It was a hell of a jam and there'd be a Dog Walloper each side with a big bamboo pole to lay into you. I'm only a little bloke, so I used to go for my life.' The civilian guards were always happy to help out.

The men were becoming human punching bags and there seemed to be no escape from the daily round of physical abuse. What's more, the guards were enjoying it. Attacking men who couldn't fight back proved to be a source of considerable amusement to the Japanese, but it was taking a heavy toll on the POWs' nerves.

As December went on, the weather had worsened and the men who worked outside were issued with what they called 'emu coats' — straw jackets that had a back but no front. They kept you dry as long as you were bent over breaking or shovelling rocks, but were useless when you stood up. Apparently the Japanese designers had not considered the possibility of slave labourers wanting to stand. Straw boots were also issued but did not last long in the wet and freezing conditions. And the headgear, a sloppy hat that measured 45 centimetres across, was always blowing off in the wind.

Coming from a warm, sunny country, the Australians were not used to cold weather and complained bitterly about the winter temperatures. Chilblains on their feet and hands were a frequent source of discomfort. Camp doctor Sandy Barrett's advice was to wash their hands in urine and wipe it on the swollen areas. Surprisingly, it seemed to work.

Given their gruelling workload and poor living conditions, it wasn't long before the men's health deteriorated further. Some suffered relapses of malaria, while others went down with bronchial pneumonia. It was not a good sign. Ten months in captivity had already weakened them. The poor diet, the hard labour and now bad weather were taking their toll and their resistance was low.

'Felt very queer today,' Signalman Don Fraser recorded in his diary. 'Too weak to lift an empty shovel really. Food less than half of what we need. Little bit of horse in the stew but only as big as a sixpence. It was an old horse at that, but lovely to chew.'

By late December, the Japanese had taken the decision to give diaries to the men. The logic behind this was not clear. Most of the entries referred to the health of inmates and the quality of the food, perhaps as a result of which the Japs decided they needed to be recalled and censored.

Some of the POWs hung on to their diaries for most if not all of their incarceration, secreting the written account of their hellish existence in special hiding places. It is thanks to their courage and determination to keep such a detailed record of life in Naoetsu that it's possible to produce a comprehensive picture of what they went through.

The diaries provide the trivial details that underscore the monotony and madness of the POWs' daily routine. And often, certainly in the case of Fraser, with great flair and wit. Death and suffering were all about them, yet it was the little things that helped them to survive, as Jimmy Houston observed on 18 December: 'Marched off straight to the works [at Stainless] and told we weren't to talk to or wink at the girls on the way. Tut, tut. As if we'd do anything like that.'

For Dudley Boughton, it was the illness and lack of food that overshadowed Christmas 1942. 'Another chap carried home tonight which brings it up to five in a row,' the Manly carpenter recorded.

'One had pleurisy and several have bronchitis. We're so terribly hungry it hurts. The Japs have said there'll be no plum puddings for Christmas and they've even taken back the aluminium mess dishes they gave us on arrival. Presumably they're needed for aeroplanes.'

To take their minds off their plight, the men were given lettercards for delivery to their families back home. Would they ever get them? It seemed unlikely, but it helped to lift the prisoners' spirits for a moment. The printed sheets were already half completed and merely required the sender to fill in the blank spaces.

> Dear….
> I am well and safe in Japan. My health is excellent. I have had no news from family since … How are you and the family especially … getting along? Remember me to … Love …

If only the printed sentiments were true. Dudley must have been near to tears on Christmas Eve as he completed the letter and then turned to his own diary to reveal the truth:

> My thoughts have been on home and what might have been. One minute I'm thinking of Molly [Mary Boughton, Dudley's wife] and the other about how much (or little) rice we will get with the next meal. We are all hungry, all day. The minute quantities of meat turned out to be whale, but it was great. Personally I wouldn't care if it was dog or cat. Arthur gave me a few smokes for Christmas and has promised to buy me a cigar and a pint for next Christmas. (We hope.) Never have felt more like a cockatoo in a cage than today. Don't think I will hang up my stocking. (I've only got one pair and someone may pinch them.)

Christmas Day 1942 was wet and cold, but at least it was a holiday. Some of the men attended a church service but others were too tired or sick to get out of bed. The highlight was a meal that surpassed their expectations. It included a mandarin, preserved fruit, half a loaf of bread, an apple and a little pork stew. Most agreed that it was their best meal for at least a year.

Jimmy Houston reckoned they owed it all to Lieutenant Colonel Robertson. 'But for our Colonel, I think we would have all been working,' he wrote. 'The Commanding Officer gave each man a packet of cigarettes and with our evening meal the Japs gave each man an apple, orange and a piece of jelly.'

In the evening they held a concert. It's amazing how prison life can bring so many disparate musical talents together. There was much singing in the camp that night and even the guards entered into the spirit of the occasion. At the end of the performance they sang the Australian national anthem. Even the Japanese stood to attention and removed their caps. This was the 2/20th's first Christmas in captivity — how strange and unbelievable it all was.

※ ※ ※

The next few weeks blurred into one as the winter weather became ever more severe and the prisoners' physical condition continued to weaken. Only those who kept a diary were able to separate one day from another. Just two days after the joyful Christmas concert, Dudley Boughton summed up his feelings thus:

> The worst day of my life. Everything's a study in white, apart from us who are a study in blue. Couldn't feel my feet all afternoon and coming home the string on my mess bag cut my fingers so I couldn't straighten them out. Socks, boots and sandshoes are wringing wet. Inside temperature 30F, so Christ only knows how cold it is outside. Bob Farley very sick now and six more cracked up today.

Like Boughton and Eric Richardson, Private Robert Farley was one of the June 1940 originals in the 2/18th Battalion. The young Brisbane-born digger would feature in a number of POW diaries and ultimately end up being an unfortunate star of the Naoetsu story.

During those final days of 1942, very occasionally there was something to live for. Men seized on good news with childlike enthusiasm, especially the prospect of better food. Finally on New Year's Eve, as the men returned from tipping crucibles of red-hot carbon and smashing the contents with sledgehammers, word got out that each POW was to receive a Red Cross parcel. For those who couldn't remember the last time they'd eaten a pie or crunched a biscuit or tasted chocolate, the anticipation was unbearable. They were not disappointed. Among the contents of each box was a steak and kidney pie, half a pound of liver paste, tins of tomatoes, bacon, margarine and treacle, a quarter pound block of chocolate, an apple pudding and a bar of soap. Their eyes were transfixed by the contents, each man savouring the thought of consuming such a feast.

Dudley reached in and took out a biscuit, a slice of cheese, a piece of chocolate and a pudding for his tea. 'For the first time in nearly a year I feel good. One is too happy to be unhappy as it were. Everyone has had a good hot bath and a good feed.' It was a dramatic change from his mood just four days before.

Throughout the first weeks of January, the snow continued to fall, the work increased and the health of the men worsened. Everybody seemed to have a hacking cough or diarrhoea. While the seriously ill were sometimes allowed to stay in camp — depending on the verdict of the medical orderly, Sergeant Aoki — many of the sick preferred to toil away in the plants, partly because of the better rations working parties enjoyed. It was also warmer inside the factories, although the discipline remained the same.

As in the 2/20th, there was a fair quota of New South Wales country boys in C Force: Henry Dietz, Cas Cook, Mick McAuliffe and the others were all used to the challenges provided by the harsh elements. And unsurprisingly, it was the men who'd previously worked outside on hard physical jobs who coped best with the hardship at first. Those who'd been office workers back in Australia, on the other hand, found the going much tougher.

Don Alchin was used to working in the great outdoors back home in southern New South Wales. And regardless of how he felt, he preferred to keep himself occupied. 'I always took the view that it was better to work. I wasn't frightened of hard work — I was born to it,' says Don of his attitude to the hard labour at Naoetsu. 'Even so, I copped a few hidings. See that scar behind my leg? ... That came from a pick handle. They didn't need much of a reason to hit you.'

Harry Julian was another one used to the outdoor life, in his case up in the north of the state, at Lismore. One day in mid January, Harry was among a party of men ordered to fetch water from the well outside camp. On the way there, the guard accompanying them appeared to lose his direction. 'One of the chaps tried to tell him,' Harry remembers, 'and as we were a lot bigger than them, I think the guard thought we were going to beat him up.'

Other guards arrived, likewise thinking that the POWs were trying to overpower their escort. Bayonets and rifle butts were used to maintain order, and in the melee another signalman, Doug Alexander from inner-west Sydney, was stabbed in the shoulder. The sight of blood calmed everyone down and the water party continued on its way. Signalman Alexander was allowed to return to camp, where his wounds were dressed.

In Sandy Barrett's makeshift hospital, a bayonet wound was one of the easier cases awaiting his attention at this time. There was just so little medicine to give to the sick and diseased, a situation made all the worse by Sergeant Aoki's habit of commandeering what few medical supplies were available via the Red Cross. Men relied on their own strength and determination to get better. In the first few months of 1943 the POWs at Naoetsu still had some fat on their bodies and most were healthy enough to fight disease. But even the fit and muscular were finding it hard to fend off illness.

Kevin Timbs went down with a bout of pneumonia and could hardly raise himself from his bed. There was no sympathy from the guards, who ordered: 'Him go to work tomorrow.' It was Kevin's mates who saved him. They got him out of bed and made him walk with two men supporting him. 'The next morning I went out with one each side of me, holding me up, because my legs just wouldn't work. Eventually I got over it, but that's the sort of thing that happened.'

Life was doubly difficult in the snow, which was almost 2 metres deep in places. Wheeled transportation was useless in these conditions, and pathways had to be cleared for sledges to get through. At the Nippon Stainless plant, workers had to shovel huge quantities of snow just to find the scrap iron for the furnaces.

Thoughout that first winter, gangs of men toiled in atrocious conditions, clearing snow from roads and railway lines, which were inevitably covered in fresh falls by the next morning. It was heartbreaking and exhausting work. Only those who worked in the cookhouse, where they could squirrel away some extra food when nobody was looking, remained reasonably healthy.

Jack Mudie came from Gilgandra originally, and had a tough farming background, but like fellow officers Harry Woods and Theo Lee, he also enjoyed certain benefits. For a start they didn't have to march to the factories every day, although all officers were made to do work around the camp. This privilege did not upset the lower ranks who, throughout their time at Naoetsu, remained extremely loyal to those above them. Unlike earlier attitudes in Singapore, the men were oddly unquestioning about the military class system. Maybe that was because the men had that common enemy again, something they'd been missing, ironically, when relations with their captors had been civil.

Maybe it was also because the Australian officers looked after the interests of their men, and were sometimes punished for doing so. While the officers did not have to go to work outside the camp, they were still subject to a vigorous physical routine, especially once a new camp commander had arrived during January to replace Shicata. The new regime under Lieutenant Oota signalled a noticeable stepping up in the hardship of all the prisoners. For Colonel Robertson and the others, this included the introduction of an 8-kilometre jog each morning. Sergeant Shibano, who looked after the day-to-day administration of the camp, and Private Kuriyama took particular satisfaction in putting the officers through their paces. In some respects, the combination of this running and the strenuous tasks they performed around the camp was as tiring as a full day's work in the factory, given that officers and men received the same small rations.

Even during the first week of March, with spring having barely arrived, the unsanitary conditions were attracting the flies. With a few cases of beri-beri already detected, the men were soon wearing face masks around the camp.

Among those who were getting steadily weaker was Andrew Robertson. The colonel had had a row with Kuriyama on the platform at Nagasaki railway station some months earlier, and there was good reason to believe that the Japanese private had been keen ever since to exact revenge. If this was payback time, it was certainly working.

By the end of March, the demands that Snake Eyes had placed on Robertson had reduced the head of C Force to a physical wreck. One day he collapsed and had to be admitted to a military hospital outside the camp. Lieutenant Colonel Robertson was critically ill with spinal meningitis.

Fearing an outbreak of the virus, Jack, Harry, Theo and the other officers were placed in isolation on 29 March, and the Japanese suspended all work at the factories in order to clean the camp and stop the disease spreading. That night the roll call was unusually quick and quiet. The next morning, everyone was sprayed with disinfectant from head to foot and quarantined for the next five days.

※ ※ ※

On Thursday 31 March 1943, Andrew Esmond Robertson died, the first member of the battalion to succumb to the inhuman treatment meted out by the Japanese since their arrival. The 46-year-old former accountant from Willoughby left behind a wife and two children.

Of all people, it was Private Kuriyama who made the official announcement in the squad rooms the next morning. The news shocked the camp more than any other event since the outbreak of war. The colonel was a much-loved and highly respected commanding officer, who had often stood up to his captors in defence of his men. Now their leader, the man who wore number 1 on his uniform, was the first prisoner to pass away at Naoetsu.

'The CO breathed his last at 5.40 p.m.,' Dudley Boughton lamented. 'The boys here are just about dumbfounded to put it mildly. We can't seem to realise it. He was very popular and it was the saddest thing that's happened since our POW days started.' Another, unknown diary writer wrote: 'This has been a very black week for us and most of the men will remember it for many a long day after this war is over.'

Lieutenant Colonel Robertson was cremated soon afterwards. His body was taken to the crematorium several kilometres away by motorcycle and sidecar. In common with Japanese tradition, the ashes were removed from the fire by three sets of chopsticks, which were handed to Captain Jim Chisholm, Captain Sandy Barrett and Lieutenant Alan Campbell, the 2/26th man who in civilian life had trained to be a church minister. The ashes were placed in a box for the Red Cross to take away and return to Australia.

A memorial service was held that evening, a bugle player sounded the Last Post, and black crepe was placed around the camp by the Japanese as a symbol of mourning. All the officers seemed to agree that the Japanese doctors on this occasion had done everything possible to save the commanding officer, but to no avail. It was a dark day for the men in C Force, and especially for those from the 2/20th. But there would be many more like it.

CHAPTER 7

DEATH, DIARRHOEA AND DOG WALLOPERS

While Andrew Robertson's death left everyone in C Force deeply dejected, their new commanding officer soon proved a worthy successor. Suave and moustachioed, James Walter Strickland Chisholm came from a farming family near Glen Innes and had a commanding presence. He had been seconded to the Johore Military Volunteer Force during the Malayan Campaign but returned to lead the 2/18th's D Company in the crazed fighting around Ama Keng. Captain Chisholm was well known to the 2/20th diggers also, having been part of Robertson's composite Y Battalion at Holland Road. He was a popular man, in other words, well before he began showing his mettle against the tyrannical Japanese at Camp 4-B. Together with Captain Sandy Barrett — whose medical studies at the University of Sydney were to prove crucial to the care and survival of so many men — Chisholm would help restore morale at a time when the future looked hopelessly bleak. As for Sandy, although he had little time for malingerers, his tact in dealing with the men under his command added considerably to the efficiency of the unit.

At least the weather was beginning to improve by the end of March. The snow had practically disappeared now, which made it easier to get to and from work, but the daily grind continued all the same. To make matters worse, in fact, the men were soon transferred to temporary accommodation in the nearby village of Arita, which turned out to be even more uncomfortable than the first camp.

The Australians moved into their new quarters on 2 April 1943, and although they had another move six months later, they would stay in Arita until their liberation, nearly two-and-a-half years hence. For much of this time they occupied a large, two-storey warehouse made from galvanised iron that had previously been used for storing salt. Its barred windows reminded the men of their status in this windswept outpost of Japan's home islands, as if a reminder was needed. Divided into squad rooms with concrete floors, the building had no heating and little in the way of washing facilities. Wind and rain would penetrate the large cracks in the flimsy corrugated-iron walls, turning the interior into an ice box during winter and an oven in the summer. Depending on the time of year, there were swarms of insects, including flies, fleas, lice and mosquitoes, to keep the prisoners company. While the relocation was no doubt intended to address the concerns regarding a possible outbreak of spinal meningitis, such conditions were never going to be conducive to maintaining a healthy workforce for the Japanese.

The walled compound had only one entrance where a guard stood on sentry duty to monitor arrivals and departures. Inside and to the right of the gatehouse was the two-storey building where the men slept. To the left was a single-storey barracks occupied by the guards. And at the far end of the compound stood the kitchen which adjoined the latrine. (No wonder the hygiene left a lot to be desired.)

Included within the walled compound was a separate guardhouse, the inside of which a number of unfortunate POWs would come to know intimately. Guardhouse punishment would be meted out at will to the prisoners here, the highest level ('severe') amounting to a death sentence for the hapless offender. The other camp facilities — mess area/assembly hall, sick room, latrines and washing area, officers' quarters, cookhouse, storeroom and administration offices — were all housed inside the compound. POW diaries also make mention of a pen that was home to two pigs.

The transfer to a different site also signalled the introduction of an even stricter and more brutal regimen. While ostensibly in charge of the place, Lieutenant Oota increasingly left much of the day-to-day running of the camp to his underlings. It meant that at night the Australians were at the mercy of orderly sergeants and their fellow psychopaths, whose reign of terror in the camp knew no limits.

'There were some real bastards among those guards,' Don Alchin confirms. 'The worst one was a medical orderly named Sergeant Aoki — the Faith Healer. Then there was his mate Sergeant Shibano — the Bull. He was about 6 feet and 23 stone and would strike you across the back with a rod of split bamboo. My, it was painful.'

Some days a man might find himself left alone, free of the abuse, but once a fortnight the guards would hit the saki and decide to have a bit of fun. 'You'd be lucky if you went a week without a clobbering,' says Snowy Collins. 'If they didn't like the look of you, they'd just lay into yer. I remember a bloke called Keith Burling, who was about 6 feet tall. One day he was mucking around and put his hands around one of the guard's shoulders. Well, did they give him a beating — they broke his jaw.'

Like Kevin Timbs, Jimmy Houston and many others in C Force, Private Burling was a big bloke and could certainly take care of himself, under normal circumstances. Along with his brother James, the youngster from Lakemba had provided formidable defence on the soccer pitch for the 2/20th, but a level playing field was never a consideration at Naoetsu.

'They thought they were superior, and they'd belt the Christ out of you,' Don explains. 'Yet you couldn't fight back — they'd shoot you.' It was true: the Japanese warrior code allowed for full honours for their enemies who died on the battlefield, but a prisoner of war was beneath contempt.

Often the men were punished for seemingly trivial accidents. If they broke a mess bowl they were made to stand outside in the cold, at attention, holding the broken pieces at arm's length; this cruel and petty treatment might go on for anything up to six hours.

Even random scribblings could unleash the guards' full fury. And unless someone owned up, the entire camp would be punished. One day the Japs discovered a message on the wall of the latrine. It read: *Chin up — be free in June.* Rather than see collective punishment inflicted on everybody, and even though he hadn't done it, Wally Lewis confessed to the crime. Justice was swift. Two of the Japanese camp staff, Privates Katayama (the Cat) and Kuriyama (Snake Eyes, again), marched him into the guardhouse and dog-walloped him to within an inch of his life. Barely conscious, he was made to stand to attention in the bitterly cold corridor for five hours.

Back at the Christmas Day concert, Private Lewis's irreverent performance had delighted his fellow Aussies, as always, but less so the prison guards. The 22-year-old from Parramatta had become a popular target from then on, with Katayama and Kuriyama in particular setting on him for no reason. There is little doubt that the regular beatings he would receive over the next twelve months contributed to his eventual death in January 1944.

Jack Mudie might have been an officer but it didn't stop him getting bashed. 'Most of the guards were quite sadistic,' he says. 'It didn't take long before it became quite clear to us that under Japanese army rule any soldier had the power to inflict physical punishment on those below him. A two-star private could belt the daylights out of a one-star private, and he in turn could do the same to us. If he didn't like the way we stood or spoke he'd lay into us, and we'd just have to live with it.'

One one occasion, Mudie had several of his teeth broken off when he was hit in the mouth, leading to frequent bouts of pain. There was no dentist in the camp to attend to his damaged jaw and every night, he admits, he cried himself to sleep from the constant toothache. Albert Yates also found that the pips on his epaulettes were no barrier for the camp guards; Jack Hepburn too, for having the temerity to quote the stipulations regarding international prisoners of war set out in the Geneva Convention.

And a misdemeanour by one man could impact on the entire camp. 'Right from the beginning, it was made very clear to us that if anything went wrong, everyone would be punished,' Jack continues.

'If someone stole some food, everybody would be punished. So you had to be very careful. You didn't do anything that would get your mates into trouble.' Most of the men got the message, but not all.

※ ※ ※

The following account of POW life from April 1943 to the end of August that year is partly drawn from the diaries of Jimmy Houston, Dudley Boughton and the recollections of a number of other former prisoners. Together, these members of C Force provide a graphic picture of a five-month period at Naoetsu that would set the template for what was to follow.

2 APRIL 1943

A Thursday, and extremely cold despite it being spring. 'While waiting for roll call I put my coat over my feet to try to get them warm,' Houston recalled. 'When it was time for roll call I left the coat on the bed — for that crime I get a couple of punches to the chin.' Boughton also remembered the beating: 'All had to bash one another on roll call because some bloody fool left their beds and gear untidy.'

The guards were keen to assert their authority again today, and quick to lash out for perceived misdemeanours. Most of the men were desperate for a smoke and there was much trading to satisfy their craving. One bloke sold his bread ration for six cigarettes. Captain Chisholm reminded them that food was 'their ticket home'. If they didn't eat properly they would die, he warned. The advice fell on deaf ears in the coming months, sadly, as the tobacco addicts continued to swap their paltry rations for a fag.

6 APRIL

A consignment of bully beef arrived from South Africa. 'It's not issued yet, but it's bloody good just to look at it,' admitted Boughton. 'Trouble is I've got diarrhoea now — think it's the water here.' By now a number of men were developing beri-beri, the result of thiamine deficiency. It's a particularly unpleasant condition associated with a poor diet. Victims suffer swollen limbs, shortness of breath, sore leg muscles and cramp, numbness of the toes and a burning sensation in the feet. Faces become bloated and it is difficult to walk and breathe.

7 APRIL

An almighty explosion in one of the furnaces at Shin-Etsu, though the cause is unclear. The furnaces were deserted by the Japs in a few seconds, Boughton noted; fearing an air raid, they ran for their lives, leaving the POWs to clear up the mess. There was talk of sabotage, but nobody could prove it.

8 APRIL

More men were suffering from diarrhoea, possibly the result of the slightly improved rations, or more likely the lack of hygiene. There was very little water in the camp at Arita and no chance of a bath. The men were so filthy that they cut off their hair, according to Boughton. With token washing facilities and no soap, it was the only way to keep their heads clean.

9 APRIL

Spring finally seemed to have arrived. 'Ideal days, the weather's grand,' reported Jimmy Houston. The Red Cross also managed to deliver more bully beef, as well as dried fruit and breakfast cereal. Nothing to satisfy the mind, though. The men were desperate for news from home, but the only papers they were given were heavily censored.

11 APRIL

Camp life was beginning to take its toll. 'There was a bit of trouble — one young chap has gone a bit queer, stealing everything about the place,' Houston revealed. 'His latest stunt is to burst a case of bully beef and take four tins. When the officers searched his pack they found a lot of stuff that had been reported missing.'

This caused a moral dilemma. If he was handed over to the Japanese he would be severely punished; on the other hand, he was one of their own and needed to be looked after. In the end, the officers decided to report him to the guards, a decision that upset Jimmy: 'This means that all he gets in the way of food is a few spoonfuls of rice and a glass of salt water to drink. What a night.' Reduced rations was just one of the deprivations.

The thief received twenty days of heavy guardhouse duty. In the current, warmer spring temperatures, there was a chance he'd survive at least. Clearly, the culprit was not thinking rationally. At night he tried to escape when taken to the latrine; later on, he was caught climbing out of the open window of the guardhouse. The Japanese were lenient with him, thankfully. Others would not be so fortunate.

24 APRIL, GOOD FRIDAY

A new squad of guards arrived in camp, and appeared to be more violent than the others. One of them punched Wally Hayson in the face for no reason whatsoever, recalled Houston. Private Wallace Hayson was another 2/20th original, from Woollahra in Sydney, close to Jimmy and George Daldry's home suburb of Darlinghurst.

Houston also recounted a drama that upset the men. Captain Chisholm informed the guards that three more cans of bully beef (courtesy of the Red Cross) had gone missing, a situation that prompted another mass appearance on the parade ground. No one would own up to the theft, so the men were kept there until midnight. And all this after a ten-hour day at work. Those who arrived back after the night shift suffered the same treatment — being made to stand for four-and-a-half hours after a fifteen-hour shift in the foundry. And still no one confessed. As the commanding officer, and therefore the one responsible for keeping the men in order, Chisholm was only following instructions in reporting the theft. But there were some among the 2/20th who questioned his judgement.

A year ago today, the men had been enjoying the fruits of the newly operational field bakery at Selarang. No hot cross buns in Easter 1943, however, and not for a while yet either.

26 APRIL, EASTER SUNDAY AND ANZAC DAY

Those not working in the furnaces were given a day off. A church parade was planned for the morning and a concert in the evening. But just in case anyone thought the Japs were going easy on them, Dudley Boughton reported that several of the men were bashed for going to the toilet before early morning roll call.

27 APRIL

The bully-beef thief was exposed and forced to stand outside on a raised platform for everyone to see. There was little sympathy for what Dudley Boughton described as 'this mongrel bastard', whose actions caused 280 men to stand out on the parade ground for several hours on Saturday and miss their tea and breakfast. The guards had suspected the culprit for a couple of days and got a confession out of the man after dragging him over to the guardhouse. As Jimmy Houston pointed out, if he'd had the courage to admit it earlier, four honest men would have escaped a bashing, including one who was badly hit in the face.

Like any institution there were a few bad apples. While most of the men kept their noses clean, there were some who were habitual thieves. John Cook's neighbour in the squad room was always getting everybody else into trouble.

'Once I got the blame for something he'd done, but I just couldn't dob him in so I had to cop it,' John said. 'He'd pinched some Jap's dinner out of the factory and word got around that the thief was from our section. Kevin Timbs came up and said, "Someone's got to take the blame for this", so I said it was me. I got belted across the face with a shoe and made to stand for hours. If you got caught thieving in camp you got taken around every squad room, forced to drop your pants and belted across the backside. By the end, your arse would be red raw.'

As the days and weeks went by, the guards devised ever more imaginative schemes to punish and humiliate their prisoners. It was one night in May that Jack Mudie suffered his worst beating, and all over something he didn't do. 'The guards just wanted some amusement and reckoned some of the men hadn't placed their shoes straight,' he remembered. 'I was one of those pulled out on the parade ground and made to crawl around on my hands and knees while I was hit by the dog wallopers. They carried on like this until we collapsed. I think I was very near death that night.'

On such occasions Jim Chisholm urged the men to be philosophical and not hit back. It was hard to accept, but it was the only way — 'Otherwise we'd have been killed,' says Mudie. 'Everyone heeded Chisholm's advice, and I'll say this for the men, they were all extremely loyal. I'm still amazed at their fidelity and their sense of brotherhood and loyalty to each other. I've nothing but the highest praise for them.'

It was no wonder that the condition of some of the prisoners had plummeted to an all-time low, with dozens of cases of pneumonia, diarrhoea and beri-beri being reported at this point. And still the work intensified. Now there were night shifts too.

From April 1943 parties of men were rostered to work in the furnaces at both factories from 5 pm to 7 am. Once a week when the night-shift workers completed their roster, they had to carry on working until midday — a staggering nineteen hours on duty. Meanwhile, those on the day shift would leave the camp at 11.30 am on changeover day and work from 12 noon to 7 am the next morning. This shift pattern continued for the rest of the war, with some men working more than 100 days without a break. It was a cruel and inhuman practice, and it took a heavy toll on the POWs.

Despite the long and demanding hours, some of the men preferred to do the night shift because it kept them away from the camp at a time when the guards were often at their worst. The factories also provided the prisoners with two rice balls, which proved another strong incentive.

Food was at a premium and the lack of it was causing great concern, and not just within the camp. There were reports of long queues outside the shops in town as well. But the starvation diet combined with hard physical labour was turning many of the men into emaciated versions of their original selves. Dudley Boughton was losing half a kilo a day and was down to 64 kilograms. Already the CO had died, and it wouldn't be long before the demands of Japanese prison life would claim further victims.

27 MAY

Dudley Boughton: 'George Beale died at 1.30 p.m. today from injuries received at work. We only had 20 minutes to go of a 24 hour shift and his leg got caught in a conveyor and was pulled up into a chute. A great tragedy. He was very popular.' Private Beale, from Gunnedah, near Tamworth, was Naoetsu's second fatality. The 38-year-old had joined up in June 1941, on the same day as his brother Fred, another member of the 2/20th and now C Force. Unlike the Daldrys, Alchins and Burlings, the two Beale brothers had made it this far together, only for George to be taken so needlessly.

It happened at one of the furnaces at Shin-Etsu. The conveyor was an endless belt with small buckets attached and a 1.2-metre gap at the bottom. As George was climbing down a ladder, he mistakenly placed one of his feet into an empty bucket, which immediately pulled him up into the machine. The Japanese foreman lurched forward and grabbed his shoulders to prevent him from disappearing into the contraption, while shouting for someone to turn the motor off. Frustratingly, none of the men knew where the switch was, because it was the first time they'd worked there, but eventually one of the Japanese employees found the lever to stop the belt. Several minutes later, George, who was screaming in agony, was extricated. But by then the damage was done. Blood pouring from his leg and stomach suggested he was in a very bad way. At the military hospital, medics staunched the blood flow but the surgery was basic, to say the least. Doctors resorted to a length of silver wire to help mend his broken pelvis. Such was the agony that George lost consciousness.

The accident deeply upset Jimmy Houston. 'Dreadful news,' he wrote. 'One of the chaps was so seriously hurt at work that he died soon after being admitted to hospital. His condition was so weak owing to the lack of decent food that he couldn't put up a fight. Word came through to the camp that they wanted men for a blood transfusion but before the truck arrived to take them to the hospital they rang to say that he had died.' In a rare display of compassion, the Japanese agreed to a ten-minute funeral service for George at the camp, before his remains were carried off for cremation.

30 MAY

Hardly had the day passed when news of another death was confirmed. Since 26 May, Corporal George Sheridan had been sick with bronchitis, which then turned to double pneumonia. A few days later, he'd reported to the sick room with a very high temperature, then subsequently rallied. Everybody assumed he was on the mend, but his resistance was so low that he died on 30 May. George, who came from Sydney, was twenty-four years of age and had lost 19 kilos since leaving Singapore. He was another 2/20th man, from D Company.

Houston's tone reflected a growing anger: 'Three men have passed away since the short time we have been in Japan and I can safely say that with proper care and the right sort of food they would all be alive here today.' To make matters worse, it emerged that the same poor standard of treatment and attention did not apply to the Japanese who fell sick. A Japanese corporal who had also developed pneumonia had two Australians looking after him day and night, washing his feet and placing ice packs on his head.

7 JUNE

A fourth man dead. Private Jack Eddison, aged twenty-eight, who had been suffering from pneumonia and pleurisy, succumbed at

6.50 am. Sandy Barrett did his utmost to revive him and managed to get him breathing again on two occasions, but Jack just wasn't strong enough to hold on. An original member of the 2/20th, Jack was in HQ Company with Bluey Firth, and specialised in transport. Like Henry Dietz, he'd also worn a lance-corporal's stripe for all of a month back in '41 before giving it away. Jack's family owned a large station out near Canberra and those who knew him well respected his soldierly qualities.

Eddison's death prompted Dr Barrett to lecture everyone about the importance of looking after their health. Captain Chisholm demanded an interview with the camp commandant to express his concerns about the deaths of three men in just over a week. Unless the food improved and the working hours were cut, the death rate would get worse, he warned; and, perhaps the guards might also go a little easier on the men, Chisholm suggested. Inevitably the plea fell on deaf ears.

8 JUNE

Jack Eddison was placed in a rough pine coffin put together by Corporal Bill Clegg for cremation the next day. It was a desperately sad way to go.

14 JUNE

With the warmer weather came more flies, which were attracted by the insanitary conditions, especially around the latrine. It measured about 9 metres long, 2 metres wide and 2.5 deep. Some of the Japanese women would arrive with buckets dangling from a bamboo pole to retrieve the contents for use as fertiliser, but the stench remained, and the flies were drawn to it in ever-increasing numbers. The Japs came up with a novel plan to combat the fly plague by making everyone catch at least ten of them a day. This instruction was taken extremely seriously by the guards, who demanded that every man hand in his quota at the end of the day. Those who failed to achieve the minimum kill were made to double-march around the parade ground for three-quarters of an hour.

Jimmy Houston, who had just returned from a nineteen-hour shift, tried to get out of the fly-swatting detail.

> I told him I had a bad knee and couldn't run so he told me to do body presses which is the worst sort of torture. I complained to the Japanese corporal twice. The first time he rushed at me with his sword and the second time he punched me in the jaw. Someone kicked me twice from behind and hit me across the head with a thick stick. I shut up after that. When I finished doing body presses I had to run around the ground for half an hour while the guards started belting me and others across the back and legs as we ran past. A couple of the chaps collapsed completely. This was the worst blitz they turned on yet — and all because we didn't hand in two dead flies each!

Harry Julian was always in trouble for not catching enough flies. He often wondered what sort of mentality drove a human being to such cruelty, but he knew it was hopeless to complain. Whatever you were doing, it was wrong. 'If you were trying to catch flies you weren't working. And I was always being accused of not pulling my weight — they weren't joking either. If they said do something, you had to do it or you'd be accused of causing trouble. The guards had a very quick temper and you didn't want to get on the wrong side of them, otherwise they'd whip you.'

27 JUNE

Perhaps it was the sickness or exhaustion, but a more reflective mood could be detected in some of the POW diaries. Boughton: 'Another month over. Terrible day yesterday. Very bloody sick. Diarrhoea, loss of weight, weakness and now Beri Beri, which causes my feet to swell enormously. Have had one holiday since starting on the furnaces nearly three months ago. Would give anything for news of the war. Even rumours have ceased. Hoping hard for peace before it's too late.'

Houston: 'Got back to camp at 12.00 noon after working 19 hours. If anyone would have told me I could work all these hours on rice I would have told him to see a doctor. Another batch of letters were issued last night with some of the chaps getting three or four, but I missed out again. How time passes. It's three years today since I joined the army and I only hope I will be out of this dump this time next year.'

28 JUNE

There was still no sign of the Red Cross food parcels that had arrived last month, and which the Japanese seemed to be keeping for themselves. Some of the men confirmed that they saw the guards steal two cases of cocoa and a bag of sugar from the Red Cross bags. Houston noted that Captain Chisholm had made a point of visiting the Japanese HQ every day to plead the men's case but they'd only laughed. 'The hospital is full of sick men who could do with that food,' Jimmy added.

Apart from the pneumonia that had recently claimed the lives of George Sheridan and Jack Eddison, beri-beri and diarrhoea were now the most common complaints. This placed an increasingly heavy burden on Captain Sandy Barrett, whose team was on duty for up to twenty hours a day. The sick room had a raised platform that lined the interior; here the five or six highly dedicated Australian medical personnel under Barrett's leadership performed some extraordinary work. Every day produced a miracle. While much has been written about the work of doctors on the Burma–Thai Railway, the standard of care that saved so many lives at Naoetsu was no less remarkable.

One of the more incomprehensible orders imposed by the Japanese on those admitted to the sick room was to place the men on one-third rations for the duration of their stay. The theory was that if they didn't work, they didn't need the food, and therefore didn't need to eat so much. It would also be an added incentive for any man who was hungry to leave the sick room as soon as possible.

The smaller rations were rigorously policed. Not only was the cook under strict orders to allocate tinier portions to the seriously ill, but Japanese army personnel such as Sergeant Aoki, the Faith Healer, and Private Taguchi, the Germ, made regular visits to the sick room to police the rules. Rarely had Australian larrikin humour been put to such appropriate use. With medicine in such short supply, faith was the only alternative in such a germ-ridden environment.

29 JUNE

More letters arrived, Houston reported. It was great news for those who received one but miserable for those who didn't. Some were keen to share their news, which lifted the spirits of others who were forgotten. A few blokes received letters dating back a year or more. How they must have relished each and every word, their eyes soaking up the blue ink and their fingers caressing the notepaper that their loved ones had probably kissed.

1 JULY

'What a day this was,' Jimmy declared. The men who normally worked in the furnace were told to shovel the slag. That meant ten hours bent double, apart from the odd few minutes for a smoko. After lunch, the afternoon Dog Walloper arrived and started shouting commands, which nobody understood. 'He did his block, stood us up, roared at us for nearly five minutes and belted each across the face with a stick,' Houston recalled.

There were ten men in the slag-shovelling party and each one received three whacks across the jaw. One of the young blokes had very tender skin — he was left with three bright red marks across his face. The point of this unprovoked assault remained a mystery.

'This animal, for he is nothing else, does some of the boys over every day,' Jimmy observed.

In the summer, the Australians preferred to do outdoor duties if they could, but there was no escape from the backbreaking nature of their work. For both the Stainless and Shin-Etsu work parties, one of the most demanding of these jobs involved unloading coal from ships anchored a kilometre or two offshore. Naoetsu had no deepwater port or docking facilities so the only way of transferring raw materials like coal was to do it by hand. Every morning, parties of men were ferried out to the colliers on half-a-dozen lighters, towed by 'Little Toot' the tugboat, which belched several hundred smoke rings into the air as its diesel motor started up.

Once the men arrived on board, they would be divided into groups of four, with one party being allotted to each coal hold. What followed can only be described as slave labour in the extreme.

From 7 am to 5 pm each group would work frantically, shovelling coal into a special sling, which, once filled, would require all four men to then haul it up to the opening of the hold. Meanwhile, the guards would run about hitting the labourers with sticks and clubs, in an effort to speed up the process. As soon as one sling was filled and hoisted up onto the deck for tipping into the lighter, another would be thrown down to replace it. And the process became even more difficult as the level of the coal gradually got lower. The work just went on in this way, hour after hour and day after day, with only thirty minutes' break for lunch. The only other opportunity the men had to straighten their backs would be when the loaded freighters or barges were replaced by an empty one — a process that lasted about twelve minutes.

It was not only tiring and filthy work, but also dangerous. Herb Lamb suffered a bad fall and broke his shoulder when a rope ladder snapped. 'I was scaling the ladder when it suddenly gave way and I plunged back down onto the barge,' he remembers. 'I fell onto my elbow and my shoulder, which was really smashed up. Of course, nothing was done to treat it and I still can't lift it properly.'

Those who weren't unloading ships at sea often found themselves on coal duty. This appealed to those who suffered from seasickness and preferred to work on the calmer waters of the river. That's not to say that the job was any easier, of course. Once the lighters were towed in with their heavy load, the coal had to be transferred to several large pens. This was done manually; there was no machinery to make the process faster and more efficient. Instead, the men would have to carry it ashore on their backs.

Eric Endacott, a 23-year-old signalman with the 2/18th Battalion, remembered lifting a long bar with a basket dangling from ropes at each end. 'We had to carry it over our shoulder and dog-trot. There seemed to be a hundredweight of coal in each basket, and you had to jog up a slippery bank. The idea was that you did a deft move and unloaded both these baskets into the coal trucks.'

John Cook describes it as the very worst kind of slave labour. 'The lighters were unloaded by men sometimes with panniers strapped to their backs, or else by two blokes carrying a large basket on a pole between them. When full, the baskets had to be carried up a steep plank to the coal pens. Here again there was no let-up on the men, whose working hours were the same as the barge party. More than a hundred tons of coal a day was moved in this manner.'

One of the occasional perks of unloading was when a ship arrived containing salt — which was then often pilfered. Salt was a desperately valuable commodity and, although it was inedible in its raw state, could be processed by boiling and evaporation. Apart from being used to flavour food, it was especially beneficial for treating 'the burning pisses'. The loss of body salt in the furnaces, combined with the lack of salt in the diet, also caused muscle cramps. Acids in the body, normally neutralised by salt, went straight to the bladder and caused the sufferer a great deal of pain.

To ease this problem, the men devised an ingenious system to clarify the stolen salt right in front of their guards, at Stainless and Shin-Etsu. Every day and at great personal risk, a quantity of raw salt would be placed in a water bottle, which would be hung around a drum containing a coke fire, in the rest room. The bottle was left there overnight, and at the first opportunity in the morning, it would then be transferred to the furnace area and hung alongside the other water bottles, which the furnace workers always kept close by, to allow them to slake their thirsts. Eventually the bottle with the salt in it would boil dry and the contents, roughly the equivalent of two tablespoons, would be salvaged from the bottom. The few ounces of rusty-looking grains that were scraped from the metal army-issue bottle may not have looked particularly palatable, but they were worth their weight in gold.

3 JULY

A day of rumour and ill-founded optimism. Dudley Boughton reported that some of the Dog Wallopers had been sent to Tokyo. 'I guess we had all sorts of ideas, especially as rumours have persisted that Germany is just about finished and we are all going to Formosa. But it died down, however.' Dudley's consolation was a decent dinner for a change, including dumplings, pork stew, cucumber and rice. 'Best day for meals for a week,' he wrote.

4 JULY

The predictability of each day was interrupted by a most unexpected invitation. Any man who wanted to could write a message for his family and record it for broadcast. It had to be no longer than 250 words and be completed in three minutes. Only fifty men accepted the offer, the others suspecting they were being used in some kind of propaganda offensive. Officially, it was against army regulations for a POW to take part in a broadcast like this, but those who agreed to participate felt that it might comfort the folks back home.

In the afternoon they were led to the Japanese headquarters and sat down in front of a microphone, where their words were recorded onto a gramophone record. It was not a comfortable experience. Some of them were nervous and fluffed their lines. But it broke up the day and, hopefully, provided some solace for those who got to hear it.

The Japanese were apparently annoyed that only fifty out of nearly 300 men took advantage of the offer to broadcast home. Next morning those who didn't co-operate had to parade for work immediately and stand for hours in the pouring rain.

Mick McAuliffe was one of those who agreed to make the broadcast, and his family was deluged by messages from people who heard it in such far-flung corners of the globe as South Africa and New Zealand. 'That was the first time my family knew where I was, and that I was alive, in a couple of years,' said Mick. 'Even people who never knew me wrote to tell my dad. A few of the blokes in the camp frowned on me making the broadcast, but it didn't worry me — I couldn't see it doing any harm.'

5 JULY

One of the medical orderlies accidentally broke a thermometer in the sick room and got knocked around terribly by the guards. 'His screams were so loud,' wrote Houston, 'that they kept most of the chaps awake.' Even Captain Yates, who just happened to be passing, got a few belts across the face. The same guard entered the sick room and ordered Private Mick Gorman, who was partially paralysed, out of bed. 'Even on good days he has to be helped outside,' Jimmy noted of the young man from Coffs Harbour. 'The guard that did this is a swine of the lowest type.'

9 JULY

In summertime the heat could become unbearable — prompting Sergeant Aoki to rule that each man had to sleep under five blankets, with a folded sheet wrapped around his stomach. Apparently, the Faith Healer reasoned, it would protect the men from contracting certain diseases.

And thus the men endured 'the Great Sheet Blitz' of summer 1943. According to John Cook, it was absolute torture. 'Apart from the heat of the blankets, as soon as you put the sheet around the stomach and got into bed under the five blankets, a mass of fleas would attack the skin under the sheet. For this reason, many men took the risk of being caught without the folded sheet.'

Frequently guards would inspect the sleeping men, and those found to have discarded their blankets would be called out onto the parade ground. On the night of 8–9 July, twenty-two men were caught without their sheets on and everyone was ordered outside. There they were told to form two circles: the inner ring consisted of those who'd disobeyed the bedclothes rule, and the outer circle comprised the rest of the men. For three long hours the men in the inner ring were made to run in a continuous circle while the guards beat them with clubs. Eventually tiring of the fun, the Japs then decided to force the men to imitate an animal as they hopped around on the palms of their hands and the soles of their feet. Cook recalled in his diary:

> 'By this time the guards had worked themselves into a frenzy, many of them making noises like dogs or hyenas. Then as a finale to the entertainment, both circles of men were ordered to pair off and beat each other. If the Japanese thought they weren't hitting each other hard enough, they would step in and demonstrate how they wanted it done. When the Japs decided they'd had enough for the night, the men would be dismissed and, after losing three hours of valuable sleep, had to climb back into bed with the five blankets and the sheet around their bodies, as there was no telling when the next raid would be.'

14 JULY

Pay day. The Japanese gave the POWs a few yen a week for their efforts — a futile exercise because there was nothing to spend it on. Now the guards decided to turn the tables and demanded the men hand over all their foreign currency. Jimmy Houston produced an

Australian pound note and a handful of coins. 'I suppose I can kiss goodbye to them,' he admitted in his diary. 'The Japs are always telling us how honest they are but they've never handed back our watches which they took some time ago.'

Only one man appeared to have a smile on his face, and he had every reason to be pleased with himself. Larry Farmer was mentally counting the cash he had stashed away deep down a hole in Singapore during the days before capitulation. A few of the blokes had heard his story and wished they'd done the same. The very thought of all that dough kept Larry going. Even the Japs couldn't steal the money or the memory.

14 JULY

Dudley Boughton had been suffering badly from beri-beri and general weakness, but he appeared to be improving. 'Last night served squid for dinner. Look like going out tomorrow. Swelling in legs gone down, but still very weak.'

Being the middle of summer, the nights recently had been like steam baths. It was almost impossible to sleep with all the flies and mosquitoes. By day some of the men were lucky to grab a five-minute swim in the river, which ran parallel to the camp. It was a bit murky but five minutes there in this sort of heat was heaven.

20 JULY

One of the POWs, who was only known to Jimmy as Gerry, was badly hurt while cleaning out the rubbish from the furnace at Stainless. A chain holding one of the slag buckets broke his nose and cut his arms and legs. Houston arrived just as he was regaining consciousness. 'We're given such dangerous jobs to do and don't get time to look around that anything's liable to happen,' Jimmy pointed out. 'The Japs don't waste any time getting out of the way, but we have to keep on working.'

24 JULY

What with the flies and the general lack of hygiene in the camp, most men had been having trouble controlling their bowels. One of the POWs, Lance Corporal John Magin, was caught short in bed and dirtied the blankets before throwing up in the corridor. He was trying to clean it up when a Jap medical private walked in and screamed abuse at him. What followed was one of the worst bashings the camp had yet seen. The incident dominated Jimmy Houston's diary entry that day:

> He made this chap take off all his clothes then laid into him with his thick leather belt. His body was a mass of bruises. After he got tired of using the belt he kicked him a number of times in the stomach, then made the poor chap do body pressing for an hour. When he finished doing that he was told to stand to attention to 5 a.m. All that happened because he was sick. This guard is nothing but an animal.

1 AUGUST

Another death. Corporal Alexander 'Jock' Kerr, from D Company of the 2/20th, was a big bear of a man and friendly with it. He came from Parramatta in Sydney's western suburbs and was married with two children. Born in Fifeshire, he loved the military life and before migrating to Australia was in the Scottish Guards Regiment. First he got a bad bout of beri-beri, which was followed by dysentery. This surprised his mates because Jock regarded cleanliness above godliness. As Dudley Boughton put it in his diary entry for that day: 'Jock was spotlessly clean and a decent bloke.'

The news hit everybody hard, but in reality Kerr didn't stand a chance. While lying sick in bed, the guards decided he was sleeping too much and ordered him to work. Jock could hardly stand, let alone shovel slag. Such was his condition the day before, he collapsed and had to be carried back to camp. Jock went on sick parade that night but Aoki classed him fit enough for work and he was sent back to the squad room. Today on arrival at the factory, he was clearly incapable of work and once again had to be carried back to camp. This time he was sent to hospital for a blood transfusion, but it was too late. At 3.30 pm word went out that Alex 'Jock' Kerr was dead at the age of thirty-six. The men were becoming unnerved by the rising death rate and wondered who would be next.

Corporal Kerr, like so many other men who were sick, had been put on so-called light duties. In reality, this meant being treated even worse than those who were classified as fit. The red ribbon that was pinned to their coat made the sick a target for the more brutal of the guards.

According to John Cook, the civilian guards were told that if the men with the ribbons didn't work hard enough at the factory, they were to be made to do so. 'As most of these men had been in camp ill and on one-third rations, on their arrival at the factory they were absolutely exhausted,' John explained. 'There was very little chance of them being able to do the work allotted to them. They were then attacked by the civilian guards, who claimed that they were loafing.'

The feeling was that Aoki, the medical orderly sergeant, ordered the civilian guards to target the light-duty men so that fewer POWs would go on sick parade. 'It soon became apparent to the men that to be given a red ribbon to wear was almost the same as getting a death sentence,' Cook continued. 'Many of the men given the ribbon to wear would beg to go on full duties again after a day or two.'

15 AUGUST

Many anniversaries had come and gone during C Force's eight-month stay so far at Naoetsu — the departure of the *Queen Mary*, the Australians' first engagement with the Japanese, the fall of Singapore. Today marked two years since the second wave of troops for the 2/20th had arrived at Sembawang, but none of the men were too excited about that landmark.

By August 1943, the camp had seen so much sickness, injury and suffering during the previous six months that the Australians were beginning to take it all in their stride. As terrible as it might sound, they were becoming hardened to the suffering of other men. It was difficult enough to look after yourself without worrying about the plight of those around you. If any affection was shared, it had to be with a really close mate. You needed a friend to watch your back and help you out in times of need; a man you could rely upon and someone whose loyalty and kindness you'd have a duty to reciprocate.

One of the August '41 arrivals, Henry Dietz soon realised he needed a mate to help him through the worst times. 'A lot of those fellas who died were big and healthy, but they just faded for no apparent reason,' he remembers. 'I found myself fading once, but thanks to my friend George Hartley, I got through. I didn't know him before we became POWs — he was in D Company and I was in C — but we joined up together. I remember him saying to me, "If you don't pull yourself together you're going to be in a little wooden box like the rest of them." So whatever we had we shared, and ended up just like brothers. Even after the war we were the same.' Henry and George saved each other's lives.

George Daldry was another one who adopted a buddy system at Naoetsu. 'I had two really good mates and I don't think any of us would have survived without each other,' he says. 'In our unit, you worked as a pair and if you got malaria or something, one of the others would go off to get the food and bring it back.'

18 AUGUST

Eight months after the men had first left camp in their work parties, there had been a lull in the violence. But it was short-lived. Just before marching off to Shin-Etsu this morning, one of the men collapsed on the parade ground. A Dog Walloper smashed him across the back with his stick as he lay unconscious on the ground.

19 AUGUST

One of the worst beatings the men had seen. This time it was POW number 300 who copped it — Henry Sweet, a 24-year-old signalman from Woollahra. He was punched in the face no fewer than 112 times (somebody actually counted the blows). It continued for several minutes. 'When I saw Sweet the left side of his face was puffed up like a balloon and he had a very black eye,' recorded Jimmy Houston.

20 AUGUST

The sadistic behaviour of the Japanese beggared belief. After returning from work this evening, all those suffering from diarrhoea were ordered to fall out and give their POW numbers. Then after tea they were lined up and beaten across the face with the buckle end of a heavy leather belt. Those whose faces didn't burst open were left with a lump the size of an egg. 'The treatment the sick men receive here is brutal' was Houston's understated comment in his diary. 'There is hardly a day that passes without some of the men collapsing. The hard work is robbing them of every bit of energy they have.'

23 AUGUST

The death of Private James Ernest Perkin, a signalman with HQ Company, 2/18th Battalion. Jimmy was the sixth man to meet his maker, and the way things were going he wouldn't be the last. He'd been suffering from a bad dose of diarrhoea but was understood to be on the mend when news came through that he'd expired. Like so many other sick men, Private Perkin had been forced to join the light-duty party and had been bashed by the civilian guards for not working once he got to the factory. Sandy Barrett's medical report concluded that he died from poor food and bad working conditions.

At almost 2 metres in height, Jim was the tallest man in the camp, which posed problems for his funeral. The boys raided the roof of the pig sty for timber to build a coffin but could only find enough to make a wooden box to cover three-quarters of his length. The indignity of it all. Some thought his trouble stemmed from a run-in he'd had in Singapore with Sergeant Susuki, who objected to him cutting down his army boots — an act that amounted to the destruction of Japanese property. Ever since then he'd been a marked man. Hoppy and Perkin were reunited at Naoetsu, where the (now ex-army) Japanese quartermaster delighted in thrashing him over the head with the heels of his boots. Jimmy Perkin, whose home was in Sydney, was still in his twenties and unmarried. It was small comfort that at least he didn't leave a wife and children behind.

30 AUGUST

Rumours persisted in the camp that the war in Europe was over, and the long faces of the Japanese guards who'd been listening to the radio reinforced the gossip. In his diary Dudley Boughton hoped and prayed that another report about the enemy landing in Sydney was 'tripe'. The problem was that no one in C Force knew the truth. Cut off from the rest of the world, they accepted that speculation often ran wild.

The high summer temperature and the heat from the furnace were making the working day almost unbearable. Coupled with the hard physical labour, the Aussies were frequently at the point of collapse. No man could take this sort of treatment indefinitely. 'Every day there are men collapsing on the job and being carried back to camp,' wrote Jimmy Houston. Those who made it back in one piece fell on their pile of blankets and dreamed. It was the one constant in their otherwise bleak lives.

CHAPTER 8

WHEN FOOD IS THE ONLY FANTASY

Most of the prisoners at Naoetsu dreamed of food, but rarely of sex. It is a fact of life that when a man is starving, his sex drive shuts down. Throughout C Force's time as prisoners of war in Japan, women didn't feature prominently in their thoughts, apart from the loving memory of wives, mothers, sisters and girlfriends left behind.

'Sex drive?' queries George Daldry. 'I never heard sex mentioned the whole time I was there. When you first go into the army, all you talk about is women. But once you're in a prison camp all you talk about is food.

'There were terrible arguments about food. It dominated every conversation. I remember one guy saying that if he ever got out he'd have a whole leg of lamb. Then another said he'd eat a whole sheep. Somebody else said they'd get a rice ball and cover it with chocolate and coconut. It was like that — food, food, food. But nobody ever talked about women. Even if the most beautiful girl in the world had walked in, they'd have preferred to put her on the barbecue and eat her! I mean that — when your life depends on food and you don't have any, you lose your sex drive. You just don't think about it.'

Amid his grief at losing his brother Charles, young George's fantasy was getting enough food to make him fighting fit again. 'I dreamed of going back to Bondi and opening a gym,' he explains. 'And I did. That's what kept me going.'

Kevin Timbs, who lost nearly 50 kilos while he was a POW, also became obsessed with eating. 'You used to get a little rice and barley but it was by no means enough. I was just skin and bone, so I thought about food all the time.'

Others started behaving oddly whenever they were given a meal. Like Kevin, Herb Lamb, as a sergeant, was used to keeping a watchful eye on the boys in his squad. He'd soon recognised such strange behaviour as one of the first signs that a man was losing the will to live. 'When I saw them start picking at their food and storing some of it away for later, I'd say to myself, "You'll be next." And sure enough they were. You see, their rations would go sour, they'd get this stomach upset, and invariably it would turn into dysentery, and that would be the end. Myself, I'd get my food, eat it, wash my dixie and — bang — finish. I'd eat anything. It was the one sure way to stay alive.'

When they weren't eating, they were thinking of eating, and usually of Mum's home-baked dinners. 'You dreamed about food every minute of the day,' John Cook claimed. 'My favourite dream was seeing my mother coming into the kitchen with a great big slab of buttered steak, which she would lay on the table. I'd pick it up and be just about to take a bite when I'd wake up.'

And even when his subconscious transported the 22-year-old back to an idyllic Australia and the sun-kissed paddocks of the family farm near Penrith, food was always central to the image. 'Where I used to live before the war, there were a lot of grapes,' John continued, 'and I'd have this dream that I'd be lying under the vine and go to take a mouthful — and then my eyes would open and there'd be nothing there. Everybody in the camp dreamed about food and we all had imaginary recipe books. I used to say I would pop out for a pound of butter and just sit down and eat it.' Such were the joys of fantasy cuisine.

'Everybody would dream of big bloody feeds,' confirms Cas

Cook, born in beautiful Springwood but later a resident of Penrith, like John. 'It was the only topic of conversation. You'd be sitting around discussing what you were going to cook once you got home and how you were going to cook it.'

'We used to have an imaginary menu and go right through it,' adds Snowy Collins. 'Meat pies, prawns and crab, though I was never a pudding man.' Even a starving POW, apparently, could afford to be fussy in the world of the make-believe menu.

Not so Don Fraser. 'All a man's thoughts are now of food and what he will eat when he gets home,' the young signalman recorded in a diary entry late in the year. 'I never thought I'd descend to begging scraps from a Japanese but it is surprising what two years of starvation will do.' The Melburnian also provided an idea of the sort of imaginary feast he had in mind: 'Dinner of curried spaghetti — rather good. Thought of eating toast with grilled cheese piled with spaghetti and tomato sauce. Been thinking of another meal today — grilled steak and buttered eggs.'

Eric Richardson of the 2/18th took the food discussions a step further, it seems. 'Hunger was extremely real,' he says, 'and to keep me going I would get hold of old recipes from the fellas and copy them out religiously every evening. It seemed to help.'

Like his old platoon mate Snowy, Henry Dietz also had his pet hates. 'I would always pass on pumpkin vines. They gave them to you because they were rich in vitamins, but I couldn't eat them for my life. I'd put them in the dixie and boil them on the slag but they never seemed to soften up. I would eat *anything* but pumpkin vines.'

Joe Byrne, who went from 80 kilos to just over 45, had never known what it was like to starve. 'Lack of food was *the* problem and it was terrible,' he admits. 'I'll never forget what it was like to go hungry. And because the Japs were feeding you less and less, the men had nothing to help them fight against the sickness.'

Fortunately Joe had also been blessed with a fighting spirit. What he lacked in nutrition he more than made up for in the will to survive. 'I wasn't prepared to give those bastards the satisfaction of dying. No way. And naturally enough, I was one of those fortunate enough to get out of the place.'

Others were not so lucky. Often it was the lust for food that got men into trouble and unleashed the full fury of the Japanese. Harry Julian remembers seeing a man accused of stealing a carrot. 'He was tied up in the parade ground and beaten savagely with a pole which they would also use to poke his eyes and nose with. Well, he was a terrible sight by the time they'd finished with him. And do you know what? I just couldn't bring myself to do anything about it. You knew that if any man tried to intervene they'd be set upon too. You might as well cut your throat. So you just shut your eyes to it.' Harry was traumatised by the memory of that incident. The man died the next day.

How could anyone do this to another person? What sort of warped mentality was capable of such violence?

As their time at Naoetsu progressed, it was obvious that the suffering was far from over — the worst was just beginning, in fact. The situation is made painfully clear in the following summary of Jimmy Houston, Dudley Boughton and John Cook's diary entries for early autumn 1943.

1 SEPTEMBER 1943

An air-raid warning cut off power to the factories. At the Shin-Etsu chemical plant, Jimmy Houston took the opportunity to kip down in the darkness. Once the all-clear sounded, the lights came on and a passing Dog Walloper spotted the bleary-eyed Scotsman on his mat. 'He rushed up to me and punched me half a dozen times on my classical dial,' wrote Jimmy.

2 SEPTEMBER

Rumours were rife that Tokyo had been bombed, which would explain the recent air-raid sirens and the blackouts.

9 SEPTEMBER

A cleaning blitz for the past three days as one of the Japanese generals from Tokyo camp administration was due to visit. The men were forced to sweep and scrub the place, even after returning from a fourteen-hour shift, Boughton reported. When the Jap officer arrived in the afternoon, he stayed for no more than seven minutes and gave the camp only a cursory glance. Three days of cleaning, tidying and polishing and he hardly looked at the place. Houston summed up everybody's feelings: 'I hope no more of them decide to visit us as the cleaning we did and abuse we had to put up with was something awful.'

Dudley was beyond exhaustion at this point and was finding it difficult to sleep for more than two to three hours a day.

13 SEPTEMBER

Another death. Signalman Jack Baker, from Drummoyne in Sydney, had been ill ever since he arrived in Japan. Most recently, he'd got beri-beri and diarrhoea and was obviously unfit for work, but that hadn't stopped Sergeant Aoki from sending him to the Shin-Etsu factory again yesterday. There, he was deliberately targeted by one of the civilian guards, who bashed him till he collapsed and then proceeded to kick the Australian all over the head and body, the camp learnt later. The date was 12 September, Jack's twenty-ninth birthday. He was carried back to camp and died today at 9.15 pm. Officially the cause of death was pleurisy, but those who knew the 8th Division signaller reckoned the cruelty of the guards had finished him off.

The treatment meted out to the light-duty party would ultimately claim nearly forty lives. From Jock Kerr's death at the start of August onwards, it always followed the same pattern. Only men who were suffering from severe complaints such as dysentery or beri-beri were given the red ribbon to pin on their coats. As they staggered to work, the civilian guards would strike them with their hands or sticks for falling behind the main party. John Cook painted a vivid picture of what usually happened next: 'As the men suffering from dysentery and severe diarrhoea were not allowed to stop on the way to the factory to go to the toilet, the men had no choice other than to defecate in their trousers. This meant that the excreta would finish in their boots and remain there for the whole day, or in some cases, until they were allowed to have a bath under the furnace prior to returning to the camp.'

And those who suffered from beri-beri found the going even tougher. 'This was a very painful and debilitating disease,' John continued. 'The whole body would swell to enormous proportions. The face would be swollen so much the eyes were just narrow slits. Walking became very painful as the thighs used to rub together, causing the skin to rub off. The testicles would be the size of tennis balls and the penis looked like a white cucumber. Men with this complaint still had to go to work. You had to be almost completely immobilised before being allowed to stay in the sick room.'

Then there was dry beri-beri, which had exactly the opposite effect. According to Cook: 'The victim of this complaint would contract severe diarrhoea and wouldn't be able to keep any food down. Eventually they'd be little more than skin and bone.'

Not surprisingly, by the time they reached the factory, the men on light duties would be incapable of work or anything else that required physical effort. This provoked the civilian guards into attacking them for idling. Invariably they'd collapse and have to be carried back to camp. The daily cycle of sickness and violence was complete. Most men would die in a few days. In the coming months, the death toll at Naoetsu would soar.

18 SEPTEMBER

Alfred 'Jack' Martin, from Hurstville in Sydney's south, passed away at 4.15 am. He was another member of the 8th Division Signals and had contracted pneumonia; 35-year-old Jack never stood a chance and suffered a lot towards the end. Neuritis had paralysed his right side and he had to use a stick to help him hobble to and from the factory. He should never have been made to work.

Jimmy Houston recorded in his diary how his old mate Jack was forced to walk through deep snow in worn-out boots. When he asked the Japanese for another pair they knocked him back and he had to make some straw shoes. In the end Jimmy gave him a spare pair of his own boots.

21 SEPTEMBER

The guards seemed to be worried, according to the men. A Japanese doctor arrived and toured the sick bay. He asked the patients what their trouble was — as if it wasn't obvious. Hard work, lack of medical attention and a starvation diet had taken their toll. A very slight improvement in rations had been marked by the arrival of some bread and Red Cross soup, though it had been somewhat watered down. Sometimes the Japanese showed an unusual level of concern for the POWs. On one occasion the men were given clogs, consisting of a wooden base and a length of canvas, to protect their feet. Jimmy Houston had his stolen, which led to yet another bashing from a guard who wanted to know why he wasn't wearing them, as he recounted in his diary:

> I couldn't tell him they'd been pinched off my sack so I said nothing … then he got busy on me. He smacked me four times on the face then he got one of the dog walloper's sticks, jammed it into my feet about a dozen times … done a bit of bayonet practice on my chest, knocked the hat off my head and gave me half a dozen blows. They were severe blows and made me feel crook for a few minutes. I had four lumps on my head and one was the size of an egg. I cursed him good and hard … also the swine who stole my clogs.

30 SEPTEMBER

An even sadder day than usual. Private Frederick 'Pop' Hawkins, from Leichhardt in Sydney, died at 10 pm from pneumonia. The oldest man in camp, at forty-seven, Pop had been sick for some time. He was a popular bloke and the entire camp was deflated.

Although everyone was used to death, it still came as a shock when a 2/20th stalwart like Pop Hawkins passed away.

1 OCTOBER

Autumn. Recent weeks saw some terrible weather, but today was better. There was sun and blue sky, but it was still freezing cold when the men rose at 5 am for roll call.

7 OCTOBER

A rare delight: the Japanese distributed bottles of beer to share, one bottle for every four men. A couple of swigs each went down a treat with dinner. It was the first alcohol the blokes had had since Singapore and it left some of them with a light head. Some doubtless wondered how they'd cope with a few schooners if they ever got home.

11 OCTOBER

The poor conditions and bad treatment continued to claim more victims. This time it was John 'Jack' Crandall's turn to meet his maker as the Naoetsu death toll reached double figures. The 37-year-old died from bronchial pneumonia at 10.30 pm. Jack was from Adelong, near Tumut in southern New South Wales, and joined the 2/20th after enlisting in June '41. Both Houston and Boughton found it hard to believe he'd gone. 'A week ago I was playing cards with him,' Jimmy wrote. Boughton: 'Poor old bugger. Jack was well known and popular with the boys.' Like Signalman Baker the month before, he'd been poorly ever since his arrival in Japan. Not for the last time, fellow Catholic Kevin Timbs was asked to recite the Rosary at the brief funeral service.

※ ※ ※

In the latter half of 1943 everybody was once more issued with notebooks by the Japanese and ordered to keep a daily diary, which was checked and stamped every week. This was part of official policy and designed to show how well the camp was being run, although the content usually differed sharply from the unofficial musings recorded by diggers like Houston and Boughton. The Japs wanted proof that the prisoners were being looked after, should Japan lose the war and have to answer for its misdeeds. Most of the blokes took the hint, although it must have been hard to be positive amid so much gloom.

The following section is a compilation of reports of life in Naoetsu from mid October that year to early January 1944. Like the POWs' secret diaries, most of the 'official' ones were written in spidery handwriting so as to get as much as possible on each tiny page. One of the Japanese-issue notebooks found its way into the Australian War Memorial in Canberra, but the author remains unknown. It is surprisingly upbeat in parts — but of course that's what the Japanese wanted and the writer clearly knew what was expected of him. The other writers here are all men whose names are now familiar: Captain Alex 'Sandy' Barrett; Don Fraser, the young 8th Division signaller who'd only joined up in September 1941; and Dudley Boughton, from the 2/18th. These largely unauthorised personal accounts provide the most detailed picture of what it was like to be in Camp 4-B during one of the darkest periods of their incarceration. It's almost impossible to believe that so many survived in such atrocious conditions.

Barrett set the scene with an entry written sometime during the second week of October '43. 'I'm very worried about the general health of the troops,' he began. 'They are in poor condition due to continued hard work, continued loss of weight, lack of news from home, insufficient food and the mental strain from these conditions. The remedying of these factors is of course beyond our control and I can see only increasing sickness among our lot during the remainder of our prison life.'

Yet in spite of the sickness and discomfort, he notes the morale and optimism that continues to flourish among the men. 'There is one thing that every man here is quite certain of and that is the inevitable victory of the allied army and the certain defeat of the axis nations. This makes our load much easier to carry. We would certainly have the stoop of Atlas if we ever had the thought of defeat in our minds.'

12 OCTOBER

Boughton: 'Won four packets of weed in raffle. Inspection by Jap colonel. Reveille 4 a.m. Mull Cook collapsed at work. Jim, Curly, Biscuit and I carried him back to camp. Bloody heavy after a mile or two.'

Fraser: 'Up at 4 a.m. to clean up for the Colonel. Japs all prepared for inspection. Colonel came on time and made us remove our shirts to inspect our skinny torsos. Dinner of boiled rice and onion stew. Starving before it and very hungry after it. Usual easy afternoon. Home to tea. Scored half a bowl of Jap rice in derby which made a welcome addition to a tea of two small pieces of boiled spud and one of pumpkin.'

13 OCTOBER

Fraser: 'Bad night. Coughed all night and bad diarrhoea. Lucky to miss barge party. Usual day at Stainless. Small earth tremor in afternoon. Most peculiar sensation. All afternoon thinking of Mother and what a great holiday I could have with her at Greensborough. I'd have the old Austin there and we'd visit all her friends. All I'd want to do would be to eat, read and loaf. I hope to God it won't be long before I see her again. This utter lack of news is very disheartening. Weak stew for tea.'

14 OCTOBER

Fraser: 'My unlucky day, as I copped the barge party. Very poor breakfast to work hard on all day. The only food I could beg or steal on the boat was a handful of burnt rice which some Jap apparently was getting for his pigs. Got home filthy dirty and covered with coal dirt to find some dirty swine had finished my last piece of soap. The petty pilfering of soap, tobacco, food or anything at all useful in the camp is disgusting. Some chaps have no principle at all.'

15 OCTOBER

Fraser: 'Barge party again. Bit of luck in that the winch broke at 10 a.m. so no work 'til after lunch. Dinner very tasty to my supersensitive palate, though I wouldn't give it to the dog at home. The fact that one eats it with dirty coaly hands does not add to its enjoyment. Very homesick lately. Thinking particularly of Mother and the times we'll have together when we get back.'

17 OCTOBER

Fraser: 'Holiday today. Greatly appreciated. Did some washing in cold water without soap. Read *Oliver Twist* and ate beri beri tablets till dinner, which consisted of the usual amount of rice and a ladle of pork and potato stew. The rice ration these days consists of army mugful. This, three times of day with a watery stew, is what we have to live and work hard on. It's no wonder a man is a walking skeleton.'

19 OCTOBER

Fraser: 'Started the day with a fair breakfast — plenty of watery green stew and the average rice. Worked pretty hard all day shovelling stone in the coke furnaces. Copious curry and very light rice for dinner. Excellent stew for tea — plenty of dumplings, spuds, onions and bean curd. Plenty, that is, for here, though actually one third of what I could comfortably eat before I had tea at home. Worked with Ron Cohen today. He is rather an interesting person to talk to and well travelled and intelligent.' Like Don, Adelaide-born Cohen was a signalman, but from Harry Julian's unit, 8 Corps of Signals.

21 OCTOBER

Boughton: 'Weigh 70 kilograms. The lightest ever. Two buns per man tonight. Beautiful and sweet. Slim Bayliss caught by guard thieving in kitchen again. Put in guardhouse for indefinite period this time. Should be duration. Very cold. Still got flu too.' Another starving man who couldn't help himself; as Dudley and others would have known, Private Bayliss's days were numbered.

23 OCTOBER

Fraser: 'Very cold and windy morning. Breakfast turnip top stew again. Cold morning spent cracking stone. Dinner of 3 pieces of spud, a small amount of squid and a little sauce. Not much to wield a sledgehammer on all day in the rain. Spent a very cold afternoon shovelling stone into a crusher. Very poor tea — cold blubber and turnips boiled plus a spoonful of miso paste.'

Boughton: 'Coldest I've ever been in bed last night. Just freezing.'

26 OCTOBER

Fraser: 'Greeted this morning with the news that Tom Comerford had died. He died of pure starvation. Once a man gets a bit weak here they are on to him and he goes down very rapidly.'

Private Comerford grew up in the inner Sydney suburb of Glebe and was thirty-nine years of age. He'd been sick with beri-beri for the past few weeks and had slowly deteriorated. During the week, a Dog Walloper had made him march at the double after the Aussie complained that he was too weak to stand. Tom never recovered — he collapsed and died during roll call at 5 am.

1 NOVEMBER

Fraser: 'Months going very quickly. Felt sick this morning. Result of eating too much rice. Meals fair potato and dargon stew. Thick fish stew for dinner and excellent spaghetti stew for tea. Didn't eat rice for dinner. Swapped rice for stew at tea time. Suffering from diarrhoea again. Nice sunny day but very cold in the morning and evening. Good news though — rumours of letters, issue of soap and newspapers and 130 bags of sweet potatoes arrived.'

Boughton: 'Five hundred letters in. Hoping hard. Also papers to be issued again. Both great news. More spaghetti in stew tonight. Great stew by contrast. Nearly froze in bed last night. Little sleep. Warmer today. Soap issue, more sweet spuds in. Certainly an eventful day.'

As the first signs of winter began to be felt, Captain Barrett was waging a one-man battle against disease. Diarrhoea continued to strike down many of the POWs and the Sydney doctor searched desperately for a cure: 'Cleary is very sick — has mucous diarrhoea. Look for amoebae during afternoon. Daniel Quinn very weak this morning. These cases are very worrying. We will lose a lot of men if they are not given an opportunity to strengthen. Look at some faecal specimens.' As Sandy suspected, Lance-Corporal Cleary and Private Quinn would not be long for this world.

3 NOVEMBER

Boughton: 'Still very cold. Terrible day. Work very hard. Knees up like footballs from beri beri. Watchman took all our pipes from us today at 9 a.m. and didn't give them back to us until 5 p.m. — for Ray getting caught smoking in the wrong place at the wrong time. Most awful day and worst, if possible, but great day for Gummy and Fishface.'

4 NOVEMBER

Fraser: 'Usual green stew for breakfast, boiled rice and fair potato stew for dinner, fish pumpkin and turnip top stew for tea. Very sick in the stomach all day and unable to enjoy meals. Glorious sunny weather — just like autumn at home, makes me very homesick. Spent all day thinking of lying in a deck chair on the back lawn with a book, wireless and a table laden with fruit, chocolates, cakes and biscuits and cigarettes. The walk home at night with the smell of wood smoke and food cooking also brings poignant memories. Ah well, it can't be long now.'

5 NOVEMBER

Boughton: 'Death Leo Cleary. POW No. 64 of Divy Signals. Died 7 a.m. Was in a very poor way for the last few weeks. They gave him a job in the kitchen to help him along. But he couldn't eat. Had been in squad since coming to Japan. A very nice fellow. Diarrhoea and beri beri.'

Leo was another school teacher, from Armidale in northern New South Wales, and was aged just twenty-seven. Jack Mudie supplied a moving verse in his memory, while George Gray noted with sadness how Lance-Corporal Cleary would now never see his young child, born after their departure from Australia.

7 NOVEMBER

Boughton: 'There is a letter for me. They have not been given out yet, but still this is my biggest day so far — also coldest and bleakest day so far. Last night was the hardest of my life. Finished exhausted at 4 a.m. Now out here again, the only one of us on it tonight. Rest on holiday.'

9 NOVEMBER

Fraser: 'Worked together with Rateye all day unloading bricks inside a shed. Very easy. Got sopping wet coming home. On picquet [guard] tonight. Cold, wet and windy. Giving breakfast rice to Frank to do it for me.'

Boughton: 'Colonel inspected factory last night. Had to stay up for inspection and 19 hours change tonight. Finished work earlier this morning but still exhausted. Dull day, not quite so cold. Shift went to bed 10 a.m. All up to stand attention in yard from 11 to 12.30 p.m. because of men thieving rice from Jap workmen. Not cleared up yet but two suspects. Fingers too stiff to write more now. Going back to bed to 3 p.m. Spaghetti and black tea. Molly's birthday. Good luck darling.'

11 NOVEMBER

Anon: 'Armistice Day but not for us. This time last year working on the road at Singapore. Hoping we would have been released by now. Breakfast green stew. Very poor.'

Fraser: 'Still suffering from diarrhoea. Fair dumpling stew for tea. Same job in afternoon and sopping wet going home.'

Boughton: 'Gale and rain storm on now. Fish rolls in stew for dinner, very tasty. Lot of men with diarrhoea again. Extra blankets issued, also toilet paper, toothpaste, brush. Five men in guardhouse for thieving. Slim Bayliss permanent fixture.'

12 NOVEMBER

Fraser: 'Cold, wet, windy miserable day outside all day. Diarrhoea very bad.' Boughton: 'Dinner time. Warm now this afternoon. Bitterly cold early. Bread issue again.'

13 NOVEMBER

Another man died. Corporal Garnett Judd from Newcastle had been seriously ill for some time. Like so many other men, he'd been sent to work when he wasn't fit enough and died from lack of proper care and attention. Judd, who was more than fifty, was a World War I veteran and had two sons in the army. He was one of the most widely respected men in the camp, and especially popular among his fellow diggers in the 2/20th. It was perhaps significant that Judd's passing wasn't recorded in Fraser's diary entry for this day; once again it was food that made the biggest impression.

Fraser: 'Red letter day — issue of 9 lollies, 2 eggs, sugar and 2 oz cocoa. Dry cocoa and sugar mixed together tasted to me like the finest dark chocolate. Just shows how hypersensitive one's taste is for anything decent.'

Boughton: 'Issued with half a cup of cocoa and three spoonfuls of sugar. Mixed it up and ate it like chocolate. Beautiful. Also had some boiled lollies. Best so far today. Today our thirteenth death with the passing of Garn Judd. Was a pioneer of 2/20th Battalion. Finally died from bronchitis and general weakness after months of beri beri and diarrhoea. The tragic part is that there are letters to be given out in a day or so and there are some for Garn after all this time.'

15 NOVEMBER

Boughton: 'Our fourteenth death today with the passing of Danny Quinn, another popular man of the 2/20th Battalion. Died at 7 a.m. from bronchitis and general weakness. Danny was over 40 years old and slept next to Norm Reed. Great fellow.'

Like Henry Dietz, Dudley had found a good mate to help him through the bleak times, in his case 28-year-old Norman Reed, a sapper with the 2/12th Field Company. As for the late Dan Quinn, the A Company original had made quite a name for himself throughout the 8th Division, having been the referee of choice for a host of soccer tournaments from inter-battalion level up to AIF–British forces matches and even the 1941 Malayan Cup Final. Born in Scotland but a resident of Wollongong, Dan Quinn had certainly had his impartiality tested during the last few months under Naoetsu's cruel regime.

Anon: 'This month appears to be very critical regarding men's health. Men who had stood up to hard going throughout the year of work, hard climatic conditions and lack of nutritional food, are feeling the strain.'

Fraser: 'Had the symptoms of flu all day. Miserable outside scratching slag. Very bucked to get two letters from home tonight. First word so far. Dated 1942, 18 months old, but nevertheless very welcome.'

16 NOVEMBER

Fraser: 'Excellent pumpkin and dargon stew for breakfast, very poor bean curd and green stew for dinner. Very dirty, but finished day with lukewarm bath. Tea of good boiled rice, boiled blubber, sweet potato and crab roll. Quite good. Beri-beri becoming very troublesome. Hands and feet becoming swollen and legs very stiff and painful. Scotty Allanson died of weakness this morning.' Geoffrey 'Scotty' Allanson was a lance-corporal with the 8th Division Signals. While his physical deterioration hardly put Scotty in rarefied company during the second half of '43, the 26-year-old from Adelaide was one of only two South Australian volunteers within C Force.

By now even the usually positive Sandy Barrett appeared to have resigned himself to many more deaths. He was particularly saddened by Garnett Judd's death a few days previously: 'He is the victim of overwork and insufficient food. He had bronchitis and cardiac failure. I am very sorry to see him go, but expect about eight per month from now on. Gloomy outlook.' Dr Barrett had no doubt who to hold responsible. 'The civilians in charge of work parties are deliberately sweating on the sick men,' he continued. 'I hold them more than half responsible for Judd's death. They will, I fear, kill many more men yet.'

21 NOVEMBER

There was still no let-up in the violence. Today one of the men, who was suffering from beri-beri, got badly beaten after going back to bed. Jimmy Houston was clearly enraged by what he'd seen: 'When all the workers had left camp this germ, as we all call him, got Reg out of bed, stood him up against the wall and started punching him all over the face. The dirty swine. Hardly a day goes by that he doesn't do some of the boys over. The hard part of it is that we will never have a chance to get some of our own back.'

24 NOVEMBER

Fraser: 'Went on gruel today in effort to cure diarrhoea. Good sweet potato and green stew for breakfast, vile blubber curry for dinner. Fine day. Same job as yesterday. Looks like repetition of last winter's work this winter. Snow heavy on mountain tops now. Gradually creeping closer. Rather tasteless spaghetti stew and light issue of gruel for tea. Very welcome hot bath after work.'

Boughton: 'Another mandarin each today. Small and rather sour, but mixed mine in issue of rice. Made something different.'

25 NOVEMBER

Fraser: 'Dargon stew and still lighter issue of gruel for breakfast. Dinner — curry with no vegetables in it. Fish roll and blubber stew for tea.'

Boughton: 'Date plum each. Papers given around for optimism. Life nearly normal in Moscow again. Theatres open. Business same as pre-war. Mussolini returned to Italy to lead new fascist party. Papers six weeks old. New flannel shirt each, long sleeves and warm. Best issue so far. Also pair of long cotton underpants. Down to 61 kgs. I didn't think I could ever lose so much weight. Sixteenth death today. Private Clarrie Kingham died this morning. Another bad beri beri case for a long while. Clarrie, who was 33, came from Tichborne near Parkes. Decent fellow.' Another 2/20th original, from D Company, Private Kingham actually passed away on the previous day, at around 4 pm.

Meanwhile, Doc Barrett was becoming increasingly frustrated by the lack of medical supplies and his inability to control the disease. 'The diarrhoea has me completely beaten,' he admitted. 'I have no idea of its real cause and do not know enough about beri beri to know if it will cause this type of death. I do hope that our captors would do something about finding the cause of the diarrhoea and let me in on it.'

28 NOVEMBER

Fraser: 'Cold day spent making rope. Breakfast — cabbage and sweet potato stew. Dinner same — with addition of a little pork. Tea — bread with mashed sweet potato and onion gravy.'

Boughton: 'Tobacco issued. Small mandarin each in camp. Date plum each at work. Big day. Still on night shift. Much easier but have to carry up a ramp and it's playing up my beri beri. All sorts of rumour as to our job in the near future.'

29 NOVEMBER

Boughton: 'Go on 19 hour shift. Bitterly cold day. Twelve months today since we left Singapore and what a year! I can only pray that we are not here for another 12 months. If we are, there are plenty who won't go the distance at the rate the boys are going. Our Jap diaries have been handed back to us after being in for a few days for inspection. As I am copying this out of mine there are a few days blank, but I think I can remember anything important.' This was the first hint that Dudley had two diaries — the official Japanese version and his own more incriminating catalogue of events.

30 NOVEMBER

Fraser: 'Very cold morning. Afternoon of wintry sunshine. Tea — brown, thick stew of bean curd. Dargon and greens. Boiled sweet potatoes again for supper. Beri-beri getting painful and diarrhoea worse. Feeling very weak.'

Boughton: 'Came in at 6 a.m after another early night. Only thing wrong is that when we finished around 2 a.m. there were no fires to warm us. Lots and lots of odds and ends in Red Cross comforts came in few parcels — cocoa, sugar, books and bully beef. But only a few of each. Must get ready soon. Just got time to glance through paper which I hear gives more good reason for optimism regarding an end to the cursed bastard of a war. The talk here consists practically solely of food, especially battered supper put on last night. Got ours this morning after night shift. Small pieces of sweet spud each. Scorchy but bloody nice, especially with light rice. Would give anything for a bath. Feel filthier than ever before in my life.'

1 DECEMBER

Fraser: 'Spuds cut out of rice, resulting in still further reduced ration. Getting very weak on it. Fine sunny day but too weak and miserable to enjoy it.'

Boughton: 'Another month starts. How many more? In carbon [at Shin-Etsu] last night, stirring molten pitch and other ingredients for half-an-hour or so, then stamp into moulds for carbon. Fumes everywhere. Suffocating, nearly vomiting all the time. Come off shift at noon almost collapsing. Only two hours sleep. None the night before. Now going to bed at 2 p.m.. Seventeenth death today. Ted Gentle, from Singleton, died this morning at three-o-clock. Had been very bad beri beri case for months. Gave me some salt the other day for nothing, which shows his character. That is a big thing here, as you pay dearly for a bean.' Again, perhaps Dudley's night-shift work led to some confusion regarding specific days. Private Gentle's death was officially recorded as being on 30 November. Ted enlisted in March '41 and joined the 2/20th up at Mersing.

3 DECEMBER

Anon: 'Health very good. In fact unless I am on very hard work I feel 100 per cent. Actually whistle and sing to myself now, a sign of being in good spirits.'

4 DECEMBER

Anon: 'Two tragedies in one day. Deaths of William Hale and Keith Ainsworth. Spent 28 hours in bed.'

Dudley Boughton was too sick to write his entry on this day but eventually recalled what happened and put pen to paper on 12 December. In it, he makes mention that his mate Norm Reed should have his diary if he dies. 'Entering this from memory,' he began. 'Entered RAP hospital on December 4 with pneumonia. Never felt so bad in all my life. Thought I was a "gonner" for sure. Saw Norm Reed re diary etc. Bill Hale POW 195 of 2/20th died approx 10 a.m. from abscess on hip, general weakness and beri beri. WO Keith Ainsworth died this morning approx 11.30 from pneumonia. Both were in beds next to me. Was in day boys and at Walgrove with Keith. Fine fellow. Very sudden, as previously OK.'

As a warrant officer first class, Joseph Keith Ainsworth (of A Company, 2/20th Battalion) was the most senior fatality in C Force since Colonel Robertson's passing at the end of March. Another soccer player, 38-year-old Ainsworth was born in Bathurst but resided in the northern Sydney suburb of Ryde. Welsh-born Private Hale was with C Company by the time hostilities commenced; Bill was another Newcastle man and, like Keith, died at the age of thirty-eight.

6 DECEMBER

Fraser: 'Total dead now 19. Looks as if only the very fittest will survive the winter. I hope to God this war soon ends. Breakfast this morning weak dargon stew.'

9 DECEMBER

Barrett: 'Very cold today. We are overcrowded with pneumonia cases. Now have six in sick room. Captain Yates has been bloody sick and is unable to eat which is a bad thing. Called up in the night to see Jack Huntington with asthma and pneumonia. He soon quietened.' Just five days before this matter-of-fact entry, Sandy Barrett had lost two patients in one day, in Hale and Ainsworth. It was the first time, but by no means the last. Albert Yates would soon pull through, but the suffering was far from over for Corporal Huntington, another man from C Company of the 2/20th.

11 DECEMBER

Fraser: 'First falls of snow today. Very cold and miserable. Sick parade in for two more days. Couldn't eat breakfast but enjoyed dinner of good pork stew.'

Anon: 'Very cold and wintry. Returning from work this evening in the dark and seeing the homes lit up and the people sitting around the fires while the snow fell outside, made me realise how such could be so at home.'

12 DECEMBER

Boughton: 'Our twentieth death today with the passing of WO Jack Hogarth, POW No. 18 of Divy Sigs, at 7.45 p.m., in bed opposite me. Died from the effects of beri beri, diarrhoea and general weakness. I've never seen anyone as thin as he was at the end. Doubt if he was five stone when he died. I am going to miss him a lot. I worked at Harbottle Brown [a liquor bottler] with him for seven years preceding my joining the army. He had only just moved to Manly before coming away and we'd planned a few good dinners together after this show. Jack was on "no duty" for quite a few weeks, mostly not improving, though always cheerful. So it is very sadly that I say goodbye. A real gentleman, a soldier and above all a very good friend.' Warrant Officer Hogarth was born in Claremont, Western Australia, and was aged thirty-six.

Houston: 'One hundred and eighty letters arrive today. I hope I get one.'

13 DECEMBER

Boughton: 'Couldn't straighten up to walk. Temperature 39.8 [Fahrenheit]. First night had to sleep in guard room and fall out in freezing cold on parade ground for Roll Call in the morning. Have been in here for over a week. Feel a lot better, but have felt awful. It's a terrible sickness, especially when you can't get your breath except with great pain, previously could do nothing for myself, but this morning have managed to write another letter card home, this one to Dad and makes about six. More mail came in yesterday too and I'm told there is one for me and it's dated July this year. I have been a very serious case. Doctor has told me I must keep quite still. Three good men have died right next to me so far. I have been getting a 5 oz bottle of thin milk daily, also about 4 ozs of bread. This is in addition to three small rice issues and three stew issues daily, about breakfast cup full of each. At first this was enough but am very hungry now, but when all said and done the whole day's issue would neither equal in quantity one meal at home. Have written all the preceding in semi dark as we are in sort of stalls. Also we are crawling with lice. Ray [Barnett] just took his flannel off and it is covered. Naturally reading is impossible so time drags between meals, you just lie here and hope for meals and recovery. Has been snowing outside for past two days. Everyone hoping for Xmas day now when we all hope for good big meals and Red Cross parcels. Jack Huntington pretty bad. Mr Kono the interpreter just brought him in six letters. From news in them they definitely know he's OK, so hope things are the same with my family.'

The lettercard to which Dudley was referring reads as follows: 'Dear Dad, Happy to say got first mail, year old from you. More in now. Think one for me. Hope my sixth got home, still smiling with the old chin up, praying for reunion and that you are all well. Am healthy and well treated. Deepest love to my darling wife and you all. Write often. Don't worry. Good luck. Dud.'

On the same day Sandy Barrett found himself emptying the Japanese latrines and pondered what might have been. 'What a shame we were not taken prisoner by a civilised people,' he wrote. 'Many of us would have disobeyed the surrender order [in Singapore] if we had known or even guessed at things we have been ordered to do here. I hope our countries decide to fight this case 'til he [Japan] is finished and not let him off lightly. Our few lives will not matter if this is well done.'

15 DECEMBER

Boughton: 'Doctor said I'm coming along fine this morning, yet my chest still feels very sore, very hungry. Changed my shirt last night, otherwise would never been able to sleep. I must be down to 9 stone now. Was 13 stone 8 lbs at one time. No news at all to break monotony. Vince Burns just passed away at approx. 11.45 am, as they brought the dinner in. He has been very low all morning and has had beri beri pretty badly for a fair while. Vince was a great sort of fellow and very popular. Always cheerful and a great fellow to do day's work with, as he cheered you up so much. Vince was POW No 94 of my squad, a furnace man since last September. He came from North Sydney and was engaged to a girl in Manly. This makes the 21st death for us.' Another 2/20th original, Private Burns was thirty-eight years old and was born in Charters Towers, Queensland, before moving south.

16 DECEMBER

Fraser: 'Another fairly fine and very easy day. Still off the food and feeling as weak as a kitten. The whole camp had to stand to attention from 8.30 p.m. till 11.45 p.m. because four galoots went outside the fence to thieve salt. Some chaps are absolutely irresponsible.'

Boughton: 'I've just been talking to Vince's best mate. Vince was the sole support of his mother, over 60, incredibly sad. I'll be the world's greatest pacifist after this show. There won't be enough money in the world to get me away from my family again, should I have the luck to get out of this. Everyone still seems confident that we'll be out of this by Easter. Sincerely hope so, otherwise who knows. Norm took my clothes to work to boil them this morning (lice). Finest mate I ever had, Norm Reed. With luck now we hope to spend a lot of time together after this. Intend to give Norm a better time than he ever even dreamt of. Jack Huntington has been moaning and groaning a bloody lot in the last hour or so, making it impossible to sleep. About six have done their business in bed this morning so that at times the room smells like a piggery. Oh well I suppose it breaks the monotony.'

17 DECEMBER

Fraser: 'Still chilled to the bone after last night's episode. Been eating two rice balls for breakfast instead of rice for last two days. Very tasty but not much. Merve Gronow behaving very decently and giving me all he can afford and more. Gave me all the bean curd out of dinner stew today, giving me a very tasty dinner. Cracking carbon this morning. So weak that after six strokes with a hammer I'm absolutely exhausted.' As with Dudley and Norm, Don found his Samaritan from outside the ranks of his original unit. Private Gronow was a Sydneysider and a 2/18th man.

Boughton: 'Disturbance here last night, some of the men went outside the Camp and brought back some salt. They weren't caught, but civilians saw the men and informed. They must have known what would happen as civilians around here are like flies, 24 hours a day. In my opinion they are bloody fools. Got bashed after owning up last night and again this morning. Did the night in the Guardhouse, work this morning. Salt is currency for rice, bread, tobacco etc. as it is very rare. Received letter from Mum and almost wished that I hadn't as Mum seemed so very sad.'

18 DECEMBER

Fraser: 'One year since we started work. Hope to God we don't have to complete another one. Comparison between conditions now and one year ago is woeful. Lost over three stone and now as weak as a kitten.'

Boughton: 'There have been several anniversaries lately, worse luck. Landing at Nagasaki, arriving here etc. Today is the anniversary of our first day's work in Japan. I'll never forget it, nor the feed we got either, through mistake. Rumours of party at Stainless and Shin-Etsu. Men may get an apple or something.'

20 DECEMBER

Boughton: 'Death of Johnny Miller, our 22nd death. Fifth death since I came in here last night. Johnny Miller went without a murmur in his sleep so no one is quite sure of the time. But was approx 1 pm. It was apparent for some days that there was no hope for him. They gave him some lollies and he said "Gee they're great." Half a dozen of them and a few drops of soup was all he had for days. There was nothing left of him when he died. Didn't know Johnny before coming in here. He died from diarrhoea and general weakness. Was too far gone to help himself when they brought him in here.' Yet another from the ranks of the 2/20th, Private Miller hailed from Sydney's Granville and was twenty-four years old.

Fraser: 'Suffering badly from pellagra [cracking of the skin]. Legs are practically useless. It's an agony walking home at night and climbing stairs is something I dread. However, I must keep on I suppose. A chap has too much behind him and too much to hope for to give in at this stage.'

21 DECEMBER

Fraser: 'Enjoyed rice balls again and managed to eat most of dinner. Weather hasn't been too bad lately and work is easy, so I'm not faring too badly. The legs are still the prime cause of my misery and self-pity though.' From this point, Don is too sick to continue writing. His birthday will come and go on 4 January without comment from the one-time AWA Beam Wireless telegraph clerk.

22 DECEMBER

Boughton: 'Good old Norm came to the rescue with a loan of a pkt. weed. Finest mate I've ever had, scolded me for smoking, but gave it to me without any mention of its return. John Hurley passed away this morning at 3.30 from effects of diarrhoea and malnutrition. His body was positively nothing more than a skeleton.

With the skin stretched taut over it. Poor old fellow. Was over 40 and put up a good fight for a long time. Was very popular [with] No 3 squad and always looking for recipes to make good things when he got home. Only in here a couple of days. I'm in his position now. Over 24 Deaths, and 7 since I came in here 16 days ago when Jack Huntington POW No 50 of the 2/20th died approx. 11am from effects of beri beri and pneumonia. Jack was a Corp. in No 2 NCO Squad and was very well known. He had been on camp duties and rations for weeks past, so entered here in pretty good condition but for last fortnight in here. He seemed to find it very hard to breathe, moaning and groaning most of the time. Tragic part was that only a week ago he got some letters from his people saying how delirious with joy they all were as they had just been informed after 18 months (Letters posted 1943) that he was alive and how they were awaiting his return.'

Corporal Huntington had finally gone. Jack was from Woolwich in Sydney and was just twenty-five years of age. C Force's other fatality this day, Private John Hurley, was close to forty and had been living across the harbour in Glebe before joining the 2/20th at Wallgrove in mid 1940.

23 DECEMBER

Boughton: 'Our death list went to 26 this morning with the passing away of Bob Chaney of Divy Sigs at 3.30 am. from the effects beri beri, and Merv Herps at 5.30 am. from diarrhoea, beri beri and general weakness. Bob was POW 136. Only three weeks ago Fishface gave Bob a belting for not working hard enough when the poor fellow was too sick for anything.' Private Merv Herps of the 2/20th hailed from Windsor, north-west of Sydney, Signalman Chaney from Wentworth Falls, in the Blue Mountains. Both Merv and Bob were still in their early twenties.

It had been a devastating day for Barrett and his team in the sick room — four deaths in just over twenty-four hours. Little wonder that after marching back from work each day, the men's standard questions were 'What's for tea?' and 'Who's died?' It wasn't that the men had stopped caring for each other, just that death was now all around them.

Dudley continued: 'Bob Farley caught in store last night, gave him a bashing and sent him to work. No pity for him as he got rest of mob punished as usual for his misdeeds. Also leading to lose us any privileges or any other little extras for Xmas. And god knows how we are all looking forward to filling up on Xmas Day. Every man here has lost 3 to 5 stone this past year, from too much work and too little food. Diarrhoea pretty bad now, seems to be running right through here as most of us have it. Hope I'm alright by Xmas Day. The Japs took Bob Farley round on the Roll Call for exhibition purposes tonight, his face is just one mass of pulp with slits where his eyes are.'

24 DECEMBER

Anon: 'Christmas Eve. On night work. My thoughts are on the busy period at home. No doubt we are temporarily forgotten in the excitement of the Christmas shopping. I expect and hope this time will see us all in our respective houses next year.'

Boughton: 'This is my second Xmas Eve in this place and I pray that it is my last. Am going to try and describe today in detail. Firstly it is raining and not very cold, by contrast with a foot or more of snow last year. We look like getting over "The Festive Season" without any more deaths although Frank Warren is not the best with pleurisy and pneumonia. Wal Lewis has had a guitar here (bought with a donation from the Pope) since last night and has been ever so feebly strumming it and crooning a few parodies. Many rumours about menu tomorrow. The latest news is that at 4 pm we are to be issued with tin Bully [beef], tin M&B [penicillin] and cocoa, sugar and salt each. But now the "great difficulty" has arisen from the fact that there is 1 Red Cross Parcel for every 15 men and the articles in a parcel are milk and choc down to soap and a small pkt of tea. Wal Lewis had previously started to give a bit of a concert asking us to join in the spirit of the occasion and sing softly if well enough. Now after about two numbers the voices have all changed over to parcel business. Now 15 of us have decided to split into 3 groups and draw 5 lots so that eliminates possibility of one getting soap and the other milk. I think it is a good idea. Got weighed a while ago. Not so light as I thought I'd be, considering I really have no legs now. Went 58 kgs. Think it's bedrock now. Stopped raining. They've put a bit of pine brush around the room, but it only makes one feel more homesick.

'P/S Jim Geddes gave me a shave today, so ends Xmas Eve. Got bully & tin M&B each. P/P/S. Would give 10 pound for a quart of Old.'

Private Warren's name would appear again all too soon in Dudley's diary, unfortunately for Frank. Jim Geddes was a member of C Company, 2/20th Battalion, from Surry Hills in Sydney.

25 DECEMBER, CHRISTMAS DAY

Anon: '3 a.m. Work finished. Have been under a degree of mild excitement for the last 15 hours awaiting the distribution of Red Cross supplies in addition to Christmas Day special meals and what today will bring forward in general. Am hoping that this day next year I will be at home looking back on the day as a POW in Japan. Quite a happy day. The atmosphere is most friendly, an unexpected and unusual episode for a POW camp with a stomach full and satisfied. Myself in a very happy mood and all in such a condition. Awakened from a very heavy and solid sleep but with stomach pains which were not entirely relieved until midday. Went to work at 6.30 p.m. While waiting to start went through a period of home sickness.'

Boughton: 'Merry Christmas and all my love to those at home. Have a couple for me. Woke up very squeamish this morning after spending most of the night on the pan. Still very bad in stomach and headache at 9 am. Been awake since 4 am. Reveille 6.30 am. All woke up singing a bit and passing the compliments of the season. Breakfast. I had a large cup of cocoa. Enough. Mixed nearly all remainder of sugar and cocoa with issue of rice, but still got it as I feel a bit queer. Looks like a great chocolate cake. Going to eat it as soon as possible, but know it will make me worse. This morning we have been issued with 1 bun, 1 pkt cigs, biscuit and 6 mandarins.

Also we are in the throes of drawing this parcel between 15 of us. Most of the men have just had a bath, but for myself I didn't think I'd better, the way I feel.

'P/S (Written five days later). Xmas Day fine and warm. Still racing for the pan every hour or so. Now just on tea time 30th December and the intervening space has been definitely the worst and most dangerous period of my life (war included). My thoughts when capable of any, have been solely on decent food and lemonade and cakes. I just can't describe how I feel, except that I can hardly move to get on the pan and if I stand up I fall over. I'll try to write now what I can remember of the latter half of Xmas Day. We had an indifferent stew for dinner, but for tea had dozen pieces of baked spud and piece of battered pork about the size of a match box, also sweet bean and an issue of bread. In the night the boys put on a very good concert, just above us in No 1 Squad attended by Japanese. MC Jack Mudie. Even with 6 feet above me on a thin wooden floor I just sort of fell asleep but woke up for Auld Lang Syne. This day I only had about 2 oz warm water and soup. Will I make it up?'

26–30 DECEMBER

Boughton: 'The past few days have been generally very cold with snow some short fine periods. All talking incessantly of our foods and cups. Bloody fools as it only makes you feel worse.'

Anon: 'Old year reflections. The year 1943 went through fairly quickly. Lost my comrade Acker [Private Joe Harper]. Last year's severe winter I weathered well considering we came from a hot tropical climate.

'New year hopes — that our remaining time spent here goes just as quickly. That my health remains the same. Will see our release.'

30 DECEMBER 1943 – 1 JANUARY 1944

Boughton: 'Been too sick to fill in diary, averaging about 20 times on the pan every 24 hours and eating practically nothing. New Year's Eve a great disappointment. All had expected something or other but just the same as any other day in the year, except no rice for breakfast. Two more deaths today, total of 28. Joe Harper of the 2/18th died approx 4 am. Only came in last night, was delirious during the night and had passed on when they found him. Joe was in the 2/18th Band, a stretcher bearer in action till wounded and one of the finest and cheeriest fellows it's ever been my luck to meet. Most others of the 18th and other units too will never forget him. Ernest Steel Rudd of the 2/20th died at 1.45 pm as Jap doctor was examining him. Looked like it all day, as his breathing was very loud.'

Joe Harper, a musician from Waterloo, Sydney, was thirty-five when he died. Corporal 'Steel' Rudd, another Newcastle recruit, was in his early forties. Steel's death marked the twentieth fatality for the battalion.

3 JANUARY

Anon: 'Len Lewis [sic] passed away.' Twenty-eight-year-old Len Louis was from Innisfail in northern Queensland. He appears to have been the only other member of the 2/26th Battalion at Naoetsu apart from Lieutenant Alan Campbell.

4 JANUARY

Boughton: 'Slim Tracey of the 2/20th died this morning from diarrhoea. Had been bad case for weeks but had improved a lot lately and was quite okay and talking to us and had a drink at 6.45 a.m. yet died at 7.15 a.m. Very sudden and most unexpected. Was in No. 1 Squad. This makes 10 per cent of our original complement.'

Another C Company man, Lance-Corporal Cecil 'Slim' Tracey hailed from Young and was thirty-three years of age.

5 JANUARY

Anon: 'Thirty dead of 300 in camp. 90 men off sick. George Lubey, 22, from Sydney and Leslie Cobban, aged 25, from Young passed away.' George and Leslie were from the 2/18th and 2/20th, respectively.

7 JANUARY

Anon: 'Frank Warren from Boorowa died. He was from the 2/18th and only 23. American doctor in camp, Dr Holiday.' It's not clear how long Holiday stayed in the camp, but a Captain I.H. Goad arrived from the Philippines the following day to allow Barrett to have a well-deserved break.

8 JANUARY

Anon: 'Passed away: A. Johnstone. Private Neville Buffett (Norfolk Island).' Another day offering multiple deaths, both from the ranks of the 2/20th. New Zealand-born Neville was one of the eleventh-hour reinforcements at Singapore Island along with Mick McAuliffe. Albert Johnson enlisted in June '41; the 25-year-old hailed from Booligal, in south-western New South Wales.

10 JANUARY

Anon: 'Examination by Jap civilian doctor. 196 Red Cross parcels arrive. Three parcels for me. Bully beef 7 ounce. Spam 12 oz, Kraft cheese 6 oz, Sugar 6 oz, Chocolate block 6 oz. Coffee 6 oz, prunes, ham and eggs, soap. Peach and powdered milk. 105 cigs. Chesterfields. Old Gold, Camel, Philip Morris.'

Here the entries end. There were several blank pages left in the unknown writer's diary, but there is no indication of the author's fate. Don Fraser died on 21 January 1944, aged just twenty-three. His personal belongings, which included his safety razor, shaving brush and diary, were later given to his family in Frankston, Victoria. Private Dudley Boughton of the 2/18th Battalion died a week later, on 28 January. He was twenty-nine years old. His best friend, Norman Reed, who cared for him in his final days, kept his promise and brought Dudley's diary back to Australia and delivered it into the safekeeping of his father, John Horace Boughton, in Sydney.

Throughout this period and right until the end, Captain Alex Sandy Barrett worked tirelessly on behalf of the men in his care. At one stage he was treating nearly 150 seriously ill men, some of them close to death. John Cook claimed that the doctor sat on his bed on three occasions and refused to let him die. Often Barrett was verbally abused and manhandled by his captors for trying to protect and treat the men. But for his devoted and untiring commitment to his men, the final death toll at Camp 4-B would have been much higher. If ever a soldier deserved a medal for his wartime service, Captain Sandy Barrett did.

CHAPTER 9

LIVING UNDER THE SHADOW OF DEATH

Outside the grim confines of the Naoetsu camp, by early 1944 there were signs that the war was beginning to turn in the Allies' favour. In Europe British and American bombers continued to pound German targets and the Allied forces had gained a foothold in Italy. Soviet troops were advancing on German-occupied Poland and Leningrad was finally relieved after a siege that had lasted 900 days.

The US military had launched major operations aimed at eliminating Japanese forces in the Pacific and were well on their way to breaching Japan's Central Pacific perimeter at the Gilbert and Marshall Islands. Soon they would attempt to retake Western New Guinea.

But for those being held prisoner, their ordeal was far from over. Many of the Australians who were captured after the fall of Singapore were being used as slave labour on the Burma–Thai Railway, including Merv Alchin. In all about half the 2/20th's total strength had been put to work on what would become one of Japan's most notorious building programs.

Amid the death and disease at Naoetsu, the camp's brutal and unforgiving regimen under Lieutenant Oota showed no sign of weakening during the first month of 1944. Random acts of violence continued. Perceived wrongdoings by the men were invariably met with savage retribution by the guards.

There was only one punishment feared more than a vicious beating, and that was severe guardhouse duty. In winter, this was invariably a death sentence. Any prisoner meriting this level of punishment (in the guards' eyes) would be confined to the guardhouse at night without an overcoat, boots or socks; in many cases, the men would have their hands tied together and chained to the wall also, forcing the poor soul to maintain a standing position. Freezing winds and snow would blow through the large cracks in the wall, so there was no shelter from the elements. Of the twelve prisoners who received this punishment during their time at Naoetsu, only two survived to tell the tale. James Downie of the 2/20th Battalion was one of them.

The 24-year-old private from Bellingen, on the northern coast of New South Wales, usually worked at Nippon Stainless but, one day in January, he was ordered to make up the numbers on the outside work party at Shin-Etsu. Working in the rain and sleet, he soon became soaked to the bone and was permitted by the guards there to dry his coat in front of one of the furnaces. In the extreme heat, the material was scorched; to make matters worse, when he returned to Stainless the next day, the battering his already unhealthy body had taken from the previous day's labour left Jim unable to perform to the civilian guards' high standards. The Australian was therefore ordered to report to the orderly sergeant's office once back at the camp. It was the Bull on duty that day — Sergeant Tadeo Shibano.

He was first made to stand outside in the snow for two hours before being interviewed by Shibano, who then proceeded to slap him across the face twenty times with a heavy canvas belt. Downie's face was cut, swollen and severely scarred. After the belting, he was made to walk into the snow until it came up to the level of his mouth. Clothed only in British battle dress, the Australian was forced to stand there for another two hours before being taken back to the guardhouse, where his boots, socks and coat were removed.

For a period of ten days, Jim would wake up each morning covered in snow and then be ordered back to work at the stainless steel plant, where he would receive the minimum daily ration of two rice balls. Every evening he would then return to the guardhouse for more of the same. There were no blankets to protect him from the cold until day six of the ordeal. Before then, the only way he'd been able to keep himself warm was by following the guards' orders to clean their boots and shovel the snow. After a week and a half, Jim had lost nearly 20 kilograms in weight and was close to death.

Surprisingly, Private Downie didn't give in. He was taken to the sick room, where he spent the next three months at death's door, before the Japanese took pity on him and sent him to Shimagawa Hospital in Tokyo for special treatment. Amazingly, he eventually recovered.

Not so Private Bob Farley, the habitual food thief from the 2/18th Battalion, who was on the receiving end of similarly barbaric treatment around this time. Having been caught stealing food at the chemical factory, the 23-year-old was sentenced to severe guardhouse duty from 25 January onwards and made to stand naked in a snowdrift for six hours before being let inside by his tormentors. There in the guardhouse, Bob was repeatedly beaten until he was screaming for mercy, pleading for an end to the agony. 'Kill me! Kill me!' he cried as the blows rained down on him.

In the morning he was sent back to work. But for the aid of his comrades, Farley would never have completed the journey. His head, which was so bruised it appeared to be double its normal size, rolled limply on his shoulders. There was to be no lunchtime meal to revive him — although Warrant Officer Williams did manage to slip him a rice ball while the guards were distracted. Then it was back to camp and another six hours of standing naked in the snow while being beaten by the guards. How he remained upright was an achievement in itself. How he survived so long was a miracle. By now, his eyes were merely slits in a badly swollen face, his mouth just a tiny opening above a bruised and battered chin. Slowly, he sank to the floor, all signs of life extinguished.

It was incidents like this that brought Snowy Collins to the conclusion that the Japanese were intent on killing as many of them as possible. 'It was depressing, but you just felt there was nothing you could do about it,' he says. 'After seeing one man go, then another, you had to get over it and carry on. You had to look after yourself if you wanted to survive.'

Frighteningly, given that Albert Johnson's death during the night of 8–9 January was the camp's thirty-fifth death, by the time Bob Farley succumbed on 27 January, Snowy and the others had seen fifty of their countrymen perish at the hands of the Japanese. Halfway through that month, the number of men listed off sick totalled 102. Few of the remainder who were sent to work in the factories could be described as fit enough for even moderate labour. Most had a temperature and were suffering from coughs and heavy colds.

The period from mid January through to the end of the month was almost certainly the blackest fortnight of the war for the Naoetsu boys. Lance-Corporal Wally Blackaby, another signaller, died on 14 January at 11.30 pm. The 2/20th's Private Frank Bunnett expired at 4.30 am the next morning. Frank was from Newcastle, New South Wales, via Haddiscoe in the English county of Norfolk, and was in his mid thirties.

On 17 January, one of the blokes who'd been on furnace duty, Thomas 'Peewee' Jones, a 2/18th man, died. Among the ranks of the 2/20th, Private John Boman succumbed to pneumonia a day later, and the same condition claimed the lives of Private Fred 'Slim' Bayliss — a permanent fixture in the guardhouse, as Dudley Boughton had put it back in November — and Lance-Corporal Tommy Edmunds, on 20 January. By this point there had been fifteen deaths since the start of the new year, and all of them could have been avoided had the right treatment and drugs been available and the Japanese generally more humane.

However, the fact was that some of the guards had a financial stake in the men's demise. While the makeshift coffins were the work of Tom Clegg, a Western Australian from 8 Corps of Signals, two civilian guards, Akira Yanagizawa and Masaji Sekihara, were paid 30 yen (about a dollar in today's money) for each of the small pine boxes that Jim Chisholm requested for the purpose of storing the deceased's ashes. Keen to boost their earnings, it was clearly in their interest to increase the body count by beating as many of the sick as possible. Yanagizawa in particular was known to target critically ill POWs and promise to make a box for them. 'No go back to Australia,' Gummy would tell them in broken English, while alluding to the brick-size bits of wood. Understandably this was often too much for the sick and dying, whose frail mental and physical health would steadily worsen after a few minutes in his company.

While the guards at Naoetsu appeared to be untroubled by the deaths, the mortality rate had not gone unnoticed by the prison administration in Tokyo. Under pressure from the factory bosses, who paid for the POWs' rations and expected a full, 24-hour workforce in return, the Japanese commanders realised that if the trend continued, there would be serious consequences for the nation's wilting war machine. Following a visit by one Dr Fuji around the middle of January, a party of local workmen moved in to knock down the officers' quarters and smoke room. Better facilities for the sick were desperately needed and so the area was to be converted into a hospital.

Until its completion, the old sick room remained the only area where heating of any sort was permitted. A single, small coke fire was the extent of this heating system. Unfortunately the conditions were ideal for lice in winter, the insects thriving and multiplying in the slightly warmer temperature. The whole camp was crawling with them, infesting blankets and clothing. Because everyone slept fully dressed to keep out the cold, any clean clothing was quickly contaminated by the bugs' onward march.

Further outbreaks of pneumonia, diarrhoea and beri-beri during the winter meant the sick room was always full to overflowing. As a result, there was only space for the critically ill. Those who were deemed less serious had to lie in their squad rooms, where the standard of care was inevitably lower. Even so, the healthy men rallied round whenever possible to change their mates' beds and bathe them.

Eric Richardson was only twenty-four years old at the start of 1944, but he'd seen a lifetime's worth of suffering since leaving the family home in south-west Sydney. Eric vividly recalls a bowl being handed round, in which men were encouraged to place a spoonful of their own food for those who were sick. 'It was pure altruism — a beam of light in a sea of darkness', as he puts it so poetically.

No amount of compassion could deal with the sub-zero temperatures and biting wind outside, however, which cut through the gaps in the walls, occasionally dusting the occupants in a film of snow. Nor the violence continually dealt out by Shibano and his fellow thugs in the guardhouse.

Not surprisingly, the sick had continued to die at an alarming rate. By the end of that month, C Force had lost a total of fifty-three men. From the 2/20th Battalion, the new names to add to that unofficial honour roll provided by Boughton and the unknown diarist up to 9 January were as follows: Frank Bunnett (age 36, from Bobs Farm), Corporal John Boman (30, Kyogle), Joseph Ianna (23, Lismore), Donald MacLeod (29, Drummoyne), Lance-Corporal Tom Edmunds (33, Castle Hill), Fred 'Slim' Bayliss (24, Enmore), Dennis Connor (26, Milsons Point), Wally Lewis (25, Northmead), Tommy Power (35, Sydney), Alan Cleasby (30, Wollongong) and Ralph Corderoy (36, Stockton).

During the same period — 10–30 January — the 2/18th had farewelled Tom 'Peewee' Jones (age 41, from Armidale), Corporal Bill Ashford (35, Coonamble), Bob Farley (23, Brisbane) and Dudley himself; while 8th Division Signals lost Lance-Corporal Wally Blackaby (37, Wagga Wagga) as well as Eric Bell (34, Harbord) and Don Fraser.

Throughout this time, as Sandy Barrett's temporary replacement Dr Goad worked tirelessly in such impossible conditions, and with the odds stacked so heavily against a patient surviving, Lieutenant Alan Campbell continued to serve as C Force's de facto chaplain and honorary padre. The funeral party would often include Kevin Timbs and Theo Lee, should a semblance of Catholic ritual be required.

As February arrived, the sick list was still growing every day. When Sergeant Eric Wannan of the 2/20th died at 8.30 on the morning of Friday 4 February, there was sadness at the young Scot's passing, but at least there would be extra space for someone else. How callous, how unfeeling. It wasn't in their nature to be like this, merely a measure of what happened to a man when surrounded by so much misery.

The day after Eric's demise, Naoetsu received a visit from the Tokyo camp commander. He appeared just on reveille and made straight for the squad rooms. It wasn't that unusual to have military top brass at Camp 4-B, but although the diggers didn't know it then, it signalled a change in Japanese treatment of the sick and weakened.

The commander, who spoke good English and had been educated in London, was accompanied by a couple of doctors. They spent twenty minutes in the squad rooms, examining every man and noting their condition. Afterwards the commander asked Captain Chisholm how everyone was being treated. The Australian officer did not hold back. Presented with the opportunity to tell the truth for once, he complained about the appalling conditions his men had been forced to live in and the virtually non-existent medical care. Chisholm fixed the Tokyo general with an angry stare and declared there was no doubt that Japanese ill-treatment was the prime cause of so many deaths; every one of the fifty-four (and counting) fatalities at Naoetsu had been a victim of the Japanese, he concluded.

The visitors wrote it all down and left. There was no immediate improvement in the men's health — indeed, the mortality rate continued to rise and the behaviour of the guards showed no sign of mellowing — but at least Tokyo would be aware of the truth and maybe, just possibly, efforts would be made behind the scenes to reduce the death toll.

On 8 February 1944, the new hospital room was finished and in the afternoon the sick were moved in. Unlike the rest of the warehouse building at Arita, the medical facility had several large windows, which brightened things up considerably. Corporal Kono, the camp interpreter, even set up a gramophone and played some music to cheer up the lads.

Sadly it all happened too late for the 2/20th's Private Alan Healy, Cowra born and bred, who died at 5 am on 9 February from pneumonia. Three days later, Signalman Jack Roberts also gave up the fight for life. Like Alan, Jack was twenty-nine years of age. He'd been suffering from a nasty eye injury caused by a small piece of steel that had half blinded him while at work in the Stainless factory. Despite his deteriorating condition, the guards insisted he return to work. Given the right rest and treatment, Jack would almost certainly have recovered, but compassion was never one of the Naoetsu regime's strong points.

This had long been a common theme in the treatment of prisoners just before they died, a precedent that had been set as far back as July the previous year. Jock Kerr had been so ill from dysentery when he got to the steel factory that the civilian guards had attacked him for being unable to work. He'd then had to be carried back to camp but, again, Sergeant Aoki had classified him as fit for light duties and sent him back to the plant.

Six weeks after Jock's demise, Signalman Jack Baker had been treated even more harshly. The Faith Healer had judged him fit for work and sent him off to Shin-Etsu as usual. Jack was suffering from beri-beri and diarrhoea. Like so many other assaults, his was not a random beating but a deliberate act of cruelty on a man who was so weak he was clearly close to death's door. Baker lay motionless for several minutes before his mates carried him back to camp and, ultimately, his death bed.

So appalled by the inhuman treatment of men who were little more than skeletons, John Cook continued to keep a detailed record of each incident in the hope that one day the perpetrators of such unwarranted violence would themselves be punished. Others in the camp were likewise kept busy by the ever-rising death toll.

Whenever someone died, the body had to be transported on a cart to the crematorium several kilometres away. With the sheer number of deaths, and wood being in increasingly short supply, funeral duty was a common task for the prisoners. And, surprisingly perhaps, it was not without its levity. Surrounded by death and disease, dark humour was often the only way to handle such harrowing situations.

One winter's morning, Lieutenant Harry Woods found himself with a team of four men, pulling one of the latest casualties up the road to the crematorium when the body fell out of the wafer-thin box onto the road. 'We were trying to negotiate a snowdrift when the side of the coffin gave way and out tumbled the corpse,' Harry recalls. 'Without another thought, we simply picked him up and put him back in the box,' he recalled.

Unfazed by the bizarre incident, the five Australians made a joke about how the person in the coffin was always causing trouble when he was alive, before continuing their journey and delivering him to the funeral pyre. It was all in a day's work for the members of C Force, who had seen so many horrific sights over the past three years that they were no longer shockable.

But it was amazing that they kept their humour. Perhaps it was part of their Aussie character, the way they always managed to see the funny side. Like civilian prisons, the deprivation of freedom at the camp inspired many comical situations. And those who imposed their power were frequently the butt of jokes.

The twice-daily roll calls were not funny — indeed, they were often the worst parts of the day — but Japanese difficulties with the English language would produce fits of stifled laughter. One story that soon became part of battalion folklore concerned an unwelcome smell while the men were on parade one night.

'Everyone was standing strictly to attention with fingers stretched down their sides and eyes looking straight ahead when someone passed wind,' remembered John Cook. 'Well, the interpreter raced in with his little translation book and demanded to know "Who break-ed the window?", as he put it.

'Of course, everybody glanced at the window and we got into trouble for moving our eyes. So then he goes back into his office, only to return a few moments later wanting to know "who make-ed the farto". Everyone immediately burst out laughing, and we got another two hours of standing to attention. Things like that happened all the time.'

Call it gallows humour, but the fact that it was still possible to laugh while others fought to stay alive said much about the Australian spirit. This was one of the many miracles of Naoetsu.

The harsh winter weather continued throughout the first three weeks of February 1944. Despite the new hospital, another two men died. Private Albert Barber suffered a fatal brain haemorrhage on the 18th, and five days later pneumonia claimed the life of Private Lloyd Ball at the age of twenty-four. Mick was another 2/18th original, born in Wagga Wagga. Young Lloyd had spent part of his early life in Sydney's Redfern and was highly regarded as a stalwart of what was left of the 2/20th's B Company.

☙ ☙ ☙

On 27 February there was the first sign of spring. Yes, the roads were still like skating rinks, but it was noticeably warmer. The sun was shining and after a week or so it looked like the worst of winter was over.

And although the sickness that had decimated the camp over the previous year continued to thrive, at least the death rate appeared to be slowing. Compared to the twenty-five deaths during January, five men had perished in the whole of the month of February. Another POW died on 13 March, but not from pneumonia, the usual killer. Private Robert Griffin, who hailed from Inverell, died from a burst abscess in his ear. Yet another 2/20th original, Bob was thirty.

Towards the end of March, four Yanks arrived at Naoetsu. They would be the first of many American, British and Dutch POWs despatched to the west coast as the Japanese closed down other camps that were now in the front line of Allied bombing. The four Americans were warmly welcomed to Arita — because one of them was a doctor and the other three were trained medical orderlies. With a large number of men off sick and no trained medical orderlies among the Australians, the Yanks' experience would be welcome.

The new American arrivals took time to adjust to Naoetsu's strict discipline. Unaware that harmless incidents could sometimes escalate into major dramas, the Yanks often found themselves in trouble. On one occasion a Japanese guard accused the American doctor of laughing at him. Seconds later, the Yank was manhandled into the passageway for what looked like a ritual beating. Instead, the guard produced a sword and ordered the doctor to commit harakiri. Unsure of how to read the situation, the American thought it better to play along; he took the sword and proceeded to walk away. Having called their bluff, he was prevented from leaving and was forced to hand the sword back. Another potentially explosive confrontation had somehow been defused.

As March rolled into April and the weather continued to improve, camp life became slowly more tolerable. The men were encouraged to hold concerts — although some of the Japanese lyrics they were taught to sing were largely incomprehensible and impossible to pronounce. That had never stopped the fun for the Aussies before.

In a further indication of the Japs' concern over the mortality rate, an interpreter arrived on 30 April to talk to the men about camp conditions. He wanted to know why so many POWs had died, and the men had no hesitation telling him. Harsh treatment, poor facilities and a starvation diet, the interpreter was told. Next question?

A doctor also arrived about this time, when some 75 per cent of the camp was bedridden. Immediately he ordered a week off work for everyone and a slight increase in the size of the meals. The dry-barley diet was substituted for a type of sorghum seed, and Red Cross food, which had been delivered to the camp but not issued, was partially distributed. The men also received new boots.

Day workers at the Shin-Etsu factory started getting a bowl of soup at lunchtime. Made from two bucketloads of pigs' intestine, it was not the most appetising of meals, but it served its purpose. Despite the evil smell and revolting taste, the soup helped to flavour the boiled barley and became a staple ingredient of midday fare. At the end of the week, men were allowed to eat the dregs from the old copper in which the soup had been cooked. By now the stewed intestines resembled pasta and they became a much sought-after commodity.

The various improvements didn't put a stop to the beatings or the slave labour, but fewer men were falling seriously ill and if you toed the line, life was almost bearable. Although many of the prisoners were still only barely alive, no one had actually passed away since Private Griffin's death.

But, as always, there was still the threat of a dog walloping. John Cook remembered that during nearly three years at Naoetsu, there was never a moment when the men were not subjected to nerve-racking and cruel treatment by the camp staff. As he later recalled, referring to the brutal Japanese guards:

> It would seem that they spent all the time the men were at work dreaming up some fresh type of torture to inflict on them when they returned to camp. No matter how exhausted or sick a man was when he returned from the factory, he would in turn be rostered for an hour on fire or water pumping duty. These two jobs had to be performed at any time of the night and the men would be under the constant supervision of the patrolling camp guards who wouldn't hesitate to punish anyone they thought was slacking.

It wasn't always the Japanese who caused trouble. A spirit of unity prevailed, but there was often tension between the diggers and their superiors. As Chisholm had shown, the officers were not averse to dobbing in their own men to the guards.

In a diary entry for 12 June 1944, Jimmy Houston recalled an occasion in which one of the camp cooks received a bashing from the Jap interpreter after one of the Australian officers complained about his behaviour. 'Our bright and brave put him in to the Japanese interpreter, hence the beating,' Jimmy wrote. 'There's no harmony between the men and the officers in camp. All they do is think of themselves. Bugger the men, that's their opinion.'

The big Glaswegian had been particularly outspoken in the past about the officer class and privilege. But unlike at Changi, this is one of the few references to the social tensions between some of the Australian officers and their men. While most of the POWs accepted that the lower ranks went to work in the factories and the officer class stayed behind to attend to less physically demanding tasks, a growing sense of injustice had developed among some of the men. It was not a major issue, but it was beginning to rankle.

By the second half of July, the stand taken by Captains Chisholm, Barrett, Gibbings and Yates and Lieutenants Mudie, Woods and Lee — all of the most senior Australians, in fact — was definitely becoming a major issue to the Japanese. The camp commander was getting so incensed by the officers' refusal to do a day's work in the factories that he decided to cut their rations by half in retribution. The tiny portions were so miserly that even the men felt sorry for them.

The class distinction between Australian officers and other ranks was never as rigid as it was in the British and American military. The Aussies witnessed the wider division first-hand when a new batch of fifty prisoners arrived on 20 June. They comprised thirty Dutchmen, fourteen Englishmen, two Scots and a US major. The Yank looked as though he'd just stepped out of West Point military academy and was not slow to assert his authority. 'He was tough,' wrote Houston. 'I'd seen these blokes at the pictures but I never thought I'd rub shoulders with a real live one.'

And the American officer was not all talk. On one occasion he intervened to stop a guard laying into a man with his dog walloper. 'Previously when these bashings were going on our own officers stood by and never did anything about it,' Houston noted. 'But this Yankee major went to the Jap NCO about hitting the men with these sticks. He must have done some good for he stopped it.'

But not for long. The bashings were a regular form of punishment at night during air-raid drill. 'At any time during the night the guards would rush into the building, calling out all men for a roll call,' John Cook recalls. 'The guards never lost an opportunity to help the slower men out of the building by using their rifle butts, fists and boots. After standing on parade for anything up to an hour, the men would be dismissed and allowed back to bed.'

And as ever, the trivial offences — the position of footwear at the bedside, for instance — could invoke the guards' wrath. At night, clogs had to be placed at precisely 90 degrees to the bed space, but they'd often end up moved slightly as men walked by and accidentally stepped on them. Accidents didn't happen at Naoetsu: any clog deemed to be out of angle to the bed usually meant the entire squad being woken up and ordered to stand to attention at the guards' pleasure.

Around this time some men were still bashed across the face for simply going to the toilet. It was not uncommon to see a short Japanese standing on a chair to hit a 6-foot-tall Aussie about the head. And, naturally, the work continued. In victory or defeat, Japan needed its stainless steel and silicon.

On Monday 31 July, Jimmy Houston noted in his diary:

> I have had many a hard day at work since I arrived in this country, but they were like holidays compared with what I had to do tonight. The work was heavy but it was the heat that nearly killed us. Three of the lads collapsed completely and had to be carried out and one was left lying out in the open as he was in a pretty bad way. Sometime afterwards a walloper came along, thought he was asleep and started kicking him. One of our chaps saw what was going on, ran downstairs and told the walloper that he was sick. That still didn't stop 'Ossie' getting a few nasty kicks in the ribs.

Other punishments that were meted out at random required offenders to kneel for an hour or more, or to stand to attention with their arms raised above their head while holding a heavy object. While such measures did not inflict physical injuries, they could be exceedingly painful, even after several minutes. But few beatings equalled the violence suffered by one of the two Scotsmen, a youngster whom everyone knew as Jock.

On 18 July a fight had broken out between a Dutchman and Jock, and Corporal Kono, the camp interpreter, decided they should settle their differences inside a ring drawn in the dirt. After exchanging several blows, the pair were separated and the Dutchman ordered to leave. The interpreter, it transpired, had other plans for Jock, whom he clearly believed to be the guilty party.

Standing him to attention, Kono set about him with a dummy rifle, which the Japanese used for training. When the Scot lost consciousness, the guard proceeded to jab him in the nose, mouth, ears and eyes. It was a merciless assault, and it was far from over. As Jock lay on the dusty surface, the interpreter began to kick him. Then, reaching down to a pile of bricks, he threw them at the Scotsman's motionless body.

A medical orderly from the 2/10th Field Ambulance, Bruce Porter, tried to intervene. 'Don't you think this man has been punished enough?' the young man from Tamworth enquired, bravely offering to take his place. The guard lashed out at Porter but missed. By now he was so enraged and Jock so badly hurt, that the assault was the talk of the entire camp. And still the bashing continued. It was another two hours before the bruised and bloodied victim was carried away. Few believed he would survive, but Jock, who had originally belonged to the Argyll and Sutherland Highlanders, was made of stronger stuff. Within days he was back at work.

In spite of the guards acting as if it was business as usual, by August 1944 it was clear that the Japanese efforts to improve the POWs' health were beginning to work. In fact, after the death of Corporal Jim Griffin on 8 August — doubly tragic, given that his brother Bob had died on 13 March — there were no more fatalities at Naoetsu. Even the officers had been put back on full rations.

After six weeks on a starvation diet, Jim Chisholm and his cadre of officers had won their right not to be used as slave labour. Their resistance had worked and had earned the grudging respect of the rest of the camp. But the Japanese had other plans for the men who'd had the courage to stand up to them. Perhaps the best thing would be to split them up.

The date was 24 August. Five of the Australian officers — Captains Jim Chisholm and Albert Yates, together with Lieutenants Harry Woods, Jack Mudie and Roger Cornforth — were to be moved elsewhere. Yates, also known as Bunny, had a knack of distracting the guards whenever his fellow officers were writing their diaries; he would be sorely missed at Naoetsu, where he was known as a witty man and convivial company. Word was that they were bound for Tokyo. What more could fate have in store for them?

That afternoon they were ordered to hand in most of their personal belongings, including books and records, although Jack Mudie hung on to his diaries. He dropped them down the back of his shirt, where the small booklets would remain hidden until he could be sure it was safe to transfer them to his army-issue backpack.

Their departure would leave Captain Barrett in charge of the men. Theo Lee and Alan Campbell would likewise be staying at Arita. That evening, with the officer party packed and ready for an early start, Sandy asked a favour of his old mate Yates: would Bunny mind taking a letter with him? It was a scribbled note to Sandy's wife Joan, just in case Naoetsu got the better of the doctor from Rose Bay and he didn't make it.

Jim Chisholm also knew how much Joan meant to Barrett and promised to look after her if anything should happen to him. It meant a lot to the doc, who recorded the generous gesture in his diary. 'That was not a promise too freely given with real intent,' he wrote.

The following morning, the departing officers were woken at 3.30 am and left an hour later. It took almost seventeen hours to reach Tokyo Main Camp at Omori, on the outskirts of the city, but this was not to be their ultimate destination. After bedding down for a few hours on the cold concrete, Harry, Jack and the others were off again, this time in the company of four dozen fellow officers. The party marched the 6 kilometres to the railway station, where they boarded a train for Kobe, in the south of Honshu. Another sixteen hours passed before they arrived at their new home, Zentsuji, after a ferry ride over to the island of Shikoku. And when they got there, Jack Victor Mudie suffered the shock of his life.

Within minutes of their arrival at the converted school building, the fifty-plus officers were ordered out onto the asphalt assembly area and told to place all their belongings at their feet and step back — Jack froze. Concealed inside his haversack were all his diaries, documenting the brutal behaviour of the Naoetsu guards and the conditions under which the POWs were forced to live. If the journals were discovered, the consequences could be severe. No man was allowed to keep an unofficial diary, because of the damning evidence it would almost certainly reveal about their captors.

Happy Jack realised the game was up. 'A guard a few feet away seemed to be watching closely and there was no opportunity to rummage for them and put them in my pocket out of sight,' he explains. The men were then marched off to their new quarters, leaving all their possessions there on the ground. Jack Mudie was scared.

'All that night I was haunted by fears of what would happen to me if the diaries were found and read,' he wrote later, 'and I prayed that the examination of my things would be cursory and the records passed over.' Jim Chisholm knew he was terrified and tried to reassure him. 'Don't worry until there's something to worry about' was his motto.

The next morning, the Australians were instructed to collect their belongings and take them inside the camp building. There in the old schoolhouse, Jack opened up his haversack and examined the contents. His mouth dropped — the diaries were missing ... They'd been found by the Japanese, and now he was for it.

Twenty-four hours passed but there was no news of his journals. Jack was haunted by terror. The dread of being discovered consumed him.

Finally the Japanese interpreter, Asabuki-san, came looking for him, the diaries in his hand. Fearing the very worst, the 37-year-old former school teacher from Naremburn stood to attention and awaited his fate.

But the expected belting didn't materialise. Instead, something happened over those next few moments that was to change Jack Mudie's hitherto negative assessment of the Japanese character for the rest of his life.

'Wonder of wonders!' Jack wrote when recalling the meeting. 'He gave me the diaries with a smile, remarking that life in Naoetsu must have been very bad. Asabuki was, of all the Japanese I had encountered in the prison years, the only one who was kind and gentle, the result, as I found out later, of his own experiences.'

A second-generation Japanese who had been born and educated in the United States, Asabuki spoke perfect English and had returned to Japan for a holiday only to be prevented from going back home. Jack suspected he was bitter about the army forcing him to stay and pressing him to work as an interpreter. As the months went by at Zentsuji, he got to know him even better.

'He told me his Tokyo home had been bombed and both his father and mother had been killed in the raid. Even then, he didn't show any anger to us,' Mudie recalled. 'I hope he found peace of mind and happiness when hostilities were over.'

Just as Dudley Boughton had been so impressed by the brief glimpse of Japanese civilian life they'd caught on the way to Naoetsu, Jack's meeting with Asabuki offered him an insight into what Emperor Hirohito's citizens had been forced to endure of late. Naturally, it was an insight that was denied prisoners of war in the brutal labour camps of Naoetsu, Omori, Yokohama, Zentsuji and the like. Such revelations suggested that the Emperor's regional 'Prosperity Sphere' had somehow bypassed the home islands.

Life was certainly far from prosperous for the Japanese workers who toiled away in the country's factories for twelve hours a day.

Even schoolchildren were being made to work in the plants, some as young as seven years old. From Kobe and Osaka north to Tokyo and Naoetsu, the picture was much the same. One morning at Naoetsu, there was a bad accident in which a boy was badly burnt while working near an industrial furnace. He was in such a critical condition when they took him away that he wasn't expected to live.

Hisao Otskuka was fourteen when he was sent to work at the chemical plant in Naoetsu. A second grader in junior high school, he was made to work eight hours a day at Shin-Etsu, striking the iron as it came out of the furnace. Like the POWs, Hisao was given two small rice balls to eat during the shift. The teenager was spared the dog walloping, of course. The prisoners were put to work in a separate section of the plant from the civilians, but whenever he saw the Australians as they pushed their little carts around, Hisao would be struck by their skeletal form. 'They were so skinny' is his one abiding impression.

His wife-to-be, Masako, was aged seven in 1944, but she has a rather different memory of the POW work parties. During the summer she used to grow herbs in her garden and the Australians would be sent to pick them up in a truck. 'They were tall and hairy and always seemed quite amiable, but we never talked,' Masako recalls. 'Sometimes we'd give them rice balls. We felt desperately sorry for them. They even ate grass for lunch. There was often a lot of shouting but I never saw the guards belting them.'

Girls who were old enough were also made to work. Yuko Ohama was seventeen when she was sent to the Nippon Stainless Steel Company's factory at Naoetsu. Her job was to use a grinder to repair defective parts of the steel bars the plant produced. 'Every morning I'd take the train to Naoetsu and walk to the factory, which took about twenty minutes. On the way we'd see the POWs marching the same route, and sometimes they'd wave to us.'

There was no sense of the prisoners being ill-treated, Yuko says. Indeed, their affable manner on the march to and from the factories gave no indication of the horrors endured in the camp. 'I thought they looked fairly healthy,' she adds. 'Don't forget there were many Japanese also starving at the time. Indeed, ten out of the eighty students at Naoetsu Women's High School died from pneumonia or poor nutrition during the war, so both sides were suffering.'

The 240 members of C Force who had survived the nightmare winter of 1943–44 might have begged to differ with this assessment. Many of the Aussies would never be able to see the Japanese people in a favourable light, be they among the civilian population or from the Emperor's military machine. For Jack Mudie, though, the valuable insight he'd gained at least offered him hope. It was the first small step on what would be a long, long road to forgiveness.

※ ※ ※

On the outskirts of Yokohama, over on the east coast of Japan's main island, an American POW by the name of Louis Zamperini was also doing it tough. Second Lieutenant Zamperini, a New York-born former Olympic runner who was actually introduced to Hitler during the 1936 Games in Berlin, had already cheated death several times. In fact, well before he would eventually arrive at Naoetsu in 1945 and join the Aussies, 'Lucky Louis' would have enough wartime adventures to fill a book in their own right.

Back in May–July '43, Zamperini had spent forty-seven days adrift after his B-24 bomber ditched in the Pacific Ocean. He'd been attacked by sharks and strafed by enemy aircraft before getting rescued by a Japanese patrol ship — only to then be threatened with beheading while imprisoned on the island of Kwajalein (now part of Kiribati). Four months later he'd found himself near Yokohama, in the prison camp at Ofuna, which was the main interrogation facility run by the Imperial Japanese Navy. Louis had been looking forward to finally joining some other Allied POWs, but instead ended up running into an old student chum from his days at the University of Southern California. The friend's name was James Sasaki, a Japanese man — and he just happened to be Ofuna's chief interrogation officer.

In an effort to boost his meagre food rations, Zamperini had then gone on to become the unofficial camp barber, coming perilously close to removing a guard's eyebrows on at least one occasion. Later in 1944, Radio Tokyo would attempt to recruit him as its chief propagandist on the airwaves.

It was safe to say that if there was a likelihood of a miraculous escape, bizarre coincidence or other strange twist of fate occurring, Louis Zamperini was likely to be involved.

From 30 September 1944 onwards, however, it seemed that the American's charmed, eventful existence could be over. That was the date when Louis was transferred to Omori, a short train ride away, and home to around 600 POWs. On arrival at the camp, the US Navy pilot and the other new prisoners were lined up on a barren quadrangle of sand and gravel to await their orders.

Ten minutes later, the Japanese sergeant who would hurt, harass and humiliate Zamperini throughout his time at the camp — a man who could have given Shibano, Aoki, Gummy and Hoppy a run for their money when it came to defining the essence of human cruelty — strutted onto the parade ground. He paced slowly along the line, staring each prisoner in the face as he did so.

The first man to incur his wrath was a submariner, who then received a swift punch in the mouth. 'You do not stand to attention!' roared the guard as he moved to unstrap his sword. For a moment it looked like the Jap was going to strike the seaman across the face with the weapon, but he seemed to think better of it.

Zamperini's turn came next. *Whack*. 'Why you no look me in the eyes?' the guard demanded, as Louis lifted himself from the ground.

Whack again. 'You no look at me.' The brute's face was contorted with rage. As Louis later described him, this Japanese NCO had 'the cruellest eyes I'd ever seen'.

Sergeant Matsuhiro Watanabe was in his mid twenties, just over 1.5 metres tall and the personification of evil. His nickname was 'the Bird', simply because no one could find it in themselves to come up with one that accurately reflected the man's repulsive character. 'Deranged, brutal beyond belief, vicious, like someone who tortured animals as a child before turning his evil talents on people' was Lieutenant Zamperini's further assessment.

Watanabe would haunt the American flyer for the rest of his life. One day soon the Aussies in C Force and the Yank would cross paths, Louis free at last from the months of hell he'd suffered at Omori.

※ ※ ※

After nearly two years in Naoetsu, and despite the improvements that had been introduced since late January, most of the men had lost almost half their weight. By now hunger had long been a way of life, each item in their make-believe menus fast becoming a distant memory, to the point that the fantasy meal might always have been a figment of their imagination — nothing more. Had they really ever tasted that leg of lamb, the chocolate and coconut, the buttered steak, the prawns and crab, all the dishes that they'd been craving for so long? Sometimes they couldn't be sure.

Often they would steal, knowing full well that if they were caught the punishment would be both extreme and, quite likely, meted out to the POWs as a whole. Some men took foolhardy risks whenever the opportunity arose. On 15 September, one of the blokes was found with forty-seven potatoes, two loaves of bread, a cup of flour and one-and-a-half issues of rice hidden in his pack. He was put in the guardhouse, where he was subjected to the usual round of beatings.

The discovery led to a crackdown on the rest of the POWs. When the day workers arrived back in camp, no fewer than forty were found with stolen food. How they obtained it was unclear, but a thorough search of their clothing revealed rice, salt, pepper, mustard and a dixie-load of baked potatoes (which had apparently been cooked near one of the furnaces). Afterwards, the offenders received several whacks over the head with the dog walloper and were made to stand to attention with their arms above their heads for two hours.

And as always, acts of violence would frequently be provoked by the most trivial misdemeanour. At five o'clock it was accepted that the billy would be lit for an afternoon cup of tea. On this occasion the men were ordered to leave their brew and stack a load of wood. A few of the lads stayed a little longer to finish their cuppa, though, and suddenly found themselves being abused by the guard, who swept their mugs off the table and laid into the man who'd made the tea, identified in Jimmy's diary as 'Jack'. Reported to the Dog Walloper, he was made to stand to attention and given a resounding blow across the face. It didn't end there. When the Japanese orderly sergeant came in, he got another bashing, which left purple welts across his cheek.

'The brutality that we have to put up with since we came to Japan, from some of the guards and the camp staff are unbelievable,' Jimmy Houston recorded in his diary. 'We've been told many a time by someone on the staff that this is the strictest POW camp in Japan. I pity the poor creatures who are in a worse place than this.'

As well as the physical pain, much of the suffering at Naoetsu was mental. Few of the men would talk openly about it, but the stress was having a major psychological effect on them. Harry Julian admits to being traumatised by the bashings he witnessed during his years as a POW, specifically his inability to help the victims while they were subjected to such devastating violence. But the painful memories could stretch back to long before C Force's formation.

Would Henry Dietz and other X Battalion survivors ever be able to sleep soundly after the slaughter they awoke to at that fuel dump outside Bukit Timah? How could Harry Woods possibly come to terms with the atrocities that took place at the Alexandra Hospital? Or John Cook after seeing his best mate, Roger Mort, die beside him in the mad dash from Kranji. And then there were George Daldry and Don Alchin, two men who had started off on this crazy adventure with a brother in tow, the nipper they'd mucked about with since childhood, yet suddenly they were cast into hell without them.

Throughout his imprisonment at both Naoetsu and Zentsuji, Jack Mudie fought his demons by trying to keep his feelings to himself. 'The first thing you learnt was to keep your mouth shut,' he states. 'You had to bottle up any feelings of resentment because if you gave the impression you were hurt in any way, you'd invite further retribution. So you had to be an introvert, most definitely. And you also learnt that your duty was not only to yourself, but to your mate.'

Jack's philosophy was probably right for the time, but it was to cause problems for him in later life. Yet he had one gift that helped himself and others thrown together by war: his poetry. Just as Wally Lewis's music had for so long, Jack's verses would inspire the men to keep going when all seemed lost. No doubt, it was a legacy of the warm familial evenings back in Windsor, when his dad would read Shakespeare and other works to the Mudie brood. Writing poetry would help to maintain his own mental balance, as well as his fellow POWs', through the discipline of concentration.

'I had to churn the poems over in my mind until they were absolutely perfect,' he explained. 'I didn't have any spare paper to correct them or anything like that, so they had to be memorised and amended in my head before I could put them to paper. I think, in great measure, that sort of mental training helped keep me sane.'

It was bad enough to forfeit your freedom, but even harder to be devoid of loved ones who might share the load. While the Naoetsu boys would encourage each other, each man acknowledged, just quietly, that their future was far from certain. The Allies seemed to have the Japs on the run now, so the rumours claimed. But what would happen to the POWs at the end of the war? Would they be executed en masse, to remove all evidence of the brutality they'd been subjected to?

Such questions would create a constant frisson of fear within the camp. 'Every day was bad because you thought you were going to die,' John Cook admitted. 'We weren't too happy about the prospect of being killed, yet amazingly there were no suicides in the camp. No nervous breakdowns. Somehow you just survived from day to day.'

Kevin Timbs felt he lived in the shadow of death throughout his captivity. 'They reckoned if the Allies landed in Japan, we would all be killed. I'd heard some camps even had graves dug ready for the bodies.'

It may have been because they felt they had nothing to lose that the men would occasionally give the Japanese a bit of lip. Once during an official inspection, a general complimented Timbs on his size and strength. 'That's because they grow men where I come from,' the dinky di New Englander retorted, much to the delight of his mates. Furious at the perceived insult to their general, four of the guards took Kevin aside and laid into him. He was not a pretty sight when they'd finished.

Part of his spiritual strength and determination to survive came from his faith. He was a good Catholic boy, and with no priest in the camp, he was often called upon to comfort the sick and dying. 'I was as rough as bags but I agreed to do it. All I could do was kneel beside them and talk. It was very, very depressing sometimes, but it also strengthened my own convictions and the will to live.' While his folks in Glen Innes might have been mourning his passing, Kevin Brendan Timbs had no intention of checking out just yet.

But he used to wonder whether there was someone watching over him. Fate intervened on one particular night, when he and a fellow D Company sergeant, Mick Hammond, were ordered to walk in a continuous circle out on the parade ground. The punishment had been going on for hours on end — and they'd had enough. 'I said to Mick, "They're going to kill us tonight if they keep this up." And he agreed. Well, Mick was a prize fighter, and we were so desperate that we hatched a plan to kill the guard.'

They were deadly serious. The idea was to complete the next circuit and then launch a surprise attack on their tormentor, bludgeoning him to death with his wooden club. Neither was thinking clearly, because killing a guard was a capital offence; besides, in their emaciated state, they were hardly likely to pull it off. But just as they got to the final turn, the guard ordered them back to bed.

'Somebody was looking out for us that night,' Kevin concludes. 'There's no doubt in the world that if we'd gone ahead with it, all the other guards would have killed the lot of us.' Who knows, perhaps that Bren gun on the *Kamakura Maru* wasn't loaded after all.

※ ※ ※

Winter arrived early that year. By November 1944, autumn had disappeared and the days became increasingly bleak. Cold winds and squally showers blew in from the Sea of Japan, lashing the camp with a frenzy that did not bode well for the months ahead.

Each day continued to produce more pain and misery, particularly once a fresh batch of army guards had arrived in December to replace Shibano's mob. Word was, the new sergeant and his underlings had previously been cracking skulls out Tokyo way — Yokohama, someone said. There was little to look forward to but Christmas, which, from past experience, produced a rare increase in provisions and a Red Cross parcel for each man. Unfortunately, there was no easing of the workload or any reduction in discipline. A misunderstanding over a trivial request had some of the men standing to attention for over an hour on Christmas morning.

Those who were on duty in the factories tried to fit their festive celebrations around their shift times, and all at least were assured of a reasonable feed. Christmas dinner 1944 may have lacked a turkey and all the traditional trimmings, but the plate of curried potato peelings, bowl of barley and jam sandwich would send most of them to bed that night with a full stomach for a change. Before then, there was an evening church service followed by a concert, but there was no denying the utter despair that prevailed throughout the camp as gale-force winds and hailstones battered the flimsy wooden structure.

Diaries from this period talk of the 'wildest days' the men had ever seen. 'The cold was intense and hailstones as big as marbles hit me in the face and stung like hell on my way to work,' Jimmy Houston noted on 27 December. 'On these sort of days I long for sunny Australia.'

Everyone suffered from homesickness, especially at Christmas, and the Naoetsu boys' wintry environment was the antithesis of what their friends and relatives down under would have been experiencing at the time. 'We hope that next Christmas will produce something better than potato peelings,' Jimmy added optimistically. And, for once, the optimism was not misplaced.

The new year started with a bashing for Sandy Barrett. As was so often the case when the guard details changed over, the new Japs on the block liked to make their presence felt. Barrett was extremely popular among the ranks, and the men did not take kindly to their doc receiving a belting. Underscoring what the new regime had to offer perhaps, this was the first time the Japanese guards had ever given C Force's medical officer a going over.

The one piece of good news to celebrate the new year was the departure of Sergeant Major Tadeo Shibano on 1 January. As Jimmy noted in his diary entry for the following day: 'The mongrel who has been in charge of us for over two years was transferred to another camp yesterday.'

All the men were encouraged to send letters home to their loved ones, although few could be sure they'd be delivered. On 27 January, Theo Lee summed up the feelings of many in the short note he was allowed to write to his girlfriend Joy: 'My Darling. I pledge again all my love and loyalty to you, Joy. In spite of the long separation sweet memories forever bind us together. Fondest love to mum and dad, both families, friends and the children. I am well. The photos are grand. God bless you my darling — Theo.'

January produced more heavy snow, making it difficult to get to work, and sufficiently deep to completely cover some of the two-storey houses in town. The weight of the snow was so great that the roof of the grinding factory at Nippon Stainless collapsed on 18 January, burying five young female workers. A feeble attempt by the Japanese workmen to free the girls was abandoned after half an hour and they were left to die. Their bodies were recovered the next morning. The Australians had long since come to the conclusion that their captors had little respect for human life, and even less for women.

As Jack Mudie was beginning to understand, life under the shadow of death extended well beyond the compound walls of prison camps like Naoetsu and Zentsuji. This was Japan at war, and the conflict was raging increasingly close to home.

By now, there were sixty small caskets containing the ashes of the men who'd died, stored in the officers' living room. And they were taking up a lot of valuable space. One morning the Japanese announced that the ashes would be removed from the camp, placed on a truck and taken to the local rubbish dump the following day. This did not go down well with the Australians, who had protected the remains of their fellow countrymen and felt powerless to prevent their disposal.

In Captain Chisholm's absence, Barrett had hoped to take the ashes back to Australia at the end of the war to give them a proper burial. To scatter them on a tip would be heart-wrenching, especially for their families. Some prayed that night for a solution and urged others to follow their example. The following morning their entreaties were answered in a most unexpected manner.

The local Buddhist priest happened to be visiting the camp and invited several of the officers to join him for tea. 'He was a cultured gentleman and spoke beautiful English,' one of them recalled.

As he was about to leave, the priest asked them if he could help with any problem. Immediately the Australians raised the issue of the ashes. He was appalled by what he heard. Turning to the camp commander, who was also Buddhist, he demanded that the truck should instead deliver the caskets to his temple, Tokuon-Zan Kakushin-ji, on the outskirts of the town. And that's where they stayed until the end of the war.

CHAPTER 10

'KILL THEM AND LEAVE NO TRACE'

Like the men in C Force, the American Second Lieutenant Louis Zamperini had learnt that the only way of surviving as a prisoner of war was to buckle down. He had spent the last three months of 1944 at Tokyo Main Camp at Omori, south of the Japanese capital. Now down to 40 kilos, he wasn't so much bothered by the lack of food — although naturally he would have liked more — but the loss of dignity. And that was largely due to the actions of one man: Sergeant Matsuhiro Watanabe, otherwise known as the Bird.

'Watanabe punched me in the face for not looking into his eyes and when I did he slapped me again,' Louis would recall in his autobiography, *Devil At My Heels*. 'You couldn't win.' It was true the Bird picked on him more than the other men and would often beat him for no reason, mostly with his fists or a stick, but occasionally with his thick webbed belt. Once when the Bird entered the barracks and walked down the centre aisle, he accused Louis of being the last man to stand to attention. Brandishing his belt like a baseball bat, he whipped him across the temple with the steel buckle, which weighed at least a pound.

The blow forced Zamperini to the floor, bleeding and in excruciating agony. And then as he got to his feet, Watanabe handed him a tissue to wipe away the blood. For a moment Louis thought the Bird had taken pity on him. But seconds later he struck him again in the same spot, leaving him unconscious on the ground.

Like those barbarians of Naoetsu, Shibano and Kuriyama (the Bull and Snake Eyes, respectively), because Sergeant Watanabe was not an officer himself, he hated those who were. Often he would deliberately target high-ranking POWs, abusing his power and taking every opportunity to humiliate them. And Louis Zamperini fitted the bill perfectly. At twenty-seven, he was the same age as the Bird, yet the American was a lieutenant.

All that Louis could take comfort from during that early winter, like the men at Naoetsu and countless other POW camps on Japan's home islands, was the sight of US military activity in the skies and the various rumours and reports that filtered their way in among the prisoners. The Japanese were losing the war and a transfer to a larger, more remote camp had to be on the cards if their captors wanted to exploit the POWs' potential as slave labour. Maybe then, Louis could escape this bastard Watanabe. He had to keep hoping.

Zamperini was right — the camps were being consolidated, away from the east coast. But the best news was that it wasn't only the prisoners who were facing the prospect of imminent transfer. The guards too were being moved around, including the monster Matsuhiro Watanabe. When news of his departure leaked out towards the end of December '44, the POWs could hardly contain themselves. Without the Bird to torment them, life would be almost bearable. Lucky Louis was back, and he enjoyed two months or more of comparative bliss.

Zamperini's own transfer came on 1 March 1945, when he was told he would be moved to Tokyo Camp 4-B at Naoetsu, on the opposite side of the country. It took some twelve hours to reach and by the time the train pulled into Naoetsu station, the weather conditions were appalling. There were 4-metre-deep snowdrifts, with houses buried up to their rooftops. Just marching through the freezing streets to the prison camp was difficult enough.

As he and other newly arrived POWs were herded into the parade ground and the gates were closed, a guard bellowed, 'Stand to attention!'

There they were made to wait for half an hour, their hands and feet like ice blocks. Eventually a door opened and the duty sergeant appeared. Walking down the line of men, his fearsome, black eyes seemed to bore into each and every prisoner he passed.

Louis Zamperini was dumbstruck. He gazed straight ahead and into the eyes of the scourge of Omori — his old enemy Sergeant Watanabe. 'Inside I gave up all hope,' Louis would later write. 'It was the lowest ebb. The cruelest joke … I realized I would never get away from the Bird.'

❉ ❉ ❉

From the Australians' perspective, the newcomers added pressure on the limited facilities at Arita. Herb Lamb, Snowy Collins, Bluey Firth and the other diggers looked out over the arctic parade ground that day and saw eighteen Americans, three Englishmen and a New Zealander. Most of them were naval and air force officers, including the commander of a US submarine.

The new arrivals were hardly a welcome sight to the men of C Force. Joe Byrne would soon find a positive in the situation, however: 'When they all arrived we got a bit of relief as the Japs had somebody else to thump and kick about …' The 25-year-old didn't always see eye to eye with the Americans.

And there was another bonus. The news they brought from the outside world was keenly sought by the Aussies, who had been starved of reliable information for so long. The officers told of Allied advances in Europe and the Pacific, and were confident that the end of the war was imminent.

They brought news of Germany's withdrawal from the Ardennes in early January, the liberation of Auschwitz later the same month and the destruction of Dresden in February. At the same time in the Pacific theatre, Japan's loss in the Philippines had effectively isolated it from much of its territory in South-East

Asia, thereby reducing access to resources essential to feed the Japanese war machine.

This certainly confirmed what little the Naoetsu boys did know first-hand — namely a noticeable increase in air activity throughout the area, and frequent air-raid drills in the camp and in the factories. In the first few months of 1945, the men learnt, the air strikes had been stepped up dramatically, with regular bombing raids on Japanese cities and airstrips.

A couple of months later, on 5 May, these optimistic views were reinforced when a Boeing B-29 was spotted over Naoetsu and dropped three bombs near the Shin-Etsu chemical factory, killing three Japanese and injuring thirty more. Soon American bombers were passing overhead two or three times a day. Although they were an encouraging sight, the prisoners had doubts about the crews' ability to hit their target, a situation that prompted the POWs to dash for shelter every time they saw US aircraft.

Lieutenant Tom Henling Wade, of the Loyal Regiment (North Lancs), was one of the three English officers in the Omori party on 1 March. A former journalist, Henling Wade was most sensitive to the position the camp's sitting tenants were now in. He'd been expecting the worst, but found a well-disciplined camp with good morale, largely thanks to the efforts of Lieutenants Theo Lee and Alan Campbell.

'I felt intensely sorry for these cheerful Australians who had spent [three] grim winters in this nightmare camp,' Wade wrote in his book *Prisoner of the Japanese*. 'They were so game and sound and reliable still; they faced the world with a united front, their discipline was uncorroded and they were not as ruthless as the mixed prisoners of Omori had become.'

However, the camp's fraternal atmosphere was about to change further. For a start, in light of his rank as a submarine commander, an American named Fitzgerald would become C Force's commanding officer. Then there was the mateship that had helped the Australians survive more than two desperate years in captivity — what Eric Richardson would memorably refer to as 'a beam of light in a sea of darkness'. This vital bond would be severely threatened by the addition of 400 more POWs to the camp's nominal roll, characters who would undermine the brotherly love that had helped to keep the diggers going. From late April through to early the following month, in preparation for their arrival, extensive building work was carried out in the camp.

Many of those who turned up on 14 May were American servicemen who had been captured on Wake Island in December 1941. They'd then been shipped to China and Thailand as slave labour, and finally despatched to Kobe and Osaka, where they were bombed out — hence their being sent to Naoetsu. Others were British who'd been put to work on the construction of the Burma–Thai Railway. All were men who had suffered the extremes of physical hardship and were shadows of their former selves. Suddenly the camp was holding over twice its normal complement and space was at a premium. The Australians, who'd had Naoetsu to themselves for two-and-a-half years, took particular exception to the Yanks. Joe Byrne and George Daldry, street fighters both, took on a couple of Marines in an attempt to lay down some ground rules.

'The Australians couldn't stand them and used to throw clogs at them as they gathered at the wooden door,' Henling Wade confirms. The former journalist's eye-witness account of the first few days after the arrival of the new batch of men said it all:

> The whole group arrived with almost no baggage, torn and dirty clothing or ill-fitting Japanese uniforms and extremely low morale. The Aussies did not care for them and tended to keep their friendships among themselves. Too many of these men were demoralised and shifty. Stealing became commonplace. Four of the new arrivals were appointed cooks, but within ten days they were thrown out for sneaking extra rations to their friends and smuggling stolen food out of the galley to trade for tobacco or clothing.
>
> Gangs of these men scuffed about the camp seeking to trade their paltry belongings for food or tobacco.

Overnight they transferred the whole appearance of the camp. They thronged corridors and blocked doorways offering their trades. They even woke men sleeping after a night shift. The place looked like a thieves' market or shoddy bazaar. There was a medieval look about these thin-nosed, grey faced men in over-large greasy overcoats and oily caps, sneaking food out of their sleeves.

If these broken men thought Naoetsu represented a soft passage, they had not bargained on the likes of Sergeant Watanabe, who was now in full control of camp discipline after replacing Sergeant Shibano shortly before Christmas. The Bird had soon made life a living hell for the Australians at Camp 4-B. It was he who had personally dished out bashings to Campbell and Captain Barrett, during the first two weeks of January. By the end of the month, a new camp commander had arrived from Tokyo, as if to put an official seal of approval on the Bird's activities.

Justice was swift under Watanabe's rule. Jimmy Houston would record on 19 May how three of the new men — a New Zealand lieutenant, an American-born Japanese and a doctor — were all beaten for perceived wrongdoings. A day or two later, an Australian and a Yank were bashed for speaking during roll call. And on 26 May, confusion over the whereabouts of a lost boot led to the man deemed responsible for its disappearance being hit about the face with the same boot when it was subsequently discovered. These were not quick taps on the head, but savage blows inflicted with severe force.

Later that same day, two of the boys who'd missed roll call were knocked to the ground and kicked in the face. One of them had already had his gums stitched up following a tooth extraction. The pain was unbearable.

Joe Byrne was one of the few POWs brave enough to stand up to the Bird. 'We called him "What-a-Bastard", because it rhymed pretty good with his name,' he remembers. 'Watanabe would measure you up with the left hand and break your jaw with the right. One day I thought he was going to kill me.'

Joe had been cornered by him for no apparent reason and Watanabe was striking him and screaming abuse. The young Aussie suddenly flipped. 'As far as I'm concerned, you're a coward, Sergeant!' Byrne blurted. 'The only reason you're hitting me is because there's a guard behind you with a bayonet and he'd kill me if I did anything. You know and I know that if we're ever let go from this hellhole, I'll knock your bloody head off!'

Ever one to acknowledge a degree of Irish hot-headedness in his make-up, Joe admits: 'It was a fit of temper and I nearly got killed over it.' Everybody knew it was pointless to lose your temper in such a situation, but Joe survived to tell the tale and even won the admiration of many of the other men.

On 29 May, Watanabe laid into the camp dentist. Soon afterwards, all the officers who'd been put to work in the garden were beaten up for not working hard enough. One of them, an American, was so badly injured that he lost consciousness and had to have a bucket of water thrown over him to bring him around. When he came to, he received another beating. Four medical orderlies endured the same treatment. By the day's end, at least a dozen men were sporting terrible black eyes.

And so it continued — day after day of random bashings. Sometimes the men would be strip-searched. On other occasions they would be clubbed with dog wallopers or made to stand to attention without movement for several hours.

Invariably the punishment was unjustified. Tom Henling Wade remembered getting back to camp one night after a hard day's work only to suffer a particularly painful and humiliating ordeal. Watanabe claimed that some of the prisoners had stolen a couple of vegetables, and he wanted to make an example of them. 'Admit now!' he bellowed across the parade ground.

One by one, POWs stepped forward until there were eight. But the Bird wasn't satisfied. He wanted more. Turning to Tom, he called, 'Wado — out front.'

Innocent though he was, the English officer was also about to be punished. What followed was extraordinary, even by Naoetsu standards. The rest of the camp was ordered to line up and slap those men who had stepped forward. 'Hit hard with arm extended and hand open,' Watanabe instructed them.

By the end of the ordeal, each of the so-called thieves had been hit 220 times across the face. 'We were all reeling at the end of it,' recounted Tom. 'Some of the British soldiers whispered "Sorry sir" as they hit us, but it was still very painful. We got a hell of a beating that day and I hadn't even taken any vegetables.'

For the rest of the Japanese staff, Sergeant Watanabe's behaviour had become a popular form of entertainment. His men all appeared from the guardhouse door, laughing at the spectacle.

Half the camp seemed to be bruised and battered as they went about their daily duties. The punishments were not only painful and demeaning, but often preceded or followed twelve hours of toil in the factories or on the coal barges. How their emaciated bodies coped with such physical discomfort and demands is almost beyond understanding. It didn't bear thinking about what this madman might have achieved had he been at Naoetsu during that winter of death in 1943–44.

Despite the slight improvements in the camp diet, the men were still weak from starvation and after some three years under the sword, they were psychologically at breaking point. The fear of an unexpected beating and the prospect of sudden death would cause nightmares and haunt their every waking hour.

Even Lieutenant Zamperini, who remained strong in mind and body, would fear for his survival, and with good reason. His old enemy, Watanabe, would take a sadistic delight in seeking out Louis, making impossible requests and threatening summary execution.

Once while on sick leave, he was ordered by Watanabe to tend the camp goat, a skinny animal that also seemed at death's door. 'Care for goat!' the Bird barked. 'Care goat. If goat die, you die!' That night the animal found its way into the grain shack and gobbled all the barley. By morning, its bloated body lay heaving on the floor. The next week it died. When Watanabe heard about it, he was furious.

'He called me out in front of all the Americans, the English and the Australians who knew I'd been warned about the consequences,' Louis recalled in *Devil At My Heels*. 'So I'm the centre of attraction waiting for whatever's going to be when the Bird draws his sword and starts walking back and forth. If he's going to kill me, he'll do it here, I thought.'

Zamperini awaited his fate with dignity, mentally preparing himself for the sword's sharp edge to slice his neck. But instead of decapitation, Watanabe had another plan in store for the young American. First he hit him, then he dragged him out to the end of the compound and ordered Louis to hold a hardwood timber beam at arm's length above his head.

For an agonising thirty-seven minutes, he was made to carry the block of wood, which measured 1.2 by 1.2 metres and close to 2 metres in length. Meanwhile, the Bird sat on a low roof nearby chatting with his fellow guards. 'The first three minutes I could hardly take the pain,' Zamperini later wrote. 'Every muscle burned and begged to collapse. Then all 100 pounds of me went numb. I froze in that position and time stood still until, seething with anger and frustration, the Bird hopped off the roof and punched me in the stomach with all his might. The beam dropped on my head and knocked me flat on my face, and out.'

※ ※ ※

Come the middle of 1945, Naoetsu's numbers had grown to around 700 POWs. With the war in Europe over, the men were hoping for an early release, but no one could be certain. The Japanese had made it plain that if the Allies landed in Japan, they would fight on. For their part, the POWs suspected rightly that their chances of survival would be slim in the event of a US invasion. Their only option would be to rise up and escape. Already there had been hushed talk of insurrection in the camp.

What the prisoners couldn't have known was that it would be every man for himself if the Japanese looked like implementing their mass-extermination program. An order dated 1 August 1944 had made the Japanese position clear. In the event of invasion or an uprising, the guards were instructed as follows: 'Whether they are destroyed individually or in groups, or however it is done, with mass bombings, poisonous smoke, poisons, drowning, decapitation, or what, dispose of them as the case dictates. In any case it is the aim not to allow the escape of a single one, to annihilate them all and not to leave any trace.'

While the men were fearful of their fate, they were encouraged by continuing US air activity. George Daldry admitted they all wondered if they'd get out of it alive. 'That's what everybody thought about. "What's going to happen to us?"' At first he assumed the planes overhead were Japanese. 'When we realised they were Yanks we flew outside, grabbed a bucket of lime and painted *POW* on the roof. We didn't want to be attacked.'

If the Japs were unnerved by the aerial display, they hid it. Don Alchin saw 'flight after flight of big bombers' high in the sky and was surprised at how the guards would not accept the truth. The civilian guard known as Hoppy was always playing things down. 'They're not Americans, they're our planes,' he would insist to Don.

As the B-29s criss-crossed the night sky on their bombing missions, both the prisoners and the guards hid in makeshift air-raid shelters. Kevin Timbs prayed that the crews wouldn't drop their cargo on the camp. 'I'd think, "Oh God. Don't drop them now", as you heard them going over.'

The next morning Watanabe would remind Kevin how lucky he'd been the previous night. 'And so were you,' Timbs replied with growing bravado. 'But not for much longer. You know they're going to hang you,' he warned.

The Bird seemed unperturbed. 'Oh, no — they won't hang me,' he insisted. 'My family name will save me. They will never get me.' Watanabe enjoyed a status within Japan's social structure that would protect him from military justice. It seemed that plans for his escape were already well advanced.

Towards the end of July it became clear that the war in the Pacific was about to reach its climax. With the war in Europe over, American bombers continued to pound Japanese cities and US submarines had stopped crucial supplies reaching the country's ports. The Japanese could not hold out much longer, and the tension in the camp was palpable. Yet the 'cattle march' to the factories, as the men described it, still continued. And for Henry Dietz, fate had one last trick to play.

After surviving Endau, Kranji, X Battalion, Holland Road, Selarang, the Singapore work camps and (he hoped) Naoetsu, Henry very nearly didn't make it. On 28 July, while working at Nippon Stainless, the young man from Botany Bay was about to place a bucket of water on the burning slag to make a cup of tea for the men in his squad when he slipped and landed on the red-hot coals. 'I was burned from my feet to my backside and was unconscious for three days,' he remembers.

It was a close thing. Afterwards the doctor told Henry: 'You've got the constitution of a draught horse. Any normal man would have been dead by now.'

Henry's worries weren't over. While he was recuperating in the hospital, he listened to the US Air Force overhead and worried about being hit by a stray bomb. He was too badly burnt to join the rest of the men in the air-raid shelter, so the former rouseabout had to take his chances in the squad room. Luckily, Dame Fortune was now on his side.

In the closing days of the war, the guards would make themselves scarce. Watanabe would disappear for a time, only to return to bark new orders and inflict more bashings. Everyone knew his reign of terror was almost over, and many were secretly conspiring to deliver their own brand of military justice.

Louis Zamperini and his mates devised just the punishment. Somehow they acquired a 100-pound rock and hauled it upstairs to a first-floor window overlooking the Hokura River, a tributary of the much wider Sekigawa. A length of thick rope was stolen from the grain store. The idea was to seize the Bird at the appropriate moment, tie him to the rock and throw him out of the window into the muddy water below. Louis's months of torment would be avenged.

CHAPTER 11

'MY GOD, WHAT HAVE WE DONE?'

Those who weren't on night shift at the factories slept soundly in their squad rooms in the early hours of 6 August 1945. The Naoetsu boys were yet to rise for roll call, but 2500 kilometres away in a remote corner of the Pacific Ocean, the pre-dawn was alive with activity as the crew of the *Enola Gay* prepared to take off from the island of Tinian. It would take six hours to reach their target. At 6 am, Colonel Paul Tibbets, who was piloting the B-29 Superfortress, announced to his men that they were carrying the world's first atomic bomb.

The *Enola Gay* was detected by Japanese radar as it cruised towards Hiroshima, in the very south-east of Honshu, at a height of 26,000 feet at about 7.25 am, but few of the civilians who were about to be incinerated took notice of the air-raid warnings broadcast on radio stations. Assisted by fine weather, the crew were lining up for their target — a T-shaped bridge where the Honkawa and Motosayu rivers join. The time was precisely 8.09 am. Six minutes later the doors in the belly of the Superfortress opened and dropped the equivalent of between 12,000 and 15,000 tonnes of TNT.

The bomb exploded nearly 600 metres above the city centre, killing an estimated 140,000 people. Hiroshima was flattened by the blast and the subsequent fireball.

In the cockpit of the *Enola Gay*, co-pilot Captain Richard Lewis gazed over the destruction and turned to the rest of the crew. 'My God, what have we done?' he asked.

The world had entered the nuclear age.

※ ※ ※

News of the dropping of the Hiroshima bomb was slow to emerge in Japan. With communications down, the size of the explosion and exactly what caused it did not filter through to Naoetsu for some days. At first the guards tried to pretend there'd been an outbreak of cholera and that Hiroshima had been quarantined.

That didn't fool Mick McAuliffe or the other prisoners for one minute. 'We knew the end was getting close and were sure there was something up, because the Japs were all very jittery.'

It was George Daldry who first found out what had really happened, courtesy of a US pilot who threw a packet of cigarettes out of the plane with a message scrawled on the front. *Back tomorrow. Atomic bomb's been dropped*, it read.

Cas Cook, Eric Richardson and Harry Julian had all led quiet, simple lives back in Australia. They had no idea what an atomic bomb was — none of the POWs did. Perhaps the officers had a better idea, being better educated, as a rule, than most of the other ranks and from respectable professions in civilian life. A diary entry of Captain Barrett's from December 1943 certainly took on a new meaning now. 'I hope our countries decide to fight this case 'til he [Japan] is finished and not let him off lightly,' Sandy had written. 'Our few lives will not matter if this is well done.' The Japanese had most definitely not been let off lightly.

For a few days by this point, there'd been an easing in camp discipline. The atmosphere was more relaxed. Some of the men had even been allowed to go down to the beach for a swim. As they splashed about in the water, an Allied torpedo bomber flew low overhead, blinking the red lights on its wing tips in Morse code fashion. The message was clear: 'The war is over.'

At noon on 15 August, nine days after Hiroshima and six after a similar bomb had been dropped on Nagasaki, Emperor Hirohito broadcast for the first time in history. Guards listened in silence with their heads bowed as he announced that there would be no more fighting.

Still the Naoetsu boys were unsure. It wasn't until the factory night shift was dismissed that the men were certain their ordeal was over. Theo Lee charged through the camp, bellowing at the top of his voice: 'It's over! The war must be over!'

It took another two days for the ending of hostilities to be confirmed by the camp commandant at Naoetsu. Dressed in full uniform, he stood on a box in the parade ground and declared: 'To avoid further bloodshed, the Emperor has made peace.'

According to John Cook, the importance of the message was somewhat lost in translation. When the interpreter repeated the announcement in English, he said, 'The war has reached the stage of cesseration.' Predictably, it caused a greal deal of amusement.

Tom Henling Wade recalled the moment slightly differently in his book. 'We stood to attention, impassive but inwardly we exulted,' he wrote. 'We've made it! We thought, My God, after three and a half years we've made it! We've survived all their brutality, all their callousness, starvation and disease. We've survived everything. We're going to live!'

Louis Zamperini was similarly relieved, though, given the enormity of the announcement, the reaction from the men as a whole was surprisingly muted. In his own published account of the day peace broke out in Naoetsu, he admitted: 'No one moved. No one cheered. I'd heard these rumours before and been disappointed too many times to take the news seriously.' Only when Corporal Kono, Watanabe's second-in-command, confirmed 'The war is over, no work today' was he finally convinced.

Significantly, there was no sign of the Bird himself that day. He'd packed up his belongings two days earlier and left, but nobody knew where he'd gone. Like all bullies, he was a coward at heart.

Worried about his fate and the reaction of the POWs once the war was over, Watanabe had bolted. Zamperini's plan to tie him to a rock and throw him out of a first-floor window into the river had been thwarted.

Such was the prisoners' discipline, nobody had sought out the guards to exact their revenge. There were reports of retribution in other camps, with some Japanese being killed or beaten up, but the Naoetsu boys left the bullies to themselves. Corporal Kono sobbed and begged for mercy, but most of the officers and civilian guards, clearly shocked by their defeat, sat in their quarters with blank stares. Once so certain of victory, now they were the vanquished.

Around the camp, nobody acknowledged or saluted them. The roles had been reversed. Now the Japs were the prisoners, and for some of them the future was especially bleak. They didn't know it then, but eight of their number would receive an appointment with the hangman for their war crimes, and several others would be sentenced to lengthy jail terms. John Cook and the other Naoetsu boys had written and remembered the evidence that would eventually be used against their captors. Every incriminating detail would be reproduced and held against them. Justice would prevail.

It would be another eighteen days before the prisoners finally left Camp 4-B, a period made bearable by the emergency supplies that were dropped at regular intervals by Allied aircraft. US Navy Hellcats and Corsairs as well as B-29s would fly low overhead, discharging drums of food, tobacco and clothing.

Occasionally the contents of the 44-gallon containers would spill open on impact, splitting and scattering cans of meat stew or fruit across rice paddies and wasteland. The hungry men, who hadn't seen or tasted such a feast in years, clawed at the food with their fingers and gobbled it whole. Unaccustomed to such culinary delights, many would unwisely gorge themselves only to throw up a few minutes later.

While the pilots tried to drop their cargo on open ground, some accidentally missed their target. On the afternoon of 28 August, three large US planes appeared over the mountains in the distance, circled over Naoetsu three or four times, and then came down for a low-level sweep over the camp. One of the aircraft had the letters *POW* painted on a wing, prompting a massive cheer from the lads who'd gathered below to witness the spectacle.

What followed can only be described as pandemonium. As dozens of drums and crates fell to ground, civilians and POWs fled for their lives. The parachutes attached to some of the containers hadn't opened, turning the drums into speeding missiles. Anybody hit by the heavy loads risked death or serious injury.

Certainly, Jimmy Houston didn't hang around.

> One drum fell right through the roof of a Japanese house, through the floor and ended up three feet into the ground. We just managed to get everything out and all the men clear when our roof fell in. While I was busy working another plane came over flying very low. Drums were coming down in all directions. I didn't waste any time getting out of the way. It was just like Singapore all over again. I don't know how I kept my pants clean as it was a nerve-racking business trying to get the food back to camp and watching the planes at the same time. The big drums were sometimes as deep as six feet in the ground. Fancy getting hit by one of these babies.

At least one Japanese woman was killed in the accidental bombardment and several other locals injured. Another casualty was Frank Hole, from Sydney, who was only sixteen when he joined the 2/20th and was one of the youngest soldiers in the camp. A large crate of boots smashed through the washroom roof and broke his leg.

Don Alchin heard that Frank had been cleaning his teeth at the time. 'Then 600 pairs of boots drop on top of him and he swallows his toothbrush,' Don recalls of his old mate from D Company. 'It bloody nearly choked him. Poor bugger. He'd been living for the day he would go home, then this happens.' Now Frank would be robbed of his first taste of freedom since February '42 while he recovered with his leg in plaster. What rotten luck.

With their stomachs full and their safety assured, the Naoetsu boys were able to take life easily for the first time since they were captured in Singapore. They were even permitted to leave the camp. Local barber shops did a roaring trade, but the Aussies could only pay for their haircuts with chewing gum. One barber put a sign in the window that read: *Closed to chewing gum. Will accept cigarettes and chocolates.*

Those with money took advantage of the lax environment to clean themselves up in the public bath houses alongside Japanese civilians. For many, it was their first proper wash in more than three years. It also provided an opportunity to ogle the opposite sex, the first fully naked female form some of them had ever seen.

No doubt stirred by the sight in the communal baths, some of the men found a brothel. Unsure whether their equipment remained in working order, they availed themselves of the facilities and duly reported back to their mates that, yes, they were still fully functioning. There was no moral outrage at their behaviour. After all they'd been through, who could deprive them of a little physical comfort? By now the entire camp was demob happy.

Mindful of the liberties that many of the men were taking, Lieutenant Commander Fitzgerald ordered them to maintain discipline. 'I want you men to be good and behave, because anything could happen until someone comes to relieve us,' he reminded the assembled throng. 'From now on, we want you to forget the past and join with us in fighting the Red menace …'

If the tone of the submariner's voice was designed to calm the men and inspire them on to new struggles, it did not have the desired effect. One war had hardly finished — now they were talking about another. The Aussies had had enough of being bossed around by other nationalities and responded in true larrikin style. John Cook recalled how, at the back of the group, a voice piped up and growled, 'Oh, why don't you just submerge, you old tin fish!'

There is no record of the commander's response, but the remark produced gales of laughter across the parade ground. Once again Australia's secret weapon — the wit that had nourished so many of the Aussies through the dark years of war — had hit the bull's eye.

The countdown to freedom was intensifying. September had just arrived and there was still no news of when they would be allowed to go. More planes came over to drop their supplies and the men began to put on weight.

With the front gates open, there was much coming and going. Prisoners from nearby camps dropped by to pass the time. Two Englishmen who were sick of their own camp caught a train to Naoetsu. One belonged to the 85th Anti-Tank Regiment and the other came from the 5th Norfolks. They brought with them news that several thousand POWs had already left the mainland bound for the Philippines. Likewise the Naoetsu boys wandered far and wide, hiking, shopping and occasionally boozing. A few bottles of saki were acquired and consumed with relish.

Meanwhile the officers struggled to maintain a sense of discipline. One of the Australians, Lieutenant Theo Lee, had to go to the railway station to apprehend a few men who'd decided to find their own way home. While he was searching the carriage, the train moved off and Theo found himself stranded at Takada, the next station, 16 kilometres up the line. Sheepishly he had to phone Fitzgerald with the news that he would not be back until the following morning.

Camp 4-B was now the second largest camp in Japan. Naoetsu had become an unofficial clearing house for POWs and it was filling up fast with many different nationalities. A Dutch serviceman caused a riot at 6 am one day when he sounded the reveille. Tempers were quick to flare and were not assuaged when it was learnt that the men in C Force would almost certainly be the last to leave.

On 2 September 1945, the formal signing of the surrender terms took place on the battleship USS *Missouri*, anchored in Tokyo Bay. Japan was officially no longer at war.

For the Aussies, the tension was unbearable. Soon they would walk out of the gates — but when? At roll call on 3 September, Lieutenant Commander Fitzgerald pleaded with the men to play the game. They would soon be free, but it was hard to contain their growing excitement. Naoetsu was like a balloon about to burst.

Some of the lads paid a final visit to the Nippon Stainless factory, where they handed out a few cigarettes to those Japanese 'who'd not been too bad', as Jimmy Houston put it. The steel plant had been the scene of so much suffering that they were in no mood to forgive. Nor would they ever forget.

As they took one last look around the furnace, the heat, the bashings and the sickness they'd all suffered over the past two-and-a-half years or more came flooding back. They did not want to linger. Back in camp, the word was of an announcement the following morning.

At 7 am on 4 September, four fighter planes roared over the parade ground, the noise and aerial acrobatics putting a premature end to the roll call. One of them came so low it only just missed the telegraph wires before dropping more supplies.

The pilot signalled to them: 'Is there anything else you need?' Grabbing some of the parachutes that had just landed, they spelled out a big *No* on the parade ground.

The men knew they would not be there for much longer. That same morning the commander revealed that US Marines were expected to arrive in the next twenty-four hours. All the inmates should be ready to leave at 6 am the following morning for the journey to Yokohama.

The Naoetsu boys didn't need telling twice. By four o'clock that Tuesday afternoon, they were packed and waiting. Next stop Yokohoma, then home. But home to what?

PART III

CHAPTER 12

LIBERATION

When the wooden gates of Tokyo Camp 4-B swung open soon after dawn on 5 September 1945, the Naoetsu boys were already assembled on the parade ground. The men of the 2/20th and the other units that comprised C Force had waited for this moment since December 1942, and they were in no mood to hang around.

It was a bright, sunny morning, a perfect autumn day. Some cast a thoughtful eye around the prison that had been their home since they'd moved there in April '43. Others laughed and joked at the prospect of imminent freedom. They'd packed their few possessions. Now it was time to form a line and make their final march across the bridge over the Sekigawa River and through the backstreets of Naoetsu to the railway station. A special train was waiting to transport them to Tokyo and on to Yokohama.

Japanese civilians came out of their homes to witness their departure. A few waved but the majority stood still, their faces devoid of any emotion. Corporal Kono was there, some of the men noticed, gazing blankly as the steam train pulled away from the platform.

If there was any sadness on that day for the Aussies, it came from the sight of the sixty little boxes that accompanied the men on their journey. It was not meant to be a victory parade, but there is little doubt that the procession of several hundred soldiers, sailors and airmen who weaved their way through the town on that Wednesday morning were also paying homage to those who had paid the ultimate price.

They wanted those who had lost their lives to be part of this triumphant moment. The ashes in those pine boxes that were so nearly dumped on a rubbish tip were being carried to their final resting place. Not all were destined for Australian soil. Some would be buried in the war cemetery that would eventually be built at Yokohama. But this would be their finest hour.

As the train approached its destination, the men got their initial glimpse of the damage caused by American bombing raids. Much of suburban Tokyo was flattened. This was a nation on its knees.

More than six decades later, those first few days of freedom remain deeply etched in the memories of those who survived. The images are as graphic now as they were then.

Tom Henling Wade climbed out of the carriage door at Yokohama and came face to face with a smiling, peroxide-blonde American girl who looked as though she'd stepped straight out of a magazine cover. 'We still hadn't seen any American soldiers by the time we got to Yokohama,' Tom notes, 'and then who should open our door but this pretty girl in red lipstick and full US uniform. It was like a dream. We didn't know what to say or think. We were all staggered.'

'Did you get much to eat?' she asked the Englishman.

If Tom was hurt by the insensitivity of the enquiry he didn't show it. At that point he was more interested in reaching the coffee and doughnut stall.

As for the Australians, they had their own stories to tell. For many it would be weeks before they completed the journey home. Some would be lucky enough to fly back, but others would sail to Darwin or Sydney. There was also a lot of catching up to do. Letters and messages that had not been delivered would slowly filter through.

Most of these men had spent the war in a vacuum, largely cut off from the outside world and family gossip. Sometimes the news was deeply upsetting.

Don Alchin was sent to the Philippines on the first leg of his journey. In Manila he learnt that his beloved mother Annie had died at home in country New South Wales. Don and his brother Merv were devoted sons. 'She kept us going through the war and we were desperate to be reunited with her,' says Don.

But where was Merv? He'd last been seen in Changi before heading off as a POW on the Burma–Thai Railway, and there'd been no word since. 'I thought he was dead. He'd been posted as missing presumed killed, but we lived in hope,' Don remembers. 'Please God that he hasn't been taken too,' he pleaded.

In the confusion that was post-war Asia, it wasn't easy to establish the fate or whereabouts of ex-prisoners. But sometimes coincidence and happenstance would also play their part. Soon after Don arrived in the Philippines, he heard that his elder brother was indeed alive. What's more — incredibly — they were in the same city. Shortly afterwards, they were reunited. Two men who feared they wouldn't see each other again fell into each other's arms and celebrated their joy. There were tears of sorrow as well, after Don told his brother about their mum. 'It was the hardest thing I've ever had to do,' the younger Alchin confides.

Within a few weeks, the brothers were making their way to Sydney on board the British aircraft carrier HMS *Formidable*. It was late September when the ship sailed through Sydney Heads to cheering families and friends.

There was a big family party back at Temora. 'Oh, did we celebrate,' says Don. He was still suffering from ulcers and hookworm, but after three months' compassionate leave he was keen to get back to work. Amazingly for a man who had just returned from four years of war and imprisonment, he decided to join up again.

Don was also in the money. He'd just received all his back pay as well as a gratuity, and he wanted some fun. Mindful of the temptation that several hundred pounds in cash held for a man in his mid twenties, the Commonwealth Bank would only give him a hundred quid at first. 'I suppose they reckoned I'd blow it — and I would have too,' he laughs. 'I was a mad punter, particularly at the dogs.' He was also something of a petrol head, and soon he was driving around in a flash sports car. 'It was a bright red Austin A90, with hydraulic windows and a hood.'

With money in his pocket and a smart car, he soon earned himself a reputation as a ladies' man. That's when his wife-to-be Mickie met him. She was a nurse at Concord Hospital, and the rest is history.

George Daldry was flown to the island of Okinawa after his release. He spent six weeks there before being transferred to the Philippines, where there were Catalinas flying direct to Sydney's Rose Bay. Any hope of catching a ride on the Catalinas was soon dispelled, however. There was a long queue and privates had to wait their turn. Instead, George was offered a berth on HMS *Striker*, a British escort carrier that had been used in anti-submarine warfare duty in the north Atlantic. Now the ship was on her way to Australia and happy to take passengers.

George knew it would take longer, but there was no hurry, and he could do with some time to himself. A slow voyage south would provide him with the opportunity to readjust to his new-found freedom. It might also help him to decide how to break the news of his brother's death to his mum and dad.

Charlie's tragic end in the mango swamps of Singapore had been troubling George. He wasn't sure how much his parents knew, but they would obviously be heartbroken. He'd tried to put his brother's death at the back of his mind as he struggled for his own survival in Naoetsu. Now he had to face the harsh reality that Charlie wasn't coming home.

George was below decks as HMS *Striker* steamed through Sydney Heads, when a voice suggested he go up. A flotilla of pleasure craft had joined the escort carrier for the last few nautical miles of her voyage, and he was keen to see if he recognised any of the faces on the water. There was no 'if' about it.

Suddenly he spotted almost his entire family in a small boat that had drawn alongside. 'There were aunties and uncles, Mum and Dad, all packed into this boat,' he remembers. George was so elated by the sight that he climbed onto the ship's rail and leapt into the tiny craft. There were hugs and kisses as his mum, Cora, held him tightly in her arms.

Then out of the corner of his eye he saw his father, also called George, sitting at the back. 'Nobody else was with him and he just looked at me. He must have known.' Young George turned to his mother, and as their eyes met she asked, 'Where's Charlie?'

'He won't be coming home, Mum. He didn't make it.'

'They had no knowledge of Charlie's death,' George explains. 'The only thing they'd heard was two lines in the *Daily Mirror* saying George and Charlie Daldry were missing. That's the only thing they ever got. It was very emotional, I can tell you.'

Others made it back to Australia in some style. Perhaps because of his rank, Senior Sergeant Herb Lamb was offered a seat in a Liberator, one of World War II's most versatile planes. More than 18,000 of them had been built for bombing and reconnaissance duties. Now they were equally useful as transport planes.

Herb weighed just 36 kilograms when he got home. When he'd left in February 1941, his weight was almost 65 kilos and he was supremely fit. Prison life had clearly taken its toll. He soon recovered, but it took time to settle down. For the first six months he would go boozing with the boys. It was all part of the healing process — he wanted to erase the memories.

Despite his former status as a squad leader, Herb had little time for reunions and Anzac Day marches. 'They were all too depressing,' he explains now. 'I made up my mind to wipe the war out of my mind as much as possible, and I made a pretty good job of that.' Later he met Thelma, who was eight years his junior. She was his rock, keeping him on the straight and narrow, especially during those early days.

Herb went on to enjoy a successful career in building and real estate, but although he tried, he could never forget his past completely. 'I kept on having these dreams. I was always running away, always being chased. And the Japs were in the treetops, throwing grenades at me …'

Snowy Collins also caught a plane back to Australia. After being transferred to Okinawa and Manila, he boarded a bomber and slept on a mattress under the rear-gunner's position all the way to Darwin. There he was handed a new paybook and a chit allowing him to buy two beers. 'You've got your own money now, so you can buy the rest yourself,' he was informed bluntly. 'That was our mob: welcome to Australia,' he thought.

Back at Sydney airport, he somehow missed his family, who were supposed to meet him, so he decided to find his own way home to Newcastle by train. After four years away, Snowy cut a lonely figure as he made his way along the platform at Newcastle railway station just before midnight. He was trying to get to Fassifern station and his parents' home at Blackalls Park, in the southern suburbs, but the local service had stopped running so he would have to sleep there.

One of the railway staff asked him where he'd come from. How do you begin to explain it? he thought. 'Via Mersing, Singapore, Naoetsu, Okinawa and Manila,' he might have said. But the porter got the idea and offered him a cup of tea instead.

For all he'd been through, dawn on Newcastle station was something of an anticlimax. There was no hero's welcome for Arthur 'Snowy' Collins, just the next day's early train to Fassifern.

The other problem facing him was that his parents had moved house and he didn't have the exact address. 'I kept on asking people on the way if they knew them, and eventually I found them. Well, of course, Mum and Dad were all over me when they opened the front door.'

Like Herb, Snowy Collins took a bit of time to find his way. He got a job on the trams and later in the building industry. He liked to drink and gamble, and when he decided to marry Jean, both sets of parents predicted it would never work. 'I'll give them six months,' said Jean's mother. Today they're still together. 'He just needed plenty of love,' offers Jean. 'Now he's just a pussy cat.'

Kevin Timbs was luckier than most of the others. He caught a Catalina flying boat all the way home, splashing down in Rose Bay, on the south side of Sydney Harbour. The welcoming party was small and there were no speeches. Then, out of the corner of his eye, Kevin saw his mum and dad, Patrick and Katherine, who'd travelled down from Glen Innes.

Sometime in late 1944, a full two-and-a-half years after he'd been reported killed by Charles Moses, a telegraph boy had driven up to the family home on a motorbike waving an envelope. In war this usually meant one thing: bad news. Kate had burst into tears, fearing the worst, only to be told, 'It's all right, Mrs Timbs. He's alive and well and a POW in Japan.'

The entire neighbourhood had called on the Timbs family that day. Friends, relatives and kids he'd gone to school with couldn't believe the news. Someone urged Patrick, a life-long teetotaller, to celebrate with a drink. 'Not now,' he insisted. 'I'll wait for him to come home.' And wait he did.

After the mix-up over his name, Kevin's parents wanted to be certain their son was alive. Nothing would keep them from travelling down to Sydney to welcome him home. 'I'd been missing for two-and-a-half years so they were obviously pleased to see me,' he says.

While in Sydney, Kevin was given a hot meal and told to report to the showground, where he'd be issued with some civilian clothes and cash. 'Mum and Dad were allowed to join me and after that we went straight to Glen Innes to catch up with the rest of the family.' Two of Kevin's many brothers and one of his sisters had all seen military service and, thankfully, had survived the war in one piece. After pledging not to have an alcoholic drink until his long-lost son came home, Patrick Timbs raised a glass in celebration.

Kevin often found himself musing on the mix-up. He always wondered whether the other man's family had been told he was alive when he wasn't. The surviving Kevin Timbs soon got a job on the railways and later became a television repair man. About four years after the war, he met Sheila, from Newcastle, where his brother had a milk run. They married and raised a family, eventually moving to Dapto, south of Sydney, but the memory of Naoetsu would never fade. What happened half a century later would also cast a shadow.

Corporal Ken Firth flew back on a Catalina on the same day. Known as 'Bluey' to his mates, he rarely spoke of the war and never about the camp. Something had happened to him while overseas and he would never be able to find peace. He worked in an alumina plant in Tasmania before returning to Sydney and marrying a woman who was older than his mother, but the relationship failed. Ken lived in a boarding house opposite the Parramatta Leagues Club for several years until his stepbrother Geoff took him under his wing.

Henry Dietz had been so badly burned on the eve of liberation that he took much longer to reach Sydney. His slow progress on a hospital ship took him to New Zealand first. Determined to make the most of the roundabout voyage, he hobbled off the liner on crutches to hit Auckland's drinking holes and continued in much the same manner when the ship reached Wellington. Henry had a lot of catching up to do and he wasn't going to allow his war wounds to interfere with his social life.

Even once back in Sydney, he couldn't stop celebrating. Although he required treatment for his burns at the military repatriation hospital, in Concord, he took every opportunity to party. 'All we did was drink and enjoy ourselves,' he says of that period. 'We'd buy lobsters and kegs of beer all on the black market.'

If he sometimes over-imbibed, it was simply to blot out the past. There were nightmares. Surprise sounds would also set him off. Once at the cinema with Jean, his wife-to-be, they were watching a war film. Snuggling up in the back row with her arm entwined in his, there was an explosion on the screen. 'All of a sudden this plane went over and suddenly a bomb went off. Well, I nearly broke her arm as I leapt up off my seat. I couldn't stay there.' Henry was in such a state of shock that they had to walk out of the cinema.

'I also got nightmares which continued long after I was married.

I'd start kicking and screaming and fighting in bed.' Like Kevin Timbs, Henry found it hard to erase the memory of war and the horror of Naoetsu. And difficult to forgive …

Mick McAuliffe very nearly didn't make it home after liberation. A serious road smash in the Philippines almost put paid to his dreams of a new life back in Australia.

Like a caged tiger suddenly released from years of captivity, Mick had hit the streets of Manila with his mates, determined to have fun and damn the risk. Somehow they acquired a car and six of them piled in for a night on the town. There were nightclubs and pretty girls, chocolate and ice-cream to gorge, and litres of booze to wash it all down. 'I often wonder how stupid we were,' he laughed. They were an accident waiting to happen. When it did, Mick's head went straight through the windscreen. Amazingly, nobody was killed that night. Mick lost a lot of blood but managed to avoid having stitches.

It was time to head home. He joined George Daldry on HMS *Striker* and marvelled at the spectacle as he sailed through Sydney Heads.

Mick wasn't sure who, if anyone, would be there to greet him. His mum had died before the war and his father, Michael, was already an old man when he joined up. 'Well, I got the surprise of my life to see Dad, who was in his eighties, waiting there to welcome me. He just got hold of me and hugged me tight.'

Inevitably there was sadness to report as well. As father and son wiped away their tears of joy, Mick senior revealed that one of Michael's brothers had died. But another brother and four sisters were still alive — and boy, did they celebrate when the family got back together again at Glen Innes, where they now lived.

Mick McAuliffe weighed 70 kilos when he went off to war. He was down to 40 after leaving Naoetsu. Although he'd regained some weight on the voyage home, he was still painfully thin.

Soon he started work on the family farm and went on to marry Ethel, but like so many of the former POWs, he couldn't get that miserable camp out of his mind. 'You'd wake up in the middle of the night yelling and screaming, reliving the horror of it all,' he recalled of those postwar years. 'You'd see the faces of the guards, and they'd frighten the hell out of you.'

Joe Byrne had some demons to put to rest, and it was going to take time. His fiancée Joyce, who'd waited faithfully for him ever since they became engaged on the day Japan attacked Pearl Harbor, helped him to readjust to civvy street. They had two sons and a daughter and Joe went on to do well for himself as an inspector with the Water Board.

No matter how hard he tried to forget, Naoetsu would always be lurking in his subconscious, the ugly memory threatening to reappear without notice in a blinding flash of terror. Even his children were not immune to his sudden fits of wild-eyed fear. On one occasion, the kids touched his face while he was asleep. 'Well, I just exploded. I frightened the hell out of them and me too. And to think it was all related to the camp.'

When Harry Julian disembarked in Sydney Harbour, there was nobody to greet him, so he met up with a few of his old mates and went on a pub crawl. Next day he caught a train back to his home in Lismore, where his mum and a couple of other relatives turned up to welcome him.

Despite his having gone through hell for more than four years, Harry's homecoming was understated. Those who hadn't shared the experience would never really understand what he'd been through. And Harry, who'd always been a bit of a loner, was in no mood to share it. Instead, he took off by himself and worked his way around Australia, spending the next forty years of his life as a bricklayer.

Jimmy Houston went back to the wharves after being demobbed in December 1945. His discharge papers revealed he had spent 1705 days on active service overseas. Private Houston loved a drink but his temper often got the better of him. Once he threw a whisky decanter at a television screen that was showing pictures of Lord Haw Haw, Britain's Nazi propagandist.

Harry Woods steamed back to Australia on the British aircraft carrier HMS *Formidable*. 'I always remember sailing through Sydney Heads. It was something we'd dreamed about, especially while imprisoned in Naoetsu. And I remember people coming out in little boats to climb aboard. My brother was there and so was my mum.'

There were some 300 Australian troops on board *Formidable* that day, and Harry couldn't help but recall the sixty they'd left behind. 'The good blokes who were beaten and starved to death in Camp 4-B were fit men who should never have died,' he stated. 'You tried not to think about it while imprisoned, but our emotional return brought the memories flooding back.'

Harry Woods, who was listed as number 13 on the camp roll, knew he was lucky not to be among the dead. He still bore the scars of his leg and shoulder bullet wounds from the fighting in Singapore. He'd miraculously escaped the Japanese massacre of nurses, doctors and patients in Alexandra Hospital. And somehow he'd survived the appalling conditions in Naoetsu. Clearly reluctant to push his luck any further, he returned to banking and married Jeanette.

Cas Cook barely tipped the scales at 35 kilos when he regained his freedom. Like so many members of C Force, he'd lost nearly half his original weight while a POW in Japan. But he took full advantage of American largesse when he was flown to Okinawa and on to the Philippines. 'Boy, did they feed us,' he remembers. 'All the cakes and pies and soft drinks you could manage. I lapped it up and soon packed on the pounds. It was terrific.'

Back in Australia, the overindulgence continued. 'I did nothing for six months apart from getting on the grog and spending my money, our deferred pay.' Eventually he found a job as a carpenter at Warragamba Dam near the family home in Penrith. 'My father and grandfather had followed the same trade, so it was sort of bred into me.'

While ostensibly Cas's life returned to normal, mentally he was still suffering. Part of the problem was his inability to talk about what had happened. His workmates knew he'd been a prisoner of war, but that was all. Cas kept everything bottled up. 'I just never spoke about it. If anybody raised the topic, I would change the subject.' He married Marjorie soon after the war, and they'd go on to have four kids, but he'd never tell them the full story.

If any man signified the spirit and invincibility of the 2/20th Battalion, it was Cas's namesake, John Cook. Never a man to big-note, he threw himself into work and family life on his return from the war. To everyone else, he was a pillar of strength who had endured the rigours of life in a POW camp and wanted to put it all behind him.

He'd only been back in Sydney a few days when he met Terri, his future wife, in the post office at Penrith where she worked. She was transfixed by his Bing Crosby looks and baby-blue eyes, and they married soon afterwards.

For a while he worked on the family farm at Orchard Hills before joining the prison service. Perhaps because he knew what it was like to lose his freedom, he earned a high level of respect from inmates and fellow officers alike. But his wartime experiences still troubled John. 'It's no use telling anybody — they wouldn't believe you anyway,' he would respond when pressed on the subject.

Later he became a recorder at the Central Criminal Court in Darlinghurst, where again he impressed those he had dealings with. But John was quietly suffering inside. One day in 1975 he suddenly lost the ability to talk in court.

'He was taken to Concord Hospital for psychiatric help but was forced to retire at the age of fifty-three,' Terri recalls. 'They had no counsellors then. Wives were the only help they had. All the men had problems.'

John Cook, who fathered three sons and two daughters, continued to enjoy the battalion reunions and Anzac Day parades, but he would always be haunted by the memory of Naoetsu.

Theo Lee, who as one of the officers in command of the men from the 2/20th had done so much to keep the survivors going through the dark days of war, arrived back in Sydney by plane on 21 September 1945. His fiancée Joy had heard about his homecoming in the newspaper and caught a cab to the airport to meet him. Wives, girlfriends and officers gathered in a Red Cross hut to wait for the plane, which was two hours late. As it touched down and came to a halt nearby, a door flap opened beneath the aircraft and an army boot appeared. Joy and the rest of the women rushed forward but there was no sign of Theo.

'Where are the officers?' she shouted. Then, noticing a set of steps placed on the other side of the fuselage, she spotted Sandy Barrett walking down. And there behind him was the familiar figure of the man she'd waited four-and-a-half years to meet again. Overcome by emotion, she screamed Theo's name.

He swung around to see the girl with whom he'd exchanged countless love letters. Their eyes fixed on each other — and at the bottom of the steps, Theo's knees began to buckle. Joy raced across the tarmac and held on to his arm to prevent him from falling. They were married five weeks later.

Theo didn't have a mark on him but the damage was inside. Within a few months, he started to show the signs of post-traumatic stress, his nerves plaguing him for the rest of his life.

Eric Richardson recalls very little about his homecoming. 'I tried to forget it all. Everyone went their own way and there was no attempt to form a Naoetsu survivors association.'

He had no brothers or sisters to meet him on his return to Sydney and, having never married, was happy to live alone. If he had any deeper thoughts or memories about Naoetsu he was content to keep them to himself. For a time he worked as a fitter's mate before working in the power industry and getting a job as a postman in Melbourne.

Dr Sandy Barrett settled into domestic bliss with his wife Joan and had three children: Bruce, Judith and Ian. After returning to Sydney, he set up practices in Crows Nest and Marrickville and later became an allergy specialist. He rarely spoke of the war or his part in it, although a memo to the Secretary of the Army in Melbourne later made reference to his considerable contribution.

Despite this, the Australian Government decided in its wisdom that there was no case for bestowing any decoration on Captain Alex Barrett MO, late of the 2/14th Royal Army Medical Corps and the 2/18th Battalion. His efforts did not go unrecognised by the United States, however, which awarded him the Legion of Merit and the Bronze Star for bravery and meritorious service.

Writing in the *Medical Journal of Australia*, his old mate Jim Chisholm would say this of Barrett's role at Naoetsu: 'In common with many other prisoners of war camps, he had no drugs, not even aspirin and with five feet of snow on the ground in winter, at one time there were 40 cases of pneumonia in the camp. It would appear he kept the men alive with willpower, as he had very little else.'

Sandy died in 1968 at the comparatively young age of fifty-six. 'Never give up' was one of his favourite mottos.

Like many returned servicemen, Jim Chisholm took time to find his feet in civilian and domestic life. He spent the immediate postwar years gathering evidence and tracking down Japanese guards for the War Crimes Commission. By the time he returned to Australia for good, his first marriage had collapsed. However, his relationship with his second wife, Gwen, provided the love and stability he deserved. The couple went on to run a farm near Goulburn, where he pioneered the use of contour farming.

Louis Zamperini, the US airman who only joined the Naoetsu story in its final chapter, would end up with perhaps the heaviest burden. For the New Yorker, his ghosts amounted to just one man — one monster — and Louis's obsession with the Bird would soon become a prison cell of its own. In his first few years back home, he hit the bottle and almost drank himself to death. But like John, Theo and Snowy, he married a good woman. Cynthia was a willowy beauty whom he met during two weeks of R & R in Miami. There is little doubt she saved his life and possibly his soul.

It was Cynthia who persuaded him to attend a Billy Graham convention, where Louis vowed to devote the rest of his life to the service of God. As a committed Christian, he wanted to spread the word of the Lord wherever and whenever he could. But he had no idea then that his mission would lead him back to the very source of the darkness that had threatened to engulf his soul — back to Japan. And into the jail cells that now housed his wartime tormentors.

Jack Mudie had been given up for dead before he returned home. When he finally set foot on Australian soil again he was penniless. He was lucky enough, though, to fall back into the arms of a loving woman. Neno, who had waited patiently for him since the intervention of the war, realised he was scarred both physically and mentally. Jack knew he wasn't much of a catch, especially as he didn't have any money. 'You could do much better for yourself than me,' he told her. 'I'm broke and I'm a physical and emotional wreck.'

Neno wouldn't hear of it. She'd waited five long years and she wasn't about to leave him in the lurch. 'Let's get married,' she replied. 'We'll face life together.'

'And from that moment she looked after me,' Jack says now. 'It took about ten years to nurse me back to normal health and we had fifty-one years of gloriously happy married life.'

Jack wasn't always easy to live with. Psychologically he had been traumatised by Naoetsu and although he eventually managed to eradicate the nightmares, he was still disturbed. Even as a school teacher he would 'go walkabout' sometimes, disappearing after lessons. If he hadn't arrived home by 6 pm, Neno would have to search for him.

If anybody needed counselling, it was Jack Mudie. But, as Terri Cook observes, there was no such support for men like him when they returned from the war. They were imprisoned in a mental cell, unable to share their thoughts. In Jack's own words: 'It was very lonely and extremely difficult to adjust.'

CHAPTER 13

'HANG THE BASTARDS'

To this day Alan Lyon doesn't know why he was chosen to sit on the War Crimes Tribunal. A member of the Allied Occupation Force sent to Japan, Captain A.B. Lyon had arrived at the southern port of Kure, near Hiroshima, on 14 February 1946. As second-in-command of C Company in the 65th Australian Infantry Battalion, he found himself in charge of escorting tens of thousands of Koreans who were being repatriated to their homeland.

Alan and his men were then sent to Tokyo, where they performed guard duty at the numerous offices that had been set up by the Allied forces. His next move was back south to Onomichi, near Kure. In early November, while he was practising on the rifle range there, a despatch rider drew up and handed him an envelope. Inside was an order to report to the offices of brigade headquarters the following morning.

At precisely 9 am the next day, Brigadier Ronald Hopkins told him to report to the Australian War Crimes Section in Tokyo where he would represent the AIF at a hearing into alleged crimes at a prisoner-of-war camp in Japan.

The decision to hunt down and prosecute those Japanese suspected of committing war crimes required Australian Government legislation, which was passed by Canberra on 24 September 1945. Although the Japanese had never signed the Geneva Conventions on war crimes, they had been party to other international agreements on the treatment of prisoners and had also accepted the terms of the Potsdam Declaration, which provided for stern justice against those who 'visited cruelties' on prisoners of war.

From May 1946 onwards, the International Military Tribunal for the Far East instigated what became known as the Tokyo Trials, which involved the prosecution of many of the higher-ranking officers in the Japanese military and members of the government under various 'classes' of crimes. The tribunal set down the laws and procedures by which the trials should be conducted.

General Douglas MacArthur had compiled a list of the most wanted Japanese and the Australians were collecting evidence of their own. Following the new federal legislation of September '45, the Australian War Crimes Commission's brief was to investigate war crimes in all those theatres of war where Australian forces had fought and been imprisoned, including Japan. Many Australian officers found themselves gathering evidence from diggers who by now had returned home. Testimony from thousands of servicemen was collected, assessed and distributed to commanders in every area of Australian responsibility. Once details of the alleged crimes and perpetrators were established, the accused men were tracked down and arrested.

By mid 1946 the stage was set for one of the most exhaustive and lengthy legal marathons in military history as nearly 6000 suspected war criminals were tried. Between May 1946 and November 1948, almost 1000 individuals were initially condemned to death, 920 were executed and around 3000 imprisoned. The remainder from that figure of 6000 were either acquitted or not brought to trial.

Although the prosecution of the Naoetsu guards, in Yokohama, was a mere sideshow in comparison to the big, headline-grabbing cases being heard in Tokyo, the style of justice was the same and the Australian War Crimes Commission was determined to carry out its brief in a right and proper manner, even though not everyone who sat in judgement had much experience in legal affairs.

Alan Lyon, for instance, had never so much as entered a courtroom. Yet now he was being asked to decide the fate of a group of Japanese soldiers who were accused of serious war crimes.

Although the order was strictly confidential, news of his appointment inevitably leaked out. The day Captain Lyon left Onomichi for Tokyo, most of the camp appeared to know about his new responsibility. And his comrades were not slow in offering their advice, which could be summed up in three words: 'Hang the bastards.'

Not that this would influence his judgement. Lyon and the rest of the judicial panel knew they had to follow the rule of law and pass judgement based on that alone. 'If we were going to do the thing properly,' he says, 'it had to be done legally, so we all took it pretty seriously.'

Captain Lyon arrived at Yokohama District Court House on the morning of 10 November 1946, a Wednesday. Seven of Naoetsu's military guards who'd been rounded up and accused of war crimes were about to be tried. (The civilian guards would have their day in court at a later date.)

Dressed in prison garb, they were led into the wooden-panelled courtroom one by one. Armed US Military Police officers in their white helmets stood guard over them as they waited to hear the charges read out.

Lieutenant Narumi Oota, who was the commander of Camp 4-B from January 1943 until January 1945, was held responsible for the deaths of sixty Australian prisoners of war and the beating and abuse of many others by his staff. He was also accused of misappropriating Red Cross supplies that should have been distributed to the prisoners.

Sergeant Tadeo Shibano (the Bull), who was often in charge of the camp at night, faced four counts of mistreatment, abuse and torture that accelerated the deaths of some of the POWs. He was also charged with committing atrocities and stealing Red Cross supplies.

Sergeant Yusu Aoki (the Faith Healer) was accused of hastening the deaths of eight POWs and failing to discharge his duty as the camp medical representative, by refusing and denying proper health care.

Private Michio Kuriyama (Snake Eyes), the camp interpreter, Private Kongo Katayama (the Cat), a former corporal and member of the camp staff, Corporal Hiroaki Kono, also one of the interpreters, and Private Yoshio Taguchi (the Germ), another guard, were all similarly charged with committing atrocities against the Australians and killing at least ten of them.

Captain Alan Lyon spent the next three months listening to a mountain of evidence about the guards' brutality at Camp 4-B. He was an accomplished shorthand writer, a skill that enabled him to make voluminous notes during the case. It also allowed him to compare prosecution witness testimony with defence submissions and helped to clarify the often murky legal waters.

With him were three US officers, two British and one from New Zealand, whose brief it also was to decide the guilt or innocence of the Naoetsu guards and impose the appropriate penalty. Knowing they had the power of life and death in their hands, they took their responsibilities seriously.

Hardly had the trial begun than the defence counsel (which consisted of an American legal team) challenged the legality of the proceedings on the grounds that the officers had no authority to convene such a hearing. For a moment it seemed the court might be adjourned, but a quiet word to the president of the court from one of the American legal representatives convinced him that the Supreme Commander Allied Forces certainly did have the power to stage the War Crimes Tribunal.

Lyon and his colleagues had mentally prepared themselves for the grim catalogue of evidence that was to follow, but even they were shocked by the detailed accounts of brutality and cruelty that the boys of C Force had endured.

Aoki, the medical sergeant whose treatment of the sick had done so much to add to their suffering and sometimes their death, looked the meanest of the bunch. Bespectacled and with an arrogant and aggressive manner, he exuded evil as he stood in the dock — 'a really bad bugger' Alan Lyon concluded in his book *Japanese War Crimes*.

By lunchtime on day one, the tribunal members were in

desperate need of a break. The president, Lieutenant Colonel McCutcheon, a giant of a Texan, turned to the other six officers and summed up everyone's feelings: 'Well, gentlemen, it sure looks like we've got one God-damn hell of a job on our hands.'

They asked themselves how such atrocities could have taken place. How men could behave in such a callous way towards their captives. Captain Lyon had seen action in Balikpapan, on the island of Borneo, so at least he was able to tell his colleagues what he'd seen with his own eyes.

That first day saw the prosecution present its case. Major Robert Hickson of the Australian Imperial Force wanted to show that the seven accused had acted as a team, singly and jointly committing atrocities that contributed to the deaths of sixty Australians and leaving the rest in a pitiful state. Live witnesses and forty affidavits drawn from those who had survived Naoetsu would support the charges against the seven Japanese, he explained.

After a week's adjournment to allow the defence team to gather more evidence in support of the guards, the trial reconvened to hear further details of the prosecution's case. Despite the appalling allegations being made against the prisoners, the court was scrupulously fair.

The prosecution acknowledged that the first commander of the camp, Lieutenant Shicata, had acted humanely towards the POWs and often took time out to talk with Lieutenant Colonel Robertson, the Australians' commanding officer, who died of meningitis at the end of March 1943. But when his successor, the frequently absent Lieutenant Oota, took over, the NCOs were allowed to run riot. The prosecution argued that each of the accused was personally implicated in the murder of the sixty Australians who died at Naoetsu, and it would demand that the supreme penalty be invoked against them.

Several affidavits were submitted as evidence. They included the case of Private Robert Farley, who in the winter of 1943–44 was stripped naked and forced to walk into a snow bank, where he was made to stand for six hours. After being carried to the sick room, he did not recover consciousness.

Then there was the Sheet Blitz of mid 1943 and the collective punishment that followed, both of which were recalled in every incriminating detail. During the summer months, it had been Sergeant Aoki's idea to make the prisoners sleep under five blankets with a single sheet tied around their stomach, despite the hot and humid weather.

Aoki explained that this was the Japanese way of preventing the spread of diseases. In reality it was just another form of torture. When the men threw off their blankets to cool their bodies, they would be beaten with sticks. One night in particular, 8–9 July, Aoki ordered 'all men out' for what turned out to be one of the greatest communal ordeals the POWs were to suffer.

The Sheet Blitz now got a further airing as the prosecution told how many of the men collapsed either from exhaustion or blows received from the guards' clubs.

The affidavit accepted as evidence in court also provided further details of how the Japanese worked themselves into a frenzy while the men were subjected to crude and demeaning demands. The Japanese barked like dogs and laughed like hyenas. 'One of the accused, Private Kuriyama, stood in the centre of the circle with an unsheathed sword, yelling: "My sword is hot, my sword will kill, I will kill,"' the affidavit alleged.

'As a final form of entertainment for this evening,' the prosecution's evidence continued, 'the prisoners were paired off and made to beat each other with their fists. A Jap would watch and if he thought the punching was not hard enough, he would slip in and demonstrate.'

A sworn affidavit from Henry Dietz added further detail to the appalling experience of Lance-Corporal John Magin, who was severely beaten by Private Taguchi, while suffering from dysentery. Because the sick room was full, Magin was confined to his own bed, where he had no alternative than to relieve himself. 'His excreta passed through the blanket he was lying on, through the floor, on to Taguchi, whose bed was immediately under Magin's room on the floor below,' the tribunal heard.

Dietz claimed that Taguchi gave Magin one of the worst beatings he had ever witnessed: 'He hit him with a stick like a mattock handle and equally as heavy. The episode lasted ten minutes, during which Magin was struck on the head about seven times, raising lumps about the size of an egg.'

Such unspeakable conduct meted out on defenceless men was beneath contempt but it was far from unusual, the tribunal was beginning to realise.

Private James Downie, who had accidentally scorched his overcoat while working at the factory furnace, was called to give his evidence in person. He told the court how in January 1944 he was summoned to Sergeant Shibano's office, where he was slapped across the face with a heavy canvas belt about twenty times.

Downie pointed to the scars from the punishment, which were still clearly visible on his face three years later. After the beating, he was made to stand in the snow for two hours, he said. The young private's account of what happened next only served to reinforce the story which had become part of battalion folklore:

> The snow was falling continuously and I was made to walk into a steep bank of snow alongside the wall of the compound until I was standing in snow up to my mouth. While standing in the snow I was clad only in shirt and English battle dress. My great coat had been taken from me. After two hours had elapsed I was taken to the guardhouse where my boots and socks were taken from me and also my tunic. While in the guardhouse I was given what the Japs called severe guardhouse punishment which entailed sleeping without blankets and a reduction to half rations consisting of two rice balls a day. The guardhouse walls had large cracks in them and in the morning when we awoke our bodies would be covered in snow.

Downie's punishment would have killed many men, and given that he was also made to continue working at the factory during the day, it's remarkable that he didn't succumb.

'The treatment I received in the guardhouse resulted in my losing 3 stone,' he revealed to the tribunal. 'I believe a stone is about 14 pounds. I was sent back to work and managed to carry on for about 10 days, after which I became so weak that I was admitted to a hospital by an American medical officer. On several occasions during my hospitalisation my life was despaired of by the doctors.'

Jim Downie's evidence was gripping. He was also able to shed light on other atrocities involving the men, including the now notorious case of Private Farley. At night he would hear Farley pleading to be killed as his Japanese tormentors laid into him with their sticks. The next day, his head was so badly bruised and his skin so tight that the marks where he had been beaten could not be detected. His eyes were closed, his mouth was a tiny hole and his face was unrecognisable. Bob Farley's head rolled around on his shoulders, but he said nothing. Soon afterwards he died.

Downie recalled the sight of starving men whose flesh was so wasted away that their skin hung on to their bones and their thighs were the width of chair legs. He remembered Corporal Garnett Judd who between 1 October and 4 November 1943, was 'severely beaten at diverse times, by forcing him to perform tasks beyond his physical capacity whilst he was ill and diseased'. Finally, Judd was made to stand for roll call and died shortly afterwards. He looked like a sick dog, unable to raise his head or straighten his knees, Downie recalled. He could still see his skeletal form and the eyes had that starry gaze, a sure sign that he was about to die.

Captain Jim Chisholm, who'd taken over as C Force's commanding officer after Lieutenant Colonel Robertson's death, and who was due to give his evidence in person at the trial, was unable to appear because he was tied up tracking down the civilian guards. Even so, his written report to the War Crimes Tribunal made graphic reading.

His overview of camp conditions referred to the 'totally inadequate' food rations, which led to severe weight loss and sickness. Unable to retain their physical condition, the men had no resistance to disease but were still made to work twelve- to eighteen-hour shifts for as long as 110 days at a time. 'The men were forced to run to work every morning and run back again every night,' Chisholm stated in his report. 'If they were too weak and fell down, as often happened, they were savagely beaten with sticks. They were also sent to work with inadequate clothing against the bitter cold.'

One of the biggest problems was caused by misunderstandings over language. With few interpreters in the camp, the POWs were 'unmercifully thrashed' for disobeying orders that they did not comprehend. 'It was very difficult to either understand them or make our requirements clear to them,' the captain explained. 'This was a source of continual misunderstanding throughout our whole period of imprisonment.'

Captain Chisholm also mentioned the light-duty tickets — the red ribbons — that sick men were given:

> These tickets proved to be more of a liability than an asset, as any man wearing a light duty ticket would be picked on and ill-treated worse than the men with no ticket. In one case a man who was supposedly on light work was shovelling coal into a furnace and he collapsed. The Japanese guard dragged him outside and stood him over a fire, so that when he collapsed again he would fall into the fire. He was saved from doing this by the intervention of some of our own men.

Chisholm then discussed the theft of Red Cross supplies intended for the POWs, but which were largely pilfered by the guards. On one occasion he was asked to sign for twenty-eight bags of sugar, when he'd only received five. 'When I refused to sign I was told that if I did not do so, no more Red Cross supplies would come into the camp.'

And he catalogued the inhuman conditions and poor medical facilities. 'Men were sent to work by the Japanese so-called doctors, often with temperatures of 102 and 103. In some cases after having worked all day, men died on their beds at night. Insufficient medicine was available and although we asked for Red Cross medicines, of which there were ample supplies in Japan, it was refused.'

Those who made it through the work shift were often subjected to cruel treatment on their return to camp, Captain Chisholm emphasised. 'Men, after coming back from work, were stood on the parade ground without any food, until midnight and this treatment would continue as a mass punishment for three or four days at a time for the smallest of crimes.'

Lack of hygiene also contributed to everyone's state of health, but the guards did nothing about it. 'The barracks were infested with lice, fleas and bugs and no attempt was ever made by the Japanese to rid the barracks of these vermin. If, at inspection, men had mud on their boots, even under the sole, notwithstanding the fact that they were given nothing whatever with which to clean their boots, they were made to crawl along and lick all men's boots as punishment.'

Such was the day-to-day indignity of life at Naoetsu. The War Crimes Tribunal had heard enough. Japan's savagery was without doubt. The question now was what to do about it.

※ ※ ※

The defence team comprised two American civilians who were attorneys back in the United States. Although they were being paid by the US Government, their responsibility was to the seven Japanese soldiers in the dock. And while they didn't have much to work with, the two lawyers did their best to represent the prisoners' interests.

They opened their case on 29 November by emphasising the role of the Japanese medic Dr Fuji, who was sent to Naoetsu early in 1944 to establish why so many POWs were dying. He had reduced their workload, ordered more clothing, improved the heating of the barracks and brought in extra food. As a result, there were no more deaths after March 1944.

Members of the tribunal were not convinced that the doctor's arrival had been as altruistic as the defence had made out, however.

During a recess, Alan Lyon and his colleagues reasoned that the Japanese were more worried about the loss of labour in the two factories than the welfare of the prisoners.

One of the first defence witnesses to take the stand was Michio Kuriyama, who had been given various nicknames by the men, including 'the Infidel', 'Freddy' and, of course, 'Snake Eyes'. A devious guard with a vicious side, Private Kuriyama was an interpreter. In court he faced two counts of causing death and nine atrocity charges. He was a deeply unpleasant man who, recalling the beatings he was accused of, preferred to describe them as mere incidents. After all, he insisted, he was considerate enough to strike a prisoner with his fingers crooked so that he wouldn't break the victim's ear drum.

Reluctantly he agreed that some of the prosecution stories were true, including the Sheet Blitz, which ended with Kuriyama standing in a circle of men, brandishing his unsheathed sword and shouting, 'I will kill!' But he was only following Sergeant Aoki's orders, he pointed out.

'With others, I was only trying to frighten the prisoners and would never have used my sword — that was only a bluff and I did not intend to hurt anyone.'

But the damage was done. The nervous little man in the dock had been contradicted by so much of the prosecution's evidence that he knew the game was over. At the end of his cross-examination, Kuriyama stepped down from the witness stand and walked solemnly to the door. His fate was all but sealed.

Next up was Hiroaki Kono, the other camp interpreter, who had served at Naoetsu between May 1943 and August 1945. He faced the highest number of atrocity charges — ten in all.

It was Kono who'd been accused of forcing the Australians to stand in the snow while beating them with heavy sticks. Again, there was the case of Robert Farley, who in January 1944 literally caught his death in the freezing conditions. 'Do you remember such an incident?' asked the prosecution.

'No, I do not remember,' Kono replied.

Pressed further, he accepted that there were some occasions when camp regulations were broken and the men had to be punished. 'Under orders from Sergeant Aoki and Sergeant Shibano, I, with others, had to punish them, but I do not remember any particular occasion.'

Kono's composure was sorely tested. He looked pale and shaken by the questioning and at the end of his cross-examination was asked whether he had anything further to say. There was a slight pause while Kono considered his response. 'Yes, I believe I was bad at that time,' he volunteered.

It was as good as a guilty plea, and the 28-year-old former guard knew it. Now his life was also on the line.

Life could have been so much different had the war not intervened in his studies. He'd just passed the entrance examination to Niigata Medical University when he was drafted into the Imperial Japanese Army in October 1942. Although, given his behaviour in Camp 4-B, he might not have been the most suitable recruit for a career in caring for the sick.

And so it continued. Yukio Nakamiya (otherwise known as Baby Face), who was in charge of the stores, agreed that he'd reduced the prisoners' rations while making sure the Japanese guards had more. And yes, the lack of food might have contributed to illness among the men.

Kongo Katayama, a former corporal, denied he ever used extreme measures when punishing the POWs. And if he did administer a beating, it would have been on the orders of his superiors. 'I never wanted to ill-treat any prisoners,' he told the court. 'One minute I would be trying to help them, then the next minute I would have to punish them when ordered to do so.'

Denial and acting on the orders of others were becoming familiar themes. Yoshio Taguchi, who was accused of accelerating the deaths of five Australians, would also feign loss of memory but would find it harder to deny specific allegations made against him.

He was the medical orderly, whose responsibility it was to administer medicine to sick prisoners. Taguchi also took it upon himself to force them to work when unfit to do so.

He was vague on the specifics but claimed under questioning that he did all he could for his patients. 'There were some occasions when I was ordered to send as many of the sick ones [as possible] to work, but I do not recall those specific names,' he added.

It was Taguchi too who had been linked to the fierce bashing of Lance-Corporal Magin. The prosecution reminded him of the attack on Magin, who was left with lumps the size of an egg about his body. 'If, as you say, you do not remember specific names of prisoners, surely you must remember this particular incident?' the prosecution enquired.

At first reluctant to acknowledge the beating, Taguchi finally admitted, 'I lost my temper at that time but did not intend to hurt the prisoner — I just got mad.'

The prosecutor, Vincent Esposito, sensed he had the prisoner on the back foot and went in for the kill. He asked about the brutal and inhuman treatment Taguchi had dealt to Privates Comerford, Hale, Farley and Hurley and Signalman Baker. 'Do you deny that sick prisoners were beaten and forced to work and made to stand in deep snow for long periods of time?'

'Orders from Sergeant Aoki, which he had received from the Tokyo Administration, were that every prisoner had to work and when some prisoners claimed that they could not work, I was told to punish them,' Taguchi explained.

'In other words you did administer beatings and other brutalities upon sick prisoners of war, including five who died,' Esposito persisted.

'When punishment was instigated by others, I was, on some occasions, ordered to join in, but do not recall all of the ones you speak of. I cannot remember specific incidents which took place three-and-a-half years ago.'

The prosecution had nailed its man. 'We have no further questions of this witness,' Mr Esposito concluded.

Tadeo Shibano, the sergeant-major who had run the camp when Lieutenant Oota was absent, was called the following morning. A senior non-commissioned officer who had served in Naoetsu from the men's arrival in December 1942 until 21 December 1944, he was implicated in numerous atrocities and faced four counts of mistreatment and torture that led to the deaths of Privates Farley, Lubey and Bayliss and Signalman Fraser.

Shibano was asked what he remembered of these incidents. His reply was abrupt and aggressive. He was clearly having difficulty coming to terms with his changed circumstances and took exception to the implied suggestion that he'd done anything wrong. 'Prisoners had to work and obey camp regulations and we had to punish those who offended,' he reminded his accusers. 'I was not responsible for any deaths in the camp.'

'What happened to the Red Cross supplies which should have been distributed to the prisoners?' the prosecution enquired.

Shibano insisted he didn't know, deflecting any blame to his number two, Sergeant Aoki.

Later that day the prosecution returned to the affidavits that clearly linked Shibano to a series of atrocities, including the inhuman treatment of Private Downie, who had already told the court how he was beaten and confined to the guardhouse for ten days in January 1944.

'It is a miracle that he survived and was able to return to Japan to testify to this court,' the prosecution observed. 'With such clear-cut evidence, how can you now deny these charges against you?'

Again, Shibano protested his innocence and ignorance of individual events. 'I deny causing any deaths,' he said. 'I had to obey orders and was forced to punish prisoners, but I do not remember any specific incidents.'

Captain Lyon thought that Shibano was merely trying to escape the noose. The prosecution was having none of it, closing its cross-examination by pointing to the overwhelming evidence against him and recommending that the court impose the highest penalty.

The following morning Yusu Aoki, the camp medical orderly whose tyrannical rule caused the POWs so much grief, took the witness stand. There were seventeen specific charges against him, eight of which accused him of abuse, mistreatment and torture that contributed to the deaths of so many men.

Sergeant Aoki refused to accept that he had accelerated the deaths of some prisoners. 'I am not guilty,' he declared.

The prosecution suggested that, as the senior medical

representative in Naoetsu, it was his duty to care for the sick and provide the proper medical supplies and attention.

'Yes, I did everything possible to help the sick, but we were often short of medical supplies,' he explained. Questioned about the alleged abuse of prisoners who were forced to go to work when they were seriously ill, Aoki said that headquarters in Tokyo had ordered all prisoners to work.

He was also asked about the Great Sheet Blitz, which he described as 'only a minor thing'. 'There were many times when prisoners refused to obey instructions and camp staff had to take action to see that orders and camp regulations were obeyed,' he added.

The prosecution was not satisfied. Aoki had a conceited look on his face, which irritated Major Hickson, the Australian officer who led the cross-examination.

'What has been described here in court has been proven by previous evidence and also admitted by your own staff,' Hickson reminded the former guard. 'There is no doubt that it was you who initiated the Great Sheet Blitz, resulting in brutal, sadistic, collective punishment of these prisoners — what have you to say to these charges?'

'I have nothing to admit,' he replied. Aoki was clearly trying to save his neck, but such was the weight of evidence against him that the prosecution insisted there was no alternative but to impose the death sentence.

Until now Aoki had shown little emotion in the witness box, but when the court president asked him if he had anything to say in his defence, the prisoner grew excited.

'I did only what I was ordered to do,' he pleaded. 'Prisoners were very bad — they were the enemy and never co-operative, refusing to obey regulations and they had to be kept working. Punishing them was the only way to try to achieve this and I did what I had to do.'

If he was trying to justify his actions, the Faith Healer had little hope of succeeding. As Aoki stepped down from the witness box in the fading afternoon light, he was almost certainly aware that his fate was sealed.

There was only one more prisoner to call, but being a Friday afternoon, the appearance of Narumi Oota, the camp commandant, would have to wait until after the weekend. Most of the POWs agreed that Oota had been a civilising influence on the camp in the early days, but he was a weak man who was not cut out for imposing military discipline. In fact, he'd worked for the Kokuryudo Book Store Company, one of the largest chains of its kind in Japan, until he was drafted into the army in 1928. Now, at the age of forty-one, the former first lieutenant would have to take responsibility for the criminal actions of his men during his two years at Naoetsu from January 1943 onwards.

Oota told the court that he was unaware of the brutal treatment of prisoners because he was usually away from the camp at night, when much of the violence was committed. He claimed to have no knowledge of sick men being sent to the factories, but agreed that every POW was required to work, even the officers. He explained to the court that soon after their arrival at Naoetsu he told the men: 'You fought for your country for being guaranteed your life and your property, but now you are under the control of Japanese army as prisoners of war. Now in Japan not a single man can pass time idly.'

While Oota admitted he was aware of some instances where prisoners were disciplined for minor breaches of camp regulations, the thrust of the prosecution's case against him was his inability to restrain his staff from committing atrocities. This was the allegation: that he had the opportunity to stop the cruelty but failed to act.

'It is therefore our contention that as the camp commandant you did unlawfully disregard and fail to discharge your duty to restrain and control members of your staff and other persons under your submission,' the prosecution stated.

Turning to Alan Lyon and the rest of the bench, Major Hickson said, 'All the evidence before the court has shown that Lieutenant Oota did violate the laws and customs of the war, and we therefore believe that the court should invoke the supreme penalty against him.' The prisoner, who was asked if he had anything further to say, shook his head and stepped down from the witness box.

It was the end of nearly three months of evidence and testimony, and the prosecution was in no doubt how the court should respond. Major Hickson urged the court to 'bring down a guilty verdict on all charges'.

On 27 January 1947, the War Crimes hearing was adjourned for a week to allow time for the tribunal to consider the guilt or innocence of those on trial for their lives. Minds would be concentrated on both sides of the judicial fence during the next seven days.

※ ※ ※

Just before 9 am on Monday 3 February, Alan Lyon glanced into the body of the court house and noted that it was standing room only. Many of the Japanese civilians who'd been curious enough to attend the early days of the hearing but then disappeared were now back in force. It was to be a day of high drama, with the near certainty that some of the accused would be condemned to death. How would they react? When a man is forced to confront his own mortality in such a public place, the pressure to break down must be immense. Would the seven former guards meet their penalty with cowardice or courage? How would the bully-boys of Camp 4-B respond when the boot was on the other foot?

The president and his panel of officers had repeatedly examined every piece of evidence over the previous week. They would discuss the validity of allegations and try to corroborate them with claims made in the affidavits. There was no room for doubt here. If a man was accused of a particular crime, there had to be proof. Captain Lyon's 110-words-a-minute shorthand came in particularly useful as he compared his own notes with the rest of the evidence before them.

Each of the seven had his say and then they would vote on the guilt or innocence of the defendant. A majority verdict was sufficient. Occasionally the vote would be marginally in favour of a conviction. Sometimes it would be unanimous. Then they'd consider the penalty. 'We took it very seriously,' Lyon would later write, 'continually re-reading the War Crimes Act before we decided on the verdict and the penalty.'

One thing they had agreed on without much discussion was the order in which the prisoners were to be brought in. Shibano and Aoki, who'd played a major role in the crimes against the prisoners, would be dealt with first.

There was a sense of foreboding in court that morning, with military personnel whispering among themselves and the occasional murmur from the public gallery. Apart from Aoki, all the prisoners appeared to be very nervous. The Faith Healer remained defiant.

Shibano was the first man to enter the court. He had a lot to answer for, including numerous random beatings and mistreatment of POWs. As second-in-charge, he virtually ran the camp and there was ample evidence to identify him as the ringleader of many of the crimes committed. He was found guilty of accelerating the deaths of Farley, Fraser, Lubey and Bayliss and misappropriating Red Cross supplies. Sentence: death by hanging.

Aoki, who was accused of initiating the Great Sheet Blitz of summer 1943, was found guilty of contributing to the deaths of Robert Farley, Don Fraser, Garnett Judd, Alfred (Vince) Burns and Thomas Comerford, as well as several other acts of violence. Sentence: death by hanging.

Katayama was next. Given the severity of the previous penalties handed down, he wore a sombre expression as he stood for sentencing. He was found guilty of mistreating some prisoners but innocent of other charges of brutality. He was also cleared of contributing to any deaths. What went in Katayama's favour was the fact that he'd given medicine to POWs who were sick. This undoubtedly saved him from the gallows. Instead, he received twenty years' hard labour.

Kono, the interpreter, was the fourth defendant to appear. While there was insufficient evidence to convict him on all charges, he was found guilty of mistreatment and abuse, but innocent of stealing Red Cross supplies. Sentence: life imprisonment with hard labour.

The fifth prisoner, Kuriyama, the other interpreter, was found not guilty of accelerating the death of Private Wally Lewis, but guilty of mistreatment and abuse. He was sentenced to life imprisonment with hard labour.

The case against the sixth Japanese guard to appear, Taguchi, the medical orderly who'd worked under Aoki, was less clear-cut. He'd ordered sick men to work under Aoki's instruction, but had this contributed to their deaths? He had also inflicted much physical abuse. In the end, Taguchi escaped the noose by one vote. Sentence: life imprisonment with hard labour.

The final prisoner to be brought before the court was the camp commandant, Narumi Oota, who was clearly expecting the worst. The central question that had to be addressed by the court was whether he should be found guilty of crimes committed by his staff. There was a significant legal precedent here. General Yamashita, the so-called Tiger of Malaya, who had led the Japanese offensive and been accused of the rape of Manila, had argued that he had not personally ordered any massacres and therefore could not be held responsible for them. The US Supreme Court ruled otherwise and upheld the death sentence imposed on him. Did Oota fall into the same category?

The War Crimes Tribunal spent many hours anguishing over this issue and ultimately decided that he was morally accountable for what had happened at Naoetsu. But whether he deserved death, that was another matter. Three members of the panel voted no and two yes. Sentence: life imprisonment with hard labour.

Alan Lyon remembered looking at Oota shortly before the sentence was handed down. 'He was certainly expecting the death penalty and was extremely nervous,' the Australian recorded in *Japanese War Crimes*. 'He was that sort of bloke, unsure of himself. When he heard he was to be spared he was pretty relieved. A lot of people thought he should have been given the big drop but I thought it was the right decision from a legal point of view.'

Oota bowed his head to the court in acknowledgement as the sentence was handed down. He was a lucky man and he knew it.

The seven convicted men were taken back to Sugamo Prison, in Tokyo, and held until the court's findings were promulgated. Those who escaped the hangman's noose were released after serving less than ten years of their sentence.

Captain Lyon's job was over. After a few days' leave, he returned to Onomochi and later boarded a troopship bound for Australia. Once home, he became a sales executive for a large international company. But nothing would compare with the job he performed for the Allied War Crimes Commission.

CHAPTER 14

SEARCHING FOR WATANABE

If there was one important name the Naoetsu boys did not see included in the newspaper reports discussing the sentences brought down in Yokohama in February '47, and dearly wished to, it was Mitsuhiro Watanabe. Even John Cook's meticulous note-keeping, Jimmy Houston's comprehensive diary and straight-down-the-line testimony from Henry Dietz couldn't convict a war criminal if he couldn't be found. General MacArthur had placed the Bird at number 23 in his list of forty most wanted men, so there was no denying that the evidence against the Japanese former sergeant was damning.

Back in March 1945, those twenty-two Allied officers who'd arrived at Naoetsu from the Omori camp had got a headstart on the Aussies when it came to experiencing Watanabe's sheer cruelty. One of those transferred POWs, Captain Tom Henling Wade, the English journalist, had seen the bastard in action enough to form quite a picture of this severely unhinged personality. To Tom, the Bird's behaviour was the result of a massive inferiority complex. He was the spoilt son of a wealthy family and an adoring mother. After university he'd gone to work for the Japanese news agency Demei, before being called up for military service. When he failed his examination for a commission, Watanabe was humiliated — particularly as his brother and brother-in-law had both been made officers. This annoyed the *hell* out of him.

Soon after the Japanese surrender, word was that Watanabe had fled to the hills and might even have committed hara-kiri. Even his mother was reported to have made a shrine in honour of her dear dead son. But was he still alive? Louis Zamperini had been intrigued by several tantalising reports regarding Watanabe's fate and could never get his tormentor out of his mind. 'All I wanted to do was strangle him,' he wrote. 'Always in my dreams I was throttling the Bird, strangling him with my bare hands.'

In October 1950, Zamperini stepped off a plane at Tokyo airport for the first stage in a lecture tour that would take him to the very prison where some of his old adversaries were serving lengthy jail terms. Aside from the Bird, he wanted to look the other Japanese guards in the eyes. It wasn't revenge that motivated him, but curiosity. By now he'd learnt to forgive and wanted to help those who'd inflicted so much pain on him.

The problem was gaining permission to enter Sugamo Prison, in the city's Ikebukuro district. Only close relatives and those on official business were allowed inside. Never a man to ignore a challenge, Louis telephoned General MacArthur's headquarters in Japan and, using every ounce of his missionary zeal, persuaded the wartime leader to let him in.

The following morning Louis walked through the gates of Sugamo jail to address the inmates. Several hundred Japanese were held there. As always on these occasions, he ended the talk by inviting those present to become Christians. A surprisingly large number raised their hands, even though they'd been assured it would not have any influence on their sentence.

Then the colonel in charge suggested that those who had known Louis as a POW might come forward. It was an electric moment. One by one they rose from their seats and shuffled down the aisle. He recognised them all — all the Jap guards from his days at Omori, and finally James Sasaki, his former student friend from USC whom he met again at Ofuna.

But where was Watanabe? Why wasn't he in Sugamo too? Zamperini couldn't leave without asking what had happened to him. Sasaki wasn't sure. Officially, the Bird was listed as missing and had a $25,000 bounty on his head. But personally, he believed Watanabe had taken his own life.

The Bird wouldn't have the guts to kill himself, and he was too devious to be caught. The truth was to prove even more improbable but it would be another forty-five years before the full story emerged.

It transpired that Watanabe had fled to the mountains of Nagano, in central Japan, where his mother owned an isolated country property. There he got a job at a hot springs resort and changed his name to Owata. After several years, he heard that the Americans were no longer seeking to prosecute those Japanese guards who had gone missing after the war. Watanabe had eluded the noose and could walk free.

He headed for Tokyo, where he found a job with an insurance agency and later set up his own business. Life was good. He married and had children and settled in a comfortable apartment in a smart Tokyo suburb. There were even rumours that he'd bought an apartment on the Queensland Gold Coast, where he intended to spend his holidays in retirement. The claims were never substantiated, however.

News of the Bird's transformation from wartime monster to affluent family man was slow to leak out. In fact, it wasn't until 1995 that word of Watanabe's survival even became public.

On 20 August that year, almost half a century to the day that the war in the Pacific ended, London's *Mail on Sunday* published the first interview the Bird had given about his life as a prison camp guard. Watanabe, then aged seventy-seven, professed his heartfelt shame at what he'd done. Sticking out his chin, the grey-haired grandfather feigned a punch with his right hand and said: 'If the former prisoners want, I would offer to let them come here and hit me — to beat me.'

'I was severe,' he admitted, 'very severe.' Then, as if to justify his behaviour, he pointed out that he was only obeying orders — the well-worn, time-honoured excuse of war criminals the world over. 'I did not use weapons, only fists and hands — I had to teach them a lesson,' the Bird added.

Watanabe told *Mail* correspondent Peter Hadfield (the one who'd tracked him down) that there were two people inside him:

> … one that followed military orders and the other one that was more human.
>
> At times I felt I had a good heart, but Japan at that time had a bad heart. In normal times I would never have done such things. War is a crime against humanity.
>
> If I'd been better educated during the war, I think I would have been kinder, more friendly. But I was taught that the POWs had surrendered, and that was a shameful thing for them to have done. I knew nothing about the Geneva Convention. I asked my commanding officer about it and he said: 'This is not Geneva, this is Japan.'

The *Mail on Sunday* exclusive carried a photograph of the Bird, who had a slightly plump face, a thick moustache and a full head of hair. Watanabe seemed relieved that he'd got it off his chest. But was he truly repentant or simply justifying his cruelty? The fact that he had hidden his secret past for so long suggested he was deeply ashamed of what he'd done.

'No one knows the details of what I did except my wife, my son and my daughter. This is the first time I've spoken to outsiders about it,' he admitted.

In fact, his children didn't know the full story and the two of them were to be further embarrassed by their father's wicked history as word of his survival spread around the world.

Back in the United States, Louis Zamperini remained blissfully unaware of Watanabe's confession for another two-and-a-half years. It was a phone call from a television producer that was to lead to news of the Bird's existence and very nearly brought the two together again. Draggan Mihailovich of CBS Sports had been carrying out some research for the American TV network's coverage of the 1998 Winter Olympics in Nagano when he came across Louis Zamperini's name in a 1945 edition of the *New York Times*.

Mihailovich was fascinated by his story and flew out to California to meet him. A while later, when researching and filming the story in Japan with his reporter, the producer managed to track down Watanabe and rang him at his home. His wife said he was away on a trip, but Mihailovich smelt a rat. He decided to keep a watch on his house, but the Bird didn't emerge. Mihailovich was about to give up when Watanabe unexpectedly telephoned the CBS bureau in Tokyo to find out what they wanted.

Draggan takes up the story: 'Mr Kikuchi, the deputy bureau chief, mentioned that a television team from CBS Sports had met Louis Zamperini and wanted to deliver a message from him. Watanabe said, "Two o'clock, Okura Hotel." We were surprised and elated, raced over to the hotel and set up a camera in a hotel room, just in case he decided to do an interview.'

When the TV crew met him in the lobby, they were surprised at how long his hair was for a Japanese man of his generation, but he was smart and had a pocket handkerchief stuffed in his sports jacket. They also noted his big hands; more like paws, in fact. Watanabe had brought along his son, who was suspicious about the producer's intentions, but eventually they all sat down and chatted.

Watanabe surprised the journalists by saying he'd been to America about five times. And the Bird remembered Zamperini immediately — he described him as 'prisoner number one'.

'He was rather quiet when we said that Zamperini and others had fingered him as being particularly brutal,' the producer continues. 'After about thirty minutes of talking in the lobby, to my great surprise, he agreed to go upstairs and sit down in front of a camera. To this day, I don't know why he did it.'

Mihailovich felt the old man must have known what was coming but seemed flattered by the interest. Perhaps it was simply a case of vanity. 'I do remember that Bob Simon, our correspondent, mentioned to Watanabe that he was number 23 on MacArthur's list of most-wanted war criminals, but he quickly corrected him by pointing out he was "actually number seven". It was almost as if he was proud of his high ranking.'

As the interview continued, Draggan noticed a physical characteristic in Watanabe that had left an impression on men in the camp. 'I'd been told by one of the former prisoners, an American named Frank Tinker, that just before Watanabe would fly into a rage, one of his eyelids would start to droop or lower at half-mast. Sure enough, halfway through our on-camera interview, this happened. It was eerie. But he never got visibly angry.'

The Bird remembered Louis as a 'good prisoner'.

'Well, if Zamperini was such a good prisoner, why did you beat the hell out of him?' Simon asked.

'He said that?' Watanabe queried.

'Zamperini and the other prisoners remember you, in particular, as being the most brutal of all the guards — how do you explain that?'

Watanabe conceded that physical violence had taken place. 'Beating and kicking in Caucasian society are considered cruel, cruel behaviour,' he acknowledged. 'However, there were some occasions in the prison camp in which beating and kicking were unavoidable … I treated the prisoners strictly as enemies of Japan. Zamperini was well known to me. If he says he was beaten by Watanabe, then such a thing probably occurred at the camp, if you consider my personal feelings at the time.'

Under further questioning, the former guard also insisted that he wasn't acting on military orders to beat up the prisoners. Rather, he did it merely because of his own feelings towards the Americans at the time. 'He kept reiterating that the Japanese military didn't force him to do this. It sounded as if he wanted to protect the military and the Emperor,' Draggan Mihailovich remembers.

Afterwards the TV crew asked if they could film him walking on the streets of Tokyo and, much to their surprise, he agreed. Mihailovich then told him that Zamperini was returning to Japan, and that while he had not forgotten what had happened, he was willing to shake hands with his old adversary. The Bird agreed to that also.

When the ex-POW arrived in Tokyo a few months later, however, he reneged. 'We called Watanabe but he said he wanted no part of a meeting. Perhaps he just didn't want to say no in person earlier at the hotel, or maybe he'd had a chance to stew it over.'

Maybe his son, who had been clearly unhappy with the original interview, had also advised Watanabe not to go ahead with the meeting.

Louis explained later in his autobiography that he would have liked to smooth things over but understood the family's reaction. 'Any son, no matter whether he was right or wrong, is going to back his father. The Bird probably wishes he'd never been interviewed, too, because it exposed his past to the family; that he was a guard accused of being the worst of all guards; that there was a reward for his capture and General MacArthur had searched for him, that he was a class A war criminal, which means execution. This was heavy stuff.'

Watanabe never revealed where he'd hidden immediately after the war, but he continued to terrify many of his old comrades.

'Every Japanese person who ever knew him was still deathly afraid of him,' Mihailovich says. 'Even fifty years after the war, one fellow guard was scared that Watanabe was going to come after him fists a-swinging. At first I thought this was far-fetched, but after a while I realised the fear was serious.'

Louis was no longer afraid of him but had often wondered what he might say to the Bird if he encountered him. He envisaged they'd pass the time exchanging pleasantries and discussing each other's family and children. They might even have lunch. But there would be no animosity. He was certain of that. If Watanabe had mentioned the war, Louis would have said it was unfortunate that it happened. But he had no intention of accusing him of war crimes.

'The one who forgives never brings up the past to that person's face,' Zamperini wrote in *Devil At My Heels*. 'When you forgive it's like it never happened. True forgiveness is complete and total.'

CHAPTER 15

THE ROPE-MAKER AWAITS HIS FATE

Eiko Kajita remembers the day well. It was 30 January 1947 and she was at home with her father, Eiichi Uishiki, in the family's little cottage near the camp. The war had been over for more than a year and life was returning to normal in Naoetsu.

Mr Uishiki had spent the morning fashioning a length of rope from some straw. 'He was a farmer, so he always needed strong rope,' Eiko, now in her late seventies, recalls. If the symbolism of his work that morning was lost on his daughter at the time, six decades later it provides a chilling memory of what was to follow.

Eiichi Uishiki was in his fifties and was better known as Whisky or Snake in the Grass to the men of Camp 4-B. As one of the civilians who imposed their iron rule on Naoetsu, he was one of the meanest and most vicious of the guards. The civilians were regarded as much worse than the army guards, often inflicting far greater punishments on the men and contributing to many more deaths.

Not that Eiko realised this then. As the second of six children, she only knew her father as a kind but strict man, who would share his lunchbox with the POWs (or so he said). 'He was always very fond of us, especially the babies. But if we ran wild at home, he would scold us.'

Uishiki had been a soldier before the war but was invalided out of military service after an injury to his right leg and was not fit enough to enlist in the army during World War II. 'When the camp was opened, he applied to become a guard because he couldn't go to war,' Eiko explains.

When the camp was about to close, her father knew he might be in trouble. Fearing that the prisoners would go after him, Uishiki hid near the river, only emerging once he was sure he was safe. After the war, he returned to his work as a farmer and had no idea that Captain Jim Chisholm was compiling a list of the Japanese he believed should be prosecuted for war crimes.

Uishiki discovered his name was among them when he was summoned to the police station for questioning in January 1947. He must have known he was in serious trouble. 'When he came home, he looked very sad,' says Eiko. 'He sat down, folded his arms, bowed his head and didn't say anything to anyone.'

A few days later, there was a knock at the front door. Eiko pulled the handle to see two policemen standing there. 'They asked if my father was in and I said yes. There were only the two of us at home.'

It was a low-key, civilised conversation, with the police appearing to be embarrassed by their intrusion. They asked whether her father had eaten his lunch and she said no. Not wanting to seem impolite, they allowed him to sit down and eat. It would be his final meal as a free man.

Eiko remembers every detail of those last precious moments with her father. 'There was a lot of snow on the ground and only a narrow path outside the front door. As they led him away one of the officers was in front and one behind. He looked so worried and didn't say anything. He just kept everything to himself. But that was my most vivid memory: my father walking between the two police officers down the snow path. That's the last time I saw him.'

Eiichi Uishiki was taken to the local police station, where he was held until being transferred to Sugamo. By now, six other civilian guards from the Naoetsu camp had also been located and rounded up: Akira Yanagizawa (Gummy), Yoshihiro Susuki (Hoppy),

Morimasa Oshima, Masaji Sekihara (Fishface), Hiroshi Obinata (Boofhead) and Yonesaku Akiyama.

The seven men had to wait until 12 November before they were brought to trial at the Yokohama District Court House. Each faced the same charges as the military guards who'd appeared at the earlier trial — that they 'did violate the laws and customs of war' by torturing, abusing and mistreating the prisoners in their charge and contributing to their deaths. As in the previous hearing, they all pleaded not guilty.

Much of the evidence was familiar to those who had followed the first trial. There were frequent references to dog wallopers, slave labour, the inhuman treatment of the sick, and the severe beatings that were inflicted on men who were already close to death. There was the torture, such as the prisoner who was made to stand in front of a blazing fire while red-hot charcoal was placed on his legs. And the man whose head was bashed against a steel railway line when he collapsed at work.

Susuki had an obsession with shoe inspections and enjoyed forcing prisoners to lick the dirt off his shoes with their tongues.

Uishiki, the 'kind but strict' father of Eiko, also enjoyed making those with dirty boots lick them clean. And he took particular delight in beating prisoners whose buttons were missing from their coats. (It later emerged that another guard went around deliberately snipping them off.)

One of Uishiki's most sickening assaults was on Private Irwin Bailey of the 2/20th Battalion, who had four huge carbuncles on his back and was unable to stand the heat from the furnace while at work. When the guard heard about Bailey's excuse one day in April 1944, he grabbed the dog walloper and beat him about the body, targeting the carbuncles. The pain was excruciating.

As well as the 127 affidavits presented to the court from the Australian prisoners, Captain Jim Chisholm, who had spent many months collecting evidence against the civilian guards and tracing their whereabouts, appeared in court to offer his personal testimony.

Chisholm did not hold back. He was determined that these Japanese who'd made life hell for so many of his men paid for their brutality. He'd kept his own private diaries, including notes from other prisoners, which provided an encyclopaedic account of individual acts of cruelty. And there were two names in particular that would receive the full force of his vitriol.

Akira Yanagizawa (Gummy) and Masaji Sekihara (Fish Face) he identified as the most ruthless of the civilian guards, persecuting the prisoners by beating and thrashing them senseless, especially anyone wearing the light-duties red ribbon on their chest. Devoid of all mercy, they tormented those men who were close to death by beating them in the hope they might hasten the payment they received for making coffins. While hitting the prisoners, they would jokingly remark '*Mo sukoshi*' (meaning 'little box').

Captain Chisholm related the story of World War I veteran Corporal Garnett Judd, who couldn't see properly because of the effects of beri-beri. One morning in November 1943 he asked why he had to wear the red ribbon, which he viewed as an open invitation for a bashing from Yanagizawa. Sure enough, Judd was duly beaten on his way to work and had to be carried back to camp. He died soon afterwards.

Such was the scale of barbarity at Camp 4-B that the court sat there, stunned by what they heard. Sick stragglers who fell behind on the twice-daily, 2.5-kilometre runs between the camp and factory were invariably beaten by the guards. Obinata (Boofhead) and Susuki (Hoppy) were the key offenders, but others also joined in.

This grim catalogue of criminal mistreatment was further reinforced when two other Naoetsu survivors took the stand: John Laughton and Watkin Parry, formerly of the 2/20th and 2/18th respectively.

Laughton described an incident where he took the place of a fellow prisoner who was not strong enough to stand while working at the furnace in the Shin-Etsu factory. This was spotted by Obinata, who subsequently ordered him to stand at attention while he slapped him with his closed fists. Unfortunately for Laughton, this didn't satisfy Obinata's sadistic streak. Next he started kicking him about the body with his army boots.

John was so bruised, battered and pushed to his limits that he confessed in court that he would have killed Obinata had the beating not stopped. Turning to the tribunal panel he explained: 'We were machines, we did not know what we were doing, just that we had to work like machines or we would be bashed.'

The most graphic part of his evidence he left to the end. It concerned Private Wallace Lewis, who had somehow smashed a window during a scuffle with another prisoner. When Oshima got to hear of it, he knocked Lewis to the ground with a vicious blow to the nose with his wooden club. Screaming in agony, Lewis was then kicked in the groin and the stomach by Oshima for a full fifteen minutes. Despite his condition, the severely injured man was then made to join the working party.

At times during the hearing, it seemed the witnesses were about to break down, such was the intensity of their emotional recall. Private Watkin Parry revealed that he'd been aching to tell someone about the injustice meted out in Naoetsu since the end of the war. In the witness box, it all came flooding back.

There was the memory of the prisoners who were forced to work in snow and rain until their bones ached with the cold. There wasn't a day when one of his mates was not beaten or a deeply scarred face didn't walk by.

When he entered Naoetsu he weighed close to 75 kilograms. When he left he was about 45, his ribs sticking out from his skeletal form and his face and legs swollen by beri-beri. But there was always someone in an even poorer state. 'The men with diarrhoea and dysentery were much worse off. The guards were beating us all the time … every day … hit hard … the agony inside. Often at times it seemed my heart would break. My only thought was to stay alive,' the 26-year-old former soldier from Tenterfield told the hearing.

It took about six weeks to complete the evidence. After a Christmas adjournment, the court reconvened on 5 January 1948 to hand down its findings. Given what the tribunal had been told about the men before them, the outcome was inevitable.

Yanagizawa was convicted of the death of seven prisoners, contributing to the death of two more and inflicting unusually severe beatings and other cruel forms of abuse. Sentence: to be hanged by the neck until dead.

Susuki was found guilty of contributing to the death of three men and six counts of inflicting severe beatings. Sentence: to be hanged by the neck until dead.

Oshima was convicted of severely beating six prisoners but not guilty of contributing to the death of two of them. Sentence: forty-six years' imprisonment with hard labour.

Sekihara was found guilty of contributing to the death of seven prisoners but not guilty of accelerating the death of three. He was also convicted of severe beatings and other cruelties. Sentence: to be hanged by the neck until dead.

Obinata was convicted of contributing to the death of five, but not guilty to the death of four. However, he was convicted of inflicting severe beatings and other cruelties. Sentence: to be hanged by the neck until dead.

Akiyama was found guilty of contributing to the death of three prisoners and not guilty to the death of four. But he was convicted of inflicting severe beatings and other cruelties on two prisoners. Sentence: to be hanged by the neck until dead.

Uishiki was also found guilty of contributing to the death of three prisoners and guilty of nine counts of inflicting severe beatings and other cruelties on prisoners. He was not convicted of contributing to the death of another. Sentence: to be hanged by the neck until dead.

At the end of the trial, the six condemned men and the seventh whose life had been spared were driven back to Sugamo to await the confirmation of their sentences.

Back at Naoetsu, Eiko, her three brothers, two sisters and her mother, never expected Eiichi Uishiki to receive the death penalty. 'We always thought he'd be reprieved and released,' says Eiko. 'He might have been guilty but the death sentence was far too harsh.'

But they never gave up hope. 'Each month my mother went to Tokyo with my younger brother, because he was too small to be left behind.'

When the day of his execution arrived, the family was unaware.

Eiko had just returned home from a local festival when she heard the news that her father had gone to the gallows at midnight on 3 September 1948.

'I was very sad when I learnt what had happened and cried a lot,' she remembers. Even in death there was no closure to the sadness that haunted the Uishiki family. When Eiko's mother went to Tokyo to collect her husband's ashes, she discovered the bodies of the executed civilian guards had been cremated together. 'So we never knew whose ashes were whose.'

It was the final indignity. But there were no tears among the ex-POWs of the 2/20th and 2/18th that day. Justice had been done and those who had perished at the hands of Uishiki and the rest of the evil mob could finally rest in peace.

The same could not be said of all those who survived Camp 4-B. Many would continue to suffer both physically and psychologically from their ordeal. However, for some there was also closure, largely thanks to one final act of reconciliation.

※ ※ ※

On 29 June 1978, thirty-three years after the end of the war in the Far East, Theo Lee sat down to write a letter. Perhaps he wanted to put the demons to rest, for the ghosts of Naoetsu continued to haunt him. Not that he harboured grudges against those who had imprisoned him. This was more a case of simple curiosity.

Theo couldn't get the image of that battered wooden shack out of his mind. Was it still there? What had happened to Camp 4-B and did anybody in Naoetsu remember it?

He decided to make enquiries and, reasoning that he was more likely to get an accurate response from a local teacher than a politician or government figure, he addressed the letter to the headmaster of Naoetsu High School.

In due course he received a reply from the headmaster, Mr Wasaburo Goto, who assured him that much remained of the original structure, although it had been largely left to go to ruin. While a few of the buildings still existed, there was no interest in preserving the site or honouring the memory of those who'd been held there.

However, Theo's letter had touched a nerve. Not too many locals in Naoetsu liked to talk about what had happened in the war, least of all the camp. But it was part of local history and Mr Goto was keen to know more.

For the next few years, the two men corresponded, and in 1982 Theo decided to take a holiday in Japan, including a short visit to the scene of his traumatic wartime experience. Accompanied by his wife Joy, he retraced his footsteps from Naoetsu railway station to Camp 4-B in the village of Arita. Gazing across the desolate site, he pointed out to Joy where he'd read her love letters — right at the fence by the riverside.

Somehow news of his return had become public knowledge. They were entertained with a sumptuous Japanese feast by the school headmaster, his wife and local dignatories. The following morning, he was greeted by a most unexpected sight. As he walked down the stairs of his hotel to breakfast, he saw a group of strangely familiar faces. A group of older men was waiting for him.

Suddenly he realised who they were. Some of the civilian guards had come to meet him. They shook hands, smiled and exchanged pleasantries, at least as much as their broken English would allow. Just before they left, one of them came forward to present him with a cigarette lighter. Theo, who hadn't smoked since he was thirty, was grateful but slightly bemused. Then the penny dropped: it was his old lighter that had been stolen from him in the camp. The guard had kept it all that time and now his conscience had got the better of him.

During that brief and emotional visit, Theo became friendly with Mrs Yoko Ishizuka and her husband Shoichi, who had himself been a prisoner of war. He had only vague memories of the Australians in Camp 4-B because he'd left Naoetsu in early 1943. Shoichi was sent to China by the Japanese military and was captured by the Americans in 1945.

Later, after meeting Theo and other Australians who visited the camp, he became the first president of the Australian–Japanese

Friendship Society. It was the beginning of a new chapter between the people of Naoetsu and the men of the 2/20th. But their relationship did not always run smoothly.

The society launched a campaign to raise money for the purchase of the land on which Camp 4-B was built and turn it into a garden in memory of those who had died there. A statue representing peace, comprising two angels with eucalyptus and cherry blossom leaves in their hair — symbolising the friendship between the two countries — was commissioned from a well-known artist. And a plaque honouring the sixty Australian soldiers who died at Naoetsu was also to be mounted on a plinth.

Sadly, Theo never lived to see the outcome. He died in August 1991 from kidney failure and several other health issues that had overshadowed his final years. Had he survived, he would no doubt have been surprised and heartened by the fruits of his early attempts at reconciliation. The peace park was to become the only memorial of its kind throughout the length and breadth of Japan. Even today, nowhere else are the POWs remembered.

It was perhaps a measure of the sensitivity surrounding Japanese war crimes and those who were punished for them that the establishment of the garden did not receive unanimous support. In a story headlined 'ROW OVER MEMORIAL TO DIGGERS', the Brisbane *Courier Mail* reported on 16 March 1995 that a bitter argument had broken out in Japan over the planned memorial: 'A group of angry residents of the Joetsu suburb of Naoetsu, the site of a prison camp of 300 Australians, has started a campaign to stop a plaque to the dead POWs. Death threats and promises to torch memorial supporters' houses have characterised the growing anti-memorial campaign as emotions near boiling point.'

The local mayor had declared a special budget of $90,000 to set up the memorial to the Australians. But in an ominous final sentence, the article reported that a prominent author, Fuyuko Kamisaka, had taken up the cause of eight Japanese guards at the camp who were later hanged as war criminals because of the brutal treatment of Australians.

Alarm bells started ringing between Tokyo and Canberra. Australia's ambassador to Japan was concerned there might be trouble if or when the peace park was finally opened.

Back in Australia plans were well in advance for several representatives of the 2/20th to travel to Naoetsu for the opening ceremony. Jack Mudie, John Cook, John Henderson (Sigs 8 Div), Laurie Hill (Sigs 8 Div), Frank Hole and Harry Barber had all accepted invitations to attend along with their wives. But other survivors of Camp 4-B were not happy about it and refused to go.

Don Alchin said he'd only accept if the steel factory that had exploited him as slave labour paid his fare. The company, which still operates in Naoetsu, did not respond but did make a donation to the memorial park.

Jack Mudie sensed there might be trouble when he heard that friends and relatives of the guards were upset that their own menfolk would not be honoured in the same way. 'I received word from Naoetsu threatening if any Australians set foot in town for the opening of the park they would be very, very roughly received.' It had all the makings of a diplomatic incident, or at the very least a return match between two warring factions.

The ceremony was arranged for 8 October 1995. The Australian ambassador, Dr Ashton Calvert, was to be there, and a host of other VIPs, including the chief of the Oceanic Section of the Japanese Ministry of Foreign Affairs, had all agreed to attend.

On the day itself, a further crisis loomed. No one had told the men of the 2/20th that they were expected to attend the unveiling of a plaque for the executed guards, who, it had been decided, should also be honoured. Understandably, the six old soldiers were enraged and refused to go to the morning ceremony. For a moment, it looked as though the entire event would be boycotted. How dare the memory of their dead mates be abused in this manner, they fumed.

Eventually they were placated. But there was no way they'd attend the unveiling of the monument for the eight guards. They'd been executed for the cruel mistreatment of the Aussies, after all. This was not negotiable.

Finally, in the soft light of a Japanese autumn afternoon, the two sides came together for the formal opening of the Naoetsu Peace Memorial Park. Thankfully, both parties realised that this was not a time for enmity but an opportunity to heal old wounds.

Shoichi Shimomura, chairman of the Executive Committee to Erect Statues, Peace and Friendship, stood to address those gathered. Acknowledging the sensitivity of the occasion, he talked of the 'immeasurable damage' suffered by both winners and losers of the war.

'Looking back on Japan in those days I realise it was an insane militaristic nation,' he admitted. 'It was an undemocratic country where the people's fundamental human rights were utterly ignored. We have planned and held today's events so that the two peoples may face the past with frankness and honesty and start healing the wounds caused by the war. By promoting friendship and goodwill between the two countries I am sure that this tragic former camp site will turn into a symbol of peace between the two nations to be cherished in our memory. I firmly believe that those who died tragically at this camp site will be remembered forever.'

Turning to the six Australian POWs who'd made the journey, Mr Shimomura praised them for their noble deeds. 'They told us, "We cannot forget, but we can forgive,"' he explained to the assembled crowd.

John Cook disputed this interpretation. 'In fact, we said, "We can never forget, never forgive, but we can *accommodate*."'

Jack Mudie, who had done so much to make the occasion possible, said the garden would 'shine like a beacon for years and years'. 'If you have children,' he told those gathered, 'bring them to this park often. Tell them that this park now belongs to the people. Tell them that there once stood here a prison camp where 300 Australian soldiers were brutally treated, not because they did anything wrong but because they were men from another nation. And tell them that out of those dark days this garden has been built as a sign to all people everywhere that war must not come again.

'If our hearts are full of love, there is no room for hatred. If our hearts are full of peace, there is no room for thoughts of war,' he added.

It was an emotional climax to a highly charged day, especially for Mudie, who was accompanied by his son-in-law. As if to reinforce the message of reconciliation, Jack's granddaughter Lynnette had married a young Japanese man, Kenji Kise. The circle was complete.

While Jack, John and their comrades believed they had done the right thing by attending the opening of the peace garden, others at home in Australia were not so sure. Anti-Japanese sentiment continued to run deep among old soldiers and there were some who felt a sense of betrayal.

For a time, some of those who'd gone back to Naoetsu were ostracised by various members of the 2/20th. 'People didn't want to talk to us at the RSL or the golf club after we went to Naoetsu,' John Cook's wife Terri recalls. 'Even people we knew well didn't want to talk to us.'

Jack Mudie was similarly treated, and openly criticised. At Anzac Day reunions and AGMs, there were one or two tense moments, which was a pity because of all the members of the 2/20th he had done most to foster Australian–Japanese relations. But that was the problem. More than half a century later, goodwill was still in short supply.

Joe Byrne thought the peace park 'a wonderful idea'. He remembers defending Mudie's actions in front of another officer who took exception to the speech he'd made in Japan. Ever the fighter, Joe told the former captain that he didn't take kindly to a fellow POW being attacked. 'I said, "The war's over — Jack Mudie owes you nothing!"'

Yet perhaps it was equally understandable that many men could never forgive the way they'd been treated by their captors. The Naoetsu experience had left some with an indelible hatred of the Japanese foe that time and penitence could never expunge. Others could pardon, even if they couldn't forget.

As for Japan itself, while successive governments have recognised the brutality of the Japanese military, it is widely felt that the apologies haven't gone far enough. In 1995 Prime Minister Tomiichi Murayama accepted that Japan had caused much damage and suffering to the peoples of many countries and expressed his 'deep remorse'. In October 2006, Prime Minister Shinzo Abe also said sorry for the hurt caused by Japan's colonial rule and wartime aggression. But the apologies were regarded as merely symbolic and not a sincere reflection of Japanese sentiment.

Even today, visitors to the Japanese war museum in Tokyo will find no reference to the Allied POWs who suffered such unbelievable cruelty at the hands of their captors. It is this perceived refusal to acknowledge Japan's unpalatable past that continues to upset those who fell victim to it.

EPILOGUE

Naoetsu residents and the Australian–Japanese Friendship Society continue to hold services for those who lost their lives as a result of what went on in Tokyo Branch Camp 4-B. On 10 October 2006, I joined a small group of Japanese including Eyuu Horisaki, a Buddhist priest from the local Kogen-Ju Temple, to remember those who'd died. In a timely reminder of ongoing international tensions, the date of the service coincided with news that the North Koreans had just tested a nuclear device. Naoetsu is barely 400 kilometres across the water from Kim Jong-il's communist state. One of the guests mentioned that the fear of war on their doorstep only helped to renew their pledge for peace.

The priest reminded the congregation that they should mourn both the Japanese and the Australian victims of war. 'Regardless of the enemies and allies, death is death and victims are victims. War is the worst folly we humans have ever done,' he added.

Eiko Kajita, daughter of Eiichi Uishiki, who had been executed for his crimes, was there. And Shizu Obinata, daughter-in-law of Hiroshi Obinata, one of the other condemned civilian guards, was also in attendance. 'I've always wanted to come here to thank all the people who made the supreme sacrifice,' Shizu said. 'We hate war very much.'

Shoichi Ishizuka, the founding president of the Friendship Society, was there as well. Now eighty-four years old, he recalled his own military service. 'Conditions were so different then. Soldiers suffered terrible discipline from their superiors, so they in turn acted in the same brutal way to others beneath them. I can understand why the guards behaved as they did, because they believed hitting made human beings tougher. The Japanese were told at the beginning of the war that some people weren't human and soldiers went to war with that in mind. They saw their comrades killed, so they had strong feelings towards the enemy. Maybe our military chiefs should have educated their men differently but they didn't.'

Like so many young military recruits of the time, Shoichi was there to serve his Emperor. 'That's all I thought about. Yet now, I can't understand why Japan did such a foolish thing.'

In those days even the schools were run by the military. Each day the children were made to recite the Emperor's military code:

Be loyal to the Emperor.
Be well-mannered and courteous.
Be brave.
Be faithful to the good deed.
Lead a simple life.

'If we'd been loyal to the five rules, there would never have been a war,' said Shoichi, who recently retired from Naoetsu High School where he was in charge of security.

He is not ashamed to discuss his early life and tell others about it. Unfortunately, few want to know. Sometimes he encourages his own school to study the history of the POW camp down the road. But none of the pupils are keen and few of the teachers. Perhaps it's all too long ago. These days only the elderly show much interest in what happened in Camp 4-B. For the rest, it is a part of history best swept under the carpet. Who wants to remember such a dark period?

Yoshika Tamura, who helped to found the Japanese POW Association in the face of much opposition, thought she understood why. 'There was no government help for the families of guards who were condemned to death. They had no breadwinner and endured a miserable life. Because of the nature of Japanese society, rumours about a family's past continued for many years and this became a form of torture for the widows.'

When they feared their menfolk would be ignored in the memorial garden, it was the final straw. This might not justify the controversy surrounding the early days of the Naoetsu Peace Memorial Park but it did begin to explain it.

'I have little doubt the peace park wouldn't have happened if the families of the executed guards had not been allowed to build their own memorial,' said Yoshika.

Raku Fusito, the daughter of the Buddhist priest who had saved the ashes of the dead POWs from being dumped, wasn't there that day but is still a regular visitor to the shrine. Now aged eighty-four, she remembers her father's generous gesture. 'He always used to observe, "There are neither enemies or allies among the dead."' It was a sentiment with which the Naoetsu boys would have doubtless concurred.

As the Buddhist ceremony drew to a close, I began to wonder how much longer these services would be held. What would happen to the park when all those who remembered the camp were dead? Would the eucalyptus trees planted in the specially transported Australian clay have their growth stunted by the biting winds that sweep in from the ocean? Would the garden become overgrown like so many churchyards where the graves are left to decay? Would the locals turn their back on this evil chapter in their history?

I hoped not because there was something very special about the Naoetsu Peace Memorial Park, a spirit best expressed by one of Jack Mudie's poems, which was read at the opening ceremony:

> With head bowed down, I murmur one last prayer,
> To those I leave upon this foreign soil;
> Whose frames consumed by cruelty and toil,
> Will never more breathe sweet Australian air.
> When days were grey, their tired yet steadfast eyes,

> Would turn to golden sands, and rolling plains,
> To wheat fields kissed by gentle summer rains,
> And gum trees nodding under azure skies.
>
> But now they dwell with dreams in realms of thought,
> Where Halls of Dawn are filled with angels' song.
> While we enjoy the freedom that they sought,
> To bear the fiery torch they passed along.
> God grant you peace, you souls who now are free
> To join our forebears in Gallipoli.

John Cook had a less romantic view: 'It's no use telling anybody, because it was so bad they'll never bloody believe you!' Like so many of the 2/20th, he went to his grave with the worst of his memories locked inside. But at least he was surrounded by his family when he passed away on 13 February 2007 at home in Maroubra, unlike his sixty mates who died in the camp.

Those who are still alive wonder how they made it this far and ponder how Naoetsu changed them. Politically incorrect as some of their diverse comments might appear today, they are the heartfelt views of old men who arguably have the right to speak their mind.

Before he died in Canberra in November 2008, Harry Woods confided that old age had left him 'hating the Japanese more than ever'. Still proud enough to show his war wounds to visitors when he lived at Nowra on the New South Wales south coast, there were frequent glimpses of the old Harry who was a hero to his men both in Singapore and Naoetsu. After all, he survived a bullet through his leg and another in the shoulder, and even managed to elude the Japanese troops when they stormed the Alexandra Hospital in Singapore and massacred so many patients and staff.

Even at the age of ninety those memories that had not been blurred by dementia continued to be painful. 'When you see sixty of your mates die, it's horrible. They went in to the camp fit and strong and twelve months later many of them were dead. It was a terrible ordeal.'

Sadly, the war placed almost as much of a burden on the wives as their menfolk. Harry's wife Jeanette, who had loved and looked after him for so many years, died a few months after we met in 2006.

Cas Cook continues to survive the aftermath to war by keeping his own counsel and trying to forget the dark days he spent in Naoetsu. Somehow he's managed to put the beatings, the hunger, the unbearable heat of summer and the numbing cold of winter out of his mind. But he also accepts that the experience may have robbed him of compassion and sensitivity. Like the rest of them, the horror of Naoetsu left him depressed and sometimes callous.

'You'd know some poor bugger would be sick and you'd say, "He'll be gone by the time we return from work." And when you got back you'd be half-disappointed if he wasn't.' It was out of character. Amazingly, when I asked Cas to unlock his memory at the age of ninety for the purposes of this book, he was doing so for the very first time.

Harry Julian's recollection of the camp is still as sharp as a tack. It's the present he has trouble with. An operation stole his short-term memory so that nowadays he can only recall the distant past.

Sitting in his retirement home now, near Lismore, he looks back on his time as a telegraph assistant sending Morse code messages from Singapore before the capitulation. Now in his late eighties, he remembers the Japanese attack, the voyage to Nagasaki, the railway journey to Naoetsu and the conditions in the camp as if they happened yesterday.

Harry doesn't dwell on the worst things he saw. He's tried to blot them out over the years, but when pressed he admits he still has a vivid picture of a man who was tied up and beaten senseless with a pole that was rammed into his eyes and nose.

He never married and didn't really settle down until he was nearly seventy, when he built his own house. 'Marriage never really worried me,' he confides. 'I just went from place to place with my workmates and travelled all over Australia. I was quite happy doing that.'

It also helped to take his mind off the horror of Camp 4-B. He didn't wish to dwell on what happened in Naoetsu.

Joe Byrne, still mentally alert and sprightly in his late eighties, also recalls the dark days of war and imprisonment in vivid detail and, perhaps surprisingly, is convinced the camp improved him as a person, instilling in him a new-found responsibility for his fellow man. 'You had to look after each other, otherwise you'd never get out of there.'

Joe, who later became president of the Ramsgate RSL in Sydney, admits he was always selfish as a young man. 'It was a case of "Bugger you, Jack, I'm all right." But the war and the prison camp changed me. I learnt to help and think of others. Strangely, I believe Naoetsu actually made me a better person.'

It was a view shared by Mick McAuliffe, whom I met a year before he died in 2007. 'I'm sure it improved you as a person,' he said. 'I learnt never to talk someone down but listen and make up your mind afterwards.'

It was the loss of freedom that affected Mick so deeply. 'When I was first taken prisoner of war I was devastated, and you could only get used to it by living each day as it came. Imprisonment was the worst thing, not so much the physical suffering but the mental torment.'

In his later years Mick surprised himself by losing the capacity to hate. 'I take a broader view in my old age,' he explained. 'I really hated them at the time, but you can't blame the present generation for what the older generation did.'

Snowy Collins, who ended up living only a stone's throw from Jack Mudie near Lake Macquarie, claims he has learnt to forgive the Japanese for what they did to him, but quietly confides, 'I'd never trust them.'

In retrospect, he also believes it was his hard childhood before the war that enabled him to survive Naoetsu. 'Only the boys who'd already done it tough came through it well,' he insists.

Don Alchin agrees. 'Some of the poor buggers who'd come from the city and didn't know how to cut wood or shovel coal were the first to go. As for me, it just made me even more determined I wanted to succeed in life, and I did.'

Don's brother Merv, who was lucky to survive his capture by Japanese forces in Malaya, never quite came to terms with his escape and the comrades he left behind who were later executed. Even just before he died he refused to speak about 'the ghosts behind him', as his wife Joan refers to her husband's dead mates. She says he couldn't bring himself to relive the details any more and still suffered the nightmares.

'You see, he had to leave them there to die,' Joan explains. 'He never forgot what the Japanese did. He dreamed about the Japs and how they treated him, but it was a closed chapter when he was awake. The only thing he'd say was how glad he was that he wasn't tied up like a kangaroo to a palm tree.'

Mervyn Hugh Alchin died at the age of eighty-five on 30 August 2008, at Tumut where he went to farm after returning from the war. He had fathered four sons and was grandfather to twelve and great-grandfather to twenty-two.

Though not one of the Naoetsu POWs, he is remembered fondly by surviving members of the 2/20th and particularly by his brother Don. They may have gone their separate ways at Singapore but the family ties made him an integral part of this story.

At his bush funeral there was talk of Merv's 'resourcefulness, courage and toughness' and how those qualities had helped him to survive as a POW.

Herb Lamb also has his ghosts. Most of the men suffered nightmares, although his were less frequent after the war. 'I'm always running, always running,' he explains. 'Sometimes the Japs would be in the tree throwing grenades at me. It was terrible, then I'd wake up.'

Even in his early nineties he dreams of being chased by the enemy. There were no counsellors to repair the psychological damage in the immediate postwar Australia, so the mental anguish has never completely disappeared.

Over the years he has tried to come to terms with the guards' behaviour. Nowadays he concedes, 'A lot of them were bad but they were only acting under instructions, I suppose.'

George Daldry, still remarkably fit in his late eighties, puts his longevity down to a positive nature, which was an essential part of surviving Naoetsu. He never married but has no regrets. 'I've had a tremendously happy life,' he says.

George has always kept himself in good shape and went on to run his own fitness classes in later life, training the likes of Kerry Packer, Prince Albert of Monaco and even the first President George Bush on a visit to Sydney. Even today he works out at the gym and is an active member of the Bondi surf club.

Medium of stature but extremely tough, he has gone through life being able to look after himself. It's how he managed to survive Naoetsu. 'I was in the boys club and I soon learnt how to throw a straight left and not leave my head open. I'm still like that today, although I may have mellowed a bit with age,' he laughs.

There are still occasional flashes of memory which suggest his wartime experiences continue to trouble him, including the picture of the Indian gunners who were burnt to charcoal during the fighting in Singapore. 'It just looked like they'd come out of an oven,' he remembers with crystal clarity.

George has returned to Japan on three occasions but never to Naoetsu. 'Why would you want to go back?' he asks. 'I only have bad memories of the place.' Yet, perhaps surprisingly, he has nothing against the Japanese. 'I think they're a marvellous race,' he declares.

For Kevin Timbs, forgiveness has never been part of his lexicon when it comes to Naoetsu. 'I was invited to the opening ceremony of the peace park but I said no. I couldn't forgive them, I didn't like them and I wouldn't go because I've seen such terrible things,' he says.

Yet there is also something about his manner that suggests he wants closure. 'The camp made me a much quieter person and taught me to assess everything. I didn't want to say anything about it because it was all so terrible. But now I realise that I'd have been better off bringing it out into the open more,' he explains.

Henry Dietz, who in early life was haunted by his German ancestry, finally found contentment at his country home near Nana Glen, close to the mid-north New South Wales coast. He's still trying to understand his captors. 'I can't figure them out — they're a funny race,' is all he'll say. But of one thing he is sure. 'I could no more go back to Naoetsu than fly.'

Like several of the other men I spoke to, Henry still harbours the occasional grudge over perceived wrongdoings and injustices perpetrated by his comrades in arms. For some the old rivalries and petty quarrels that broke out between the POWs are as alive today as they were sixty years ago. Even issues such as the exchange of tobacco for food and those who exploited the weaknesses of others for their own ends continue to rankle. Henry won't name names but the behaviour of some who should have known better clearly left a bitter taste.

For others, however, the Naoetsu experience was not all bad. Eric Richardson of the 2/18th, who now lives in retirement in Cairns, still talks eloquently about what he learnt.

In his late eighties and still remarkably fit both mentally and physically, he vowed to put his wartime experiences behind him after being demobbed. 'I even threw away the diary I kept at the time because all I wanted to do was go back home and get on with my life,' he explained.

Like most of his fellow prisoners, it was the starvation that he will never forget. Eric was fortunate enough to avoid most of the beatings, although he did once get bashed by the dog walloper. But he also learnt many lessons including compassion and mateship. He still remembers the communal gesture of diggers chipping in whatever they could from their own meagre rations to keep a mate alive. 'It also taught me to co-operate. Unfortunately a lot of the Aussies were too macho and didn't understand we were in another part of the world. It seemed like a never-ending struggle for survival. We had to cope with extraordinary conditions for which we were unprepared by training or inclination. A lot of men wanted to condemn the Japanese, but you can't condemn an entire race for the actions of a few.'

They are sentiments with which the late Jack Mudie would have agreed. He always felt sorry for his mates who hated the Japs. Shortly before he died, he told me that it saddened him to think they still had 'bitterness within their hearts'.

'Such bitterness not only makes them unhappy, but their loved ones too,' he once told me. 'And that wasn't a price I was prepared to pay.'

Jack Mudie's willingness to forgive and forget may have got him into trouble with some of his men in later years, but he felt, if that was the price he must pay for reconciliation, then so be it. He had hated the Japanese as much as the rest of the Naoetsu boys during his imprisonment. How could anyone forgive the cruelty and the humiliation they were subjected to? But more than half a century later, maybe it was time to bury the hatchet, he reasoned.

Other old soldiers continued to disagree with Jack's stance, sparking a feud that simmered right up until his death in March 2007. It was old age that took him. Sixty-six years after he sailed out of Sydney Harbour on the *Queen Mary*, he collapsed without warning in his daughter's car. The doctor couldn't establish a cause of death. He was just a month short of his one-hundredth birthday.

Jack Mudie had never wanted to be cold or hungry again after returning from the war. That and his family had nourished and rebuilt him. His daughter Jenny had continued to ensure he lived in comfort after his beloved Neno died.

For some the war never really ended. Jimmy Houston, who died in 1981 at the age of seventy-eight, couldn't forgive his wartime adversaries, and while working as a wharfie once threw a crewman from a Japanese merchant ship into Sydney Harbour. Much of the port came out on strike when he was sacked over the incident and he was quickly reinstated.

But while he held grudges, he could also be generous to a fault. Friends and family said he'd have been a rich man if he hadn't given so much away. Fortunately, he held on to his diaries, which provide an extraordinarily detailed account of his life, from the fall of Singapore to his liberation in Japan. Jimmy wasn't an educated man and never aspired to greatness but his daily record of his experiences as a prisoner of war are a priceless legacy.

Theo Lee, who died some ten years later, never really recovered from the war. 'He was always such a likeable man but at times he could be morose,' says Joy, whose love and memory of her late husband shines as brightly now as it did on the tarmac at Sydney airport.

Theo's physical health began to deteriorate in the 1970s but not before he was able to instigate that one last act of reconciliation. He did not know it then, but as a result of his inquisitive nature, a casual enquiry would go on to ensure the men who lived and died at Naoetsu would not be forgotten. Once described as the camp that never was, thanks to Theo's efforts to build a peace park on the site, it will always be remembered.

Ken 'Bluey' Firth died in a Sydney nursing home in 1993 at the age of seventy-three. His stepbrother Geoff says he lost his short-term memory, didn't eat properly and existed on a couple of cans of beer a day. 'Finally everything just packed up.'

Like so many of his mates, Bluey ended his final years troubled, confused and consumed by ill-health. It is a sad end for men who gave so much.

※ ※ ※

In a few years all the Naoetsu boys will be gone. John Cook, who inspired this book, died just over a year after he attended the 2006 Sydney memorial service to mark the fall of Singapore. Australia owes an enormous debt to John and the members of the 2/20th and 2/18th who lived to tell the tale and those who didn't. Theirs was an appalling yet amazing experience, which deserves to be told but which history might easily have overlooked. This is their story. The heroes of a living hell which took them from the shores of Sydney Harbour to the jungles of Malaya, the capitulation of Singapore and the horror that was Camp 4-B. No matter how they tried they would never forget their battle for survival and those who didn't make it. Even in old age they would be enslaved by the nightmares of the past.

Louis Zamperini, perhaps the greatest survivor of them all and still active in his early nineties, says he has gone through life drawing from his experiences, both positive and negative, in an effort to influence others for the good. There was never room in his life for sitting still and apart from a term of imprisonment courtesy of the Japanese, he has spent most of his nine decades on the go. Even now he continues to enjoy trail-bike riding at his home in Los Angeles. In the nicest possible way, Louis Zamperini is and always has been a man on the run.

Ultimately an even greater truth emerges about the spirit of the Naoetsu boys. What really made them so remarkable was their ability to survive against such seemingly insurmountable odds. Essentially ordinary blokes who endured an extraordinary ordeal, they went through hell and emerged as heroes.

And what of Larry Farmer, the pseudonym I have given to the 2/20th soldier who reportedly dug a hole in which to hide all the money he appropriated in Singapore? Word is that after the war he returned to find his secret stash of cash and, amazingly, discovered the wad of notes still there.

Although I have been unable to corroborate this story, I am told Larry scooped up his ill-gotten gains and carried the money back to Australia. For the rest of his life he made weekly trips to different banks, handing over a few dollars at a time in exchange for more legal tender. His explanation was always the same: he'd brought some foreign notes home from the war and had forgotten they were there until he stumbled across them in his attic. No one ever queried him. After all, he was a veteran whose word was his bond.

Those foreign dollars kept him in beer and tobacco for the rest of his life. Larry Farmer, like the rest of the survivors of the 2/20th, had got the better of the bastards.

I'm assured it happened. I like to think it's true.

NAOETSU ROLL CALL

Name	Number	Rank	POW
1	NX34912	Lt Col	Robertson, A.E.
2	NX35102	Capt	Barrett, A.K.
3	NX34713	Capt	Chisholm, J.S.
4	NX34807	Capt	Chown, R.H.
5	NX34840	Capt	Gibbings, C.C.
6	NX35007	Capt	Hepburn, J.
7	NX35004	Capt	Yates, A.I.
8	NX59134	Lieut	Cornforth, R.G.W.
9	QX12107	Lieut	Campbell, A.W.
10	NX34682	Lieut	Hiley, E.V.
11	NX57412	Lieut	Lee, T.M.
12	NX56164	Lieut	Mudie, J.V.
13	NX56116	Lieut	Woods, H.A.
14	NX26448	W01	Chapman, M.B.
15	NX30287	W02	Ainsworth, J.K.
16	NX40846	W02	Finlay, J.K.
17	NX59245	W02	Gray, G.
18	NX50310	W02	Hogarth, J.C.
19	NX25563	W02	Lothian, W.A.
20	NX46353	W02	Williams, F.D.
21	NX52556	SSgt	Lamb, H.B.
22	NX45895	SSgt	Swanston, W.G.
23	NX40820	Sgt	Carter, E.I.K.
24	NX32714	Sgt	Beed, H.A.
25	NX45941	Sgt	Cooksey, R.O.
26	NX55797	SSgt	Chaplin, F.A.

Name	Number	Rank	POW
27	NX53676	Sgt	Hammond, J.T.L.
28	QX1452	Sgt	Hallam, H.V.
29	NX41007	Sgt	James, B.S.
30	NX30178	Sgt	McClure-Brown, S.
31	NX56921	Sgt	Martin, R.A.
32	NX25600	Sgt	O'Brien, V.
33	NX51652	Sgt	Puddephatt, J.J.
34	NX26674	Sgt	Slater, S.
35	NX26485	Sgt	Sheumack, C.
36	NX65873	Sgt	Timbs, K.B.
37	NX29177	Sgt	Wannan, E.S.
38	NX25965	Cpl	Ashford, W.L.
39	NX34303	Cpl	Borrowdale, A.G.
40	NX32851	Cpl	Bush, R.T.W.
41	NX52088	Cpl	Barnett, J.L.
42	NX45700	Cpl	Brisby, H.
43	NX46180	Cpl	Bowman, C.E.
44	NX45677	Cpl	Barber, H.L.
45	WX6857	Cpl	Clegg, W.J.
46	NX26833	Cpl	Firth, K.W.
47	NX30092	Cpl	Frazer, A.T.
48	NX46075	Cpl	Griffin, J.A.
49	NX26551	Cpl	Hopson, M.
50	NX54096	Cpl	Huntington, J.B.
51	NX65716	Cpl	Jackson, R.
52	NX19774	Cpl	Judd, G.L.
53	NX50861	Cpl	Kerr, A.
54	NX51467	Cpl	Keyes, E.F.
55	NX45868	Cpl	Redman, J.K.
56	NX26499	Cpl	Robertson, J.R.
57	NX56127	Cpl	Sheridan, G.
58	NX31688	Cpl	Warren, F.H.
59	NX59157	Cpl	Williamson, G.
60	NX53757	LCpl	Allery, R.F.
61	NX45661	LCpl	Blanchard, G.P.
62	SX7428	LCpl	Allanson, G.G.
63	NX35251	LCpl	Blackaby, W.
64	NX57723	LCpl	Cleary, L.S.
65	NX65393	LCpl	Edmunds, T.
66	VX25612	LCpl	Lester, W.G.
67	NX26254	LCpl	Magin, J.H.
68	VX29437	LCpl	McCarthy, E.
69	NX45897	LCpl	Tracey, C.T.
70	SX8121	LCpl	Whitington, R.L.
71	QX23007	Pte	Alexander, W.
72	NX45859	Pte	Allingham, C.E.

Name	Number	Rank	POW
73	NX31508	Pte	Alchin, D.J.
74	NX45925	Pte	Arnott, M.C.
75	NX55764	Pte	Armstrong, G.E.
76	NX72394	Pte	Allen, V.H.
77	NX41559	Pte (Sig)	Alexander, D.
78	NX32579	Pte	Barrett, R.
79	NX25786	Pte	Brown, M.W.
80	NX58805	Pte	Boughton, D.
81	NX40777	Pte	Brennan, J.C.
82		Pte	Barber, H.
83	NX33980	Pte	Baldwin, L.
84	NX31736	Pte	Beale, F.
85	NX31660	Pte	Beale, G.
86	NX57411	Pte	Beazley, C. (Tim)
87	NX51071	Pte	Betteridge, R.H.
88	NX43948	Pte	Bunnett, F.
89	NX68810	Pte	Bray, W.C.
90	NX4405	Pte	Bluhdorn, C.B.
91	NX34000	Pte	Burling, K.W.
92	NX2588	Pte	Buck, A.J.
93	NX73683	Pte	Buffett, N.
94	NX52946	Pte	Burns, A.V.
95	NX51728	Pte	Ball, L.E.
96	NX51966	Pte	Bayliss, F.D.
97	NX10520	Pte	Barwick, L.J.
98	NX7279	Pte	Byrne, H.K.
99	NX57316	Pte	Barnett, A.
100	NX51474	Pte	Bassford, H.R.
101	NX73131	Pte	Bailey, I.
102	NX54565	Pte	Blackie, J.
103	NX33600	Pte	Boman, J.
104	NX26425	Pte	Baker, J.H.
105	QX13837	Pte	Britton, R.
106	NX32841	Pte	Birse, C.A.
107	NX10331	Pte	Bell, E.
108	NX46155	Pte	Cook, A.
109	NX72603	Pte	Choice, B.
110	NX45755	Pte	Corderoy, R.S.
111	NX53403	Pte	Carr, W.E.
112	NX52129	Pte	Charlton, H.E.
113	NX48140	Pte	Clarke, R.C.
114	NX55755	Pte	Cole, R.A.
115	NX71982	Pte	Cleasby, A.F.
116	NX1692	Pte	Crandall, J.
117	NX59142	Pte	Cobban, L.W.
118	NX51530	Pte	Charlton, A.W.

Name	Number	Rank	POW
119	NX53066	Pte	Clift, M.L.
120	NX2108	Pte	Cook, J.W.
121	NX71632	Pte	Couldwell, J.
122	NX30930	Pte	Cooper, A.W.
123	NX68637	Pte	Costello, J.F.K.
124	NX54767	Pte	Connor, D.L.
125	NX45655	Pte	Cashman, L.J.
126	QX9549	Pte	Cullen, S.
127	NX52406	Pte	Clinton, K.F.
128	NX10905	Pte	Cook, J.E. (Cas.)
129	NX10941	Pte	Collins, A.
130	NX55519	Pte	Comerford, T.M.
131	NX33244	Pte	Carroll, J.R.
132	NX2175	Pte	Coss, H.A.
133	NX2163	Pte	Cohen, R.
134	NX41564	Pte	Coppin, T.
135	QX19268	Pte	Cox, D.
136	NX30417	Pte	Chaney, R.C.
137	NX54141	Pte	Downie, J.W.
138	NX19361	Pte	Doyle, E.L.
139	NX47787	Pte	Donnelly, C.G.
140	NX71913	Pte	Donnelly, R.J.
141	NX45703	Pte	Davies, A.R.
142	NX59197	Pte	Daldry, G.A.
143	NX55624	Pte	Douglas, E.A.
144	NX72590	Pte	Dietz, H.
145	NX10969	Pte	Diamond, J.
146	NX72005	Pte	Drover, A.
147	NX71542	Pte	Devlyn, C.J.
148	NX71812	Pte	Duncan, F.C.R.
149	NX41458	Pte	Dillon, N.C.
150	NX58298	Pte	Dawson, L.R.
151	NX52755	Pte	Endacott, E.M.
152	NX40457	Pte	Easy, H.C.
153	NX50532	Pte	Eilersen, O.F.
154	NX60320	Pte	Eddison, J.O.
155	NX40909	Pte	Francis, F.
156	NX27268	Pte	Farley, R.G.
157	NX40898	Pte	Fulloon, C.G.
158	NX27153	Pte	Faust, H.
159	NX26611	Pte	Fardy, T.
160	NX55102	Pte	Fowler, N.
161	NX33585	Pte	Ford, H.J.
162	NX27123	Pte	Fowler, S.W.
163	NX50328	Pte	Flicker, F.H.
164	VX63754	Pte	Frazer, D.

Name	Number	Rank	POW
165	NX40784	Pte	Gallagher, C.C.
166	NX56689	Pte	Gronow, M.
167	NX54198	Pte	Gaffney, B.
168	NX71986	Pte	Gentle, E.
169	NX71933	Pte	Griffin, L.G.
170	NX47400	Pte	Griffin, R.W.
171	NX10898	Pte	Grayndler, C.M.
172	NX44508	Pte	Gorman, M.
173	NX72010	Pte	Greatorex, T.
174	NX50286	Pte	Graves, J.L.
175	NX2910	Pte	Geddes, J.R.
176	NX32057	Pte	Grant, R.A.
177	NX33524	Pte	Hole, F.
178	NX50558	Pte	Harper, J.
179	NX2118	Pte	Hartley, R.
180	NX52492	Pte	Hair, S.M.
181	NX71574	Pte	Healy, A.
182	NX49544	Pte	Hann, A.O.
183	NX33607	Pte	Hurley, J.
184	NX53143	Pte	Hancock, R.A.
185	QX18333	Pte	Hassell, L.
186	NX65721	Pte	Hanslow, W.J.
187	NX72535	Pte	Herps, M.
188	NX55782	Pte	Hamburger, C.
189	NX51696	Pte	Houston, J.
190	NX57901	Pte	Hams, L.
191	NX36981	Pte	Hosler, R.
192	NX25993	Pte	Hayson, W.
193	NX20926	Pte	Hawkins, F.
194	NX51764	Pte	Hinder, T.
195	NX45213	Pte	Hale, W.
196	NX32382	Pte	Hewitt, A.
197	NX55267	Pte	Hollis, K.R.
198	NX57865	Pte	Henderson, J.
199		Pte	Holden, L.
200	VX58193	Pte	Hill, L.L.C.
201		Pte	Harris, C.J.
202	WX6875	Pte	Hennessy, H.
203	NX43407	Pte	Ianna, J.L.
204	NX49086	Pte	Jones, L.T. (Pinhead)
205	NX45960	Pte	Jeffries, C.
206		Pte	Johnstone, A.
207	NX32450	Pte	Jones, P.T. (Peewee),
208	NX55407	Pte	James-Barnes, N.
209	NX53809	Pte	Jolly, R.
210	NX57419	Pte	Jennings, R.A.

Name	Number	Rank	POW
211		Pte	Jones, W.J. (Buck)
212	NX46812	Pte	Julian, H.B.
213	NX73637	Pte	Kelloway, E.G.
214	NX65732	Pte	Kent, W.
215	NX6967	Pte	Kean, H.J.
216	NX72204	Pte	Kendall, F.C.
217	NX30860	Pte	Kingham, C.
218	NX73014	Pte	Kelly, T.W.
219	NX19968	Pte	Kitchener, J.
220	NX33496	Pte	Kellner, D.R.
221	NX78086	Pte	Kelly, P.F.O.
222	NX42344	Pte	Kinsey, H.T.
223		Pte	King, R.E.
224	NX49939	Pte	Lubey, G.P.
225	NX59201	Pte	Laws, E.
226	NX19962	Pte	Law, R.
227	NX21529	Pte	Langborne, F.
228	NX1852	Pte	Levett, J.
229	NX50447	Pte	Lewis, W.
230	NX50739	Pte	Lawrence, G.
231	NX73682	Pte	Luster, L.
232	NX31857	Pte	Logan, F.
233	QX15560	Pte	Louis, L.A.
234	NX45734	Pte	Loadsmen, C.D.
235	NX50611	Pte	Laughton, J.T.
236	NX57883	Pte	Leary, C.W.
237	NX53383	Pte	Marsh, J.C.
238	NX50530	Pte	Mansell, F.
239	NX1171	Pte	Micallef, C.
240	NX25192	Pte	Molloy, C.
241	NX56070	Pte	Morgan, G.K.
242	NX56156	Pte	Miller, J.J.
243	NX32110	Pte	Matherson, A.
244	NX52447	Pte	Margison, J.
245	NX51560	Pte	Moffitt, J.
246	NX29875	Pte	Martin, A.K.
247	NX72413	Pte	Mitchell, F.
248	NX22957	Pte	McDonald, R.G.
249	NX23259	Pte	Macdonald, D.
250	NX26807	Pte	MacDonald, I.G.
251	NX49439	Pte	McAuliffe, M.
252	NX54305	Pte	McDermott, E.
253	NX8350	Pte	Macleod, D.
254	NX56393	Pte	McDonald, R.D.
255	NX60091	Pte	McBurney, E.
256	NX5753	Pte	McDonald, C.

Name	Number	Rank	POW
257	NX26042	Pte	Nicol, C.
258	NX29590	Pte	Nichols, John,
259	NX1781	Pte	O'Sullivan, W.
260	NX635	Pte	O'Neill, T.N.
261	NX52011	Pte	Orchard, J.E.
262	NX10780	Pte	O'Malley, J.J.
263	NX39617	Pte	Oates, K.M.
264	NX32657	Pte	Porter, B.R.
265	NX30412	Pte	Power, R.
266	NX40700	Pte	Parry, W.J.
267	NX48211	Pte	Pearce, C.C. (Shorty)
268	NX26341	Pte	Patterson, J. (Banjo)
269	NX39761	Pte	Pollock, G.
270	NX25095	Pte	Perkin, J.E.
271	NX58585	Pte	Power, T.A.
272	NX49869	Pte	Phillips, A.R. (Jockey)
273	NX47010	Pte	Plater, O.T.
274	NX33393	Pte	Pegrum, R.O.
275	NX73690	Pte	Price, A.
276	NX50737	Pte	Patching, E.
277	NX43440	Pte	Perry, E.J.
278	NX31729	Pte	Pepper, V.
279	NX56913	Pte	Peake, P.E.
280	NX56335	Pte	Polkinghorne, H.R.
281	NX20485	Pte	Quinn, D.
282	NX33953	Pte	Ryan, M.L.
283	NX20257	Pte	Reed, N.K.
284		Pte	Richens, T.E.
285	NX40499	Pte	Richards, T.W.
286	NX43423	Pte	Rosser, R.T.
287	NX26389	Pte	Richardson, E.A.
288	NX40217	Pte	Ryan, L.J.
289	NX58507	Pte	Ross, P.
290	NX676	Pte	Ritchie, E.J.
291	NX43510	Pte	Rankin, T.E.
292	NX52105	Pte	Roberts, B.J.
293	NX4329	Pte	Rudd, E.
294	NX10307	Pte	Rodway, R.H.
295		Pte	Roberts, F.J.
296	VX43503	Pte	Robinson, W.E.
297	NX42459	Pte	Rainbow, R.K.
298	NX40158	Pte	Sutton, S.J.
299	NX40168	Pte	Sutton, G.A.
300	NX69992	Pte	Sweet, H.J.F.

SOURCES AND REFERENCES

CHAPTER 1

Sydney historic details, films, entertainment listings, job vacancies drawn from the *Sydney Morning Herald*, 29 July 1941.

Prime Minister Robert Menzies on British and Australian relations with Japan, as reported by the *Sydney Morning Herald* on 29 July 1941.

Seer's astrology forecast from *Sydney Sun*, 29 July 1941.

Property sales, clothing and electric goods as advertised in the *Sydney Morning Herald*, 30 July 1941.

'Japan Mobilises for War' – headline from *Sydney Sun*, 30 July 1941.

Background to the formation of the Citizen Military Force, military recruitment, the Eighth Division of the Australian Infantry Brigade, battalions including the 2/20th and training facilities and the general preparation for war is drawn from the following sources:

Singapore and Beyond by Don Wall, published in Australia by the 2/20 Battalion Association in 1985.

James Keady, secretary of the 2/20 Battalion.

The Australian War Memorial.

Biographical details provided by the following:

Andrew Robertson – John and Marjorie Robertson (son and daughter).

Harry Woods – interviews with Harry in May 2006 and his wife Jeanette (since deceased).

Albert (Innes) Yates and Jim Chisholm – Roderick Yates.

Alex (Sandy) Barrett – Bruce Barrett.

Don Alchin – interviews with Don, wife Mickie in Temora, July 2006 and Lindy Cooper (daughter).

Merv Alchin – thanks to Don and Merv's wife Joan.

Henry Dietz – interview with Henry in June 2006.

Kevin Timbs – interview with Kevin at Dapto in May 2006.

Cas Cook – interview with Cas and wife Marjorie in Penrith in May 2006.

Harry Julian – interview in Lismore in June 2006.

Herbert (Herb) Lamb – interview at home in Engadine, May 2006.

Arthur (Snowy) Collins – interview at Fennell Bay, NSW, June 2006.

George Daldry – interview in Bondi, 2006. Also Deb Callaghan.

Charles Daldry – interview with George Daldry, 2006.

Harold (Joe) Byrne – interview Ramsgate, Sydney, June 2006.

Mick McAuliffe – interview at Lismore, June 2006. Died 12 July 2007.

Jack Mudie – interview at home in Toronto, NSW, May 2006.

John Cook – interview Maroubra, April 2006. Also John's diaries and interviews with wife Terri.

Ken 'Bluey' Firth. Interview with Geoff Firth, stepbrother.

Eric Arthur Richardson – interview with author in 2007.

Don Fraser – based on personal diary.

David Thompson, who provided names and addresses of survivors and other biographical material.

History/background: Major General Gordon Maitland, *The Battle History of the New South Wales Regiment: Volume II 1939–1945*, Kangaroo Press, Sydney, 2002

2/20th Battalion war diary:
www.awm.gov.au/diaries/ww2/folder.asp?folder=474

re Ingleburn:
www.raemensw.com/articles/Military/ingleburn_army_camp.htm

re Ingleburn: www.awm.gov.au/units/place_1039.asp

re Bathurst: www.bathurstregion.com.au/visitors/817/Army_camp.PDF

CHAPTER 2

Factual details about the Queen Mary's journey based on interviews with survivors of the 2/20th Battalion and *Singapore and Beyond* by Don Wall.

I have also drawn from the same book for some of the background history to Singapore, as well as visits to the Raffles Museum in Singapore, The *Straits Times* library, the old Ford Motor factory and extensive interviews with the survivors of the 2/20th.

Legendary incident about B Company mess food recounted by Don Wall on page 15 of *Singapore and Beyond*.

Description of 2/20th Battalion's deployment and the Australian influence on the camp is based on interviews with survivors and Battalion records.

2/20th Battalion war diary:
www.awm.gov.au/diaries/ww2/folder.asp?folder=474

Queen Mary: www.queenmary.com/index.php?page=queenmarystats

February voyage: www.geocities.com/batt2_20/history.htm

Arrival at Singapore (2/18th's war diary):
www.awm.gov.au/diaries/ww2/folder.asp?folder=471

CHAPTER 3

General developments in the theatre – partly drawn on the *Australia in the War of 1939–45, Volume IV, The Japanese Thrust* (First Edition), by Lionel Wigmore.

Churchill quote: 'In my whole experience…'

The British Prime Minister in a statement to the House of Commons on 11 December 1942.

General Wavell's message to General Percival sent 19 January 1942.
Published in *Australia in the War of 1939–45*, Volume IV, Chapter 13.

Sir Shenton Thomas instruction: Circular issued to the Malayan Civil Service in mid-January, 1942, published in *Australia in the War of 1939–45*.

Message from Percival to Wavell on 27 January 1942, from *Australia in the War of 1939–45*, Chapter 13.

Gordon Bennett: 'There was the usual crowd …' quoted from *Why Singapore Fell*, first published by Angus and Robertson in 1944.

John Varley swimming the river – drawn from *Singapore and Beyond*.

Merv Alchin/Capt Cope drawn from interviews with Don Alchin, Merv's wife Joan and *Singapore and Beyond* by Don Wall.

Jimmy Houston's recollections based on his personal diaries.

2/20th Battalion war diary:
www.awm.gov.au/diaries/ww2/folder.asp?folder=474

Major General Gordon Maitland, *The Battle History of the New South Wales Regiment: Volume II 1939–1945*, Kangaroo Press, Sydney, 2002

2/18th Battalion war diary:
www.awm.gov.au/diaries/ww2/folder.asp?folder=471

Allied strength in Malaya:
orbat.com/site/history/historical/malaysia/malayan1941.html

CHAPTER 4

General developments in the theatre based on interviews with 2/20th survivors and *Australia in the War of 1939–45*.

Deployment of Australian units based on battalion records and *Singapore and Beyond*.

Churchill quotes: 'The hideous spectacle …' *Australia in the War of 1939–45*, Chapter 14.

Brig. I. Simson memo from *Australia in the War of 1939–45*, Chapter 14.

Straits Times observations: 'The real trouble…' 26 January 1941 edition of newspaper.

'A scraggy waste…' Lt. Col. R. F. Oakes, Singapore Story, made available to Lionel Wigmore for the *Australia in the War of 1939–45*.

General Percival quotes: 'I had personally selected …' etc, *The War in Malaya*, Published by Eyre and Spottiswood.

Bennett: 'We'll blow them all away tomorrow,' from *Australia in the War of 1939–45*.

Charles Moses quote: 'He was a very good soldier …' as recalled by Kevin Timbs in May 2006.

Wavell orders: 'We must defeat them …' Order issued by Wavell on 10 February 1942 quoted in the *Australia in the War of 1939–45*.

Gen. Yamashita note: 'My sincere respect …' Message dropped to Allied forces on 11 February 1942.

Bennett: 'There were holes in the road …' as recalled in his book *Why Singapore Fell*, first published by Angus and Robertson in 1944.

Churchill to Wavell: 'You are of course sole judge …' *Churchill, Vol IV*, page 92.

Sir Shenton Thomas: 'There are now one million people…' Cable to the Colonial Office, 14 February 1942. Quoted in *Australia in the War of 1939–45*. Also quoted in *Churchill, Vol IV*, page 90.

'What really caught Ray Potts' attention …' Recalled by Don Wall in *Singapore and Beyond*.

Opinions re Bennett's escape from Singapore. As recalled by Bennett in *Why Singapore Fell*.

'Ill-advised' quote by General Sturdee, Chief of General Staff, as recalled by Bennett in *Why Singapore Fell*.

Prime Minister John Curtin paid tribute to Bennett in a press statement issued after the officer's return to Australia after a War Cabinet meeting as recorded in *Australia in the War of 1939–45*, Chapter 17.

2/20th Battalion war diary:
www.awm.gov.au/diaries/ww2/folder.asp?folder=474
Major General Gordon Maitland, *The Battle History of the New South Wales Regiment: Volume II 1939–1945*, Kangaroo Press, Sydney, 2002
Dispositions and battle: en.wikipedia.org/wiki/Battle_of_Singapore

CHAPTER 5

General developments and background are based on interviews with survivors of the 2/20th Battalion. *Australia in the War of 1939–45.* Photographic captions and records at Old Ford Motor Factory, Singapore, The Battle Box, Fort Canning and World War II Interpretive Centre, Reflections of Bukit Chandu.

Houston recollection based on personal diary.

Australian units at Changi. Interviews with survivors of the 2/20th Battalion, Jimmy Houston's diary and *Australia in the War of 1939–45.*

Houston diary extracts courtesy of Pam Nielsen (stepdaughter).

Boughton diary extracts courtesy of David Boulton and members of the Boughton family.

Quotes from David Griffin: *Meanjin*, an Australian literary magazine. Published in the autumn of 1954.

Official order re black market: 'There can be no moral justification...' Changi camp order issued on 24 July 1943 and recorded in the *Australia in the War of 1939–45, Vol IV.* Taken from Part 3, Prisoners of the Japanese, written by A. J. Sweeting.

Escape and execution of four servicemen including Australians Corporal R. E. Breavington, VX63100, of Fairfield, Victoria and Private V. L. Gale, VX62289, of Balwyn, Victoria. Based on *Australia in the War of 1939–45, Vol IV.* Taken from Part 3, written by A. J. Sweeting.

Robertson's row with Japanese interpreter based on recollections of survivors who witnessed the incident.

2/20th Battalion war diary:
www.awm.gov.au/diaries/ww2/folder.asp?folder=474

Changi details: www.diggerhistory.info/pages-battles/ww2/changi/0-changi-cat-index.htm

Changi details:
www.cofepow.org.uk/pages/asia_singapore_changi_story.htm

Syonan Shinto Shrine: infopedia.nl.sg/articles/SIP_236_2004-12-24.html

SOURCES AND REFERENCES | 345

Some details about the voyage to Japan remain disappointingly vague and it is possible that some of the 550 men from C Force aboard the *Kamakura Maru* may have been selected for Kobe in a manner that differs from my conclusions in Chapter 5. Records kept by Australian commanders were often confiscated and destroyed by the Japanese and the recollections of the men sometimes contradicted each other.

CHAPTER 6

General developments and background based on interviews with survivors.
Dudley Boughton's diary extract courtesy of David Boughton and family.
Diary extract: 'This has been a very black week …' – Jimmy Houston, 29 March 1943.
All Houston diary extracts courtesy of Pam Nielsen.
'Felt very queer today' diary extract Don Fraser, no known relatives or estate.
Kuriyama announcement and black letter card text based on recollections of John Cook and other survivors.
POW details (World War 2 Nominal Roll): www.ww2roll.gov.au

CHAPTER 7

General developments and background based on diaries of Dudley Boughton, Jimmy Houston, Don Fraser, John Cook and interviews with survivors. Also research at Naoetsu Peace Park museum.
Latrine wall graffiti/Wallace Lewis. Recalled in Jimmy Houston's diary and confirmed in interviews with other survivors.
POW details (World War 2 Nominal Roll): www.ww2roll.gov.au

CHAPTER 8

General developments and background drawn from interviews with survivors.
James Downie's ordeal, based on testimony given by Downie to the War Crimes Commission in Japan, and quoted in *Japanese War Crimes*, by Alan B. Lyon, published by Australian Military History Publications, 2000.
Sandy Barrett's diary entry kindly provided by his son Bruce Barrett.
Anonymous diary entries courtesy of Australian War Memorial PR90/065. Commonwealth copyright.
POW details (World War 2 Nominal Roll): www.ww2roll.gov.au

CHAPTER 9

General developments, background and specific incidents based on author interview with Louis Zamperini and drawn from *Devil at My Heels* by Louis Zamperini and David Rensin, published by HarperCollins, New York, 2003.

POW details (World War 2 Nominal Roll): www.ww2roll.gov.au

CHAPTER 10

General development and background based on author interviews with survivors.

Visit by Tokyo commander recalled in Jimmy Houston's diary entry for 5 February 1944.

Jack Baker's ordeal based on interviews with survivors as well as Alan B. Lyon's book, *Japanese War Crimes*.

Guard's treatment of American doctor, Jimmy Houston's diary, 21 April 1944.

Jock's beating, recalled in Jimmy Houston's diary entry, 18 July 1944.

Chisholm quote, recalled by Jack Mudie in interview with author.

John Cook quote, interview with author.

Theo Lee letter, courtesy of Joy Lee (widow).

Houston diary extracts courtesy of Pamela Nielsen (stepdaughter).

Background on Asabaki, author interview with Jack Mudie, May 2006.

Background and quotes from Hisao Otskuka and Yuko Ohama based on interviews with author at Naoetsu in October 2006.

POW details (World War 2 Nominal Roll): www.ww2roll.gov.au

CHAPTER 11

General developments and background based on interview with Louis Zamperini and drawn from Devil at My Heels. Also interview with Tom Henling Wade and *Prisoner of the Japanese* by Tom Henling Wade, published by Kangaroo Press, Kenthurst, 1994.

Specific incidents and conversations based on interview with Louis Zamperini and drawn from *Devil at My Heels*.

Tom Henling Wade's recollections based on interview with author and *Prisoner of the Japanese*.

Zamperini's radio broadcast and other quotes from *Devil at My Heels*.

'Records show that …' – based on Jimmy Houston's diary extract for 19 May 1945.

POW details (World War 2 Nominal Roll): www.ww2roll.gov.au

CHAPTER 12

Background and general developments based on interviews with survivors and Louis Zamperini.
Tibbets on board Enola Gay, based on numerous historic accounts of the event gathered by the author.
Catching a train to Takada – Tom Henling Wade interview and *Prisoner of the Japanese*.
General recollections – based on interviews with survivors, including John Cook and Tom Henling Wade, as well as Jimmy Houston's diary entries.
'Why don't you submerge, you old tin fish ...' recalled by John Cook.
Louis Zamperini on Hiroshima – from *Devil at My Heels*.
Quote from Lt. Com. Fitzgerald recalled by Jimmy Houston in his diary and by other survivors.

CHAPTER 13

General background and recollections based on interviews with the survivors, including John Cook, Louis Zamperini and Tom Henling Wade, as well as *Devil at My Heels* and *Prisoner of the Japanese*.
Jimmy Houston, based on diary, courtesy of Pamela Nielsen.
Theo Lee, interview with Joy Lee (widow).
Sandy Barrett, interview with Bruce Barrett (son).
Jim Chisholm, interviews with Bruce Barrett, Roderick Yates and Joy Lee.
Memo to Secretary of the Army re Sandy Barrett, Barrett family.

CHAPTER 14

General developments and background based on interview with Louis Zamperini and *Devil at My Heels*.
CBS Sports coverage of the 1998 Winter Olympics, Robin Brendle, Executive Director, Communications, CBS Sports documentary on Louis Zamperini and interviews with him.
Peter Hadfield, *Mail on Sunday*, 20 August 1995.
Interview with Draggan Mihailovich, CBS, December 2007.

CHAPTER 15

General background – interview Alan B. Lyon, *Japanese War Crimes*, Kangaroo Press.
Australian Archives – MP 742 – 1

336/1/207, 336 1/217, 336/1/1123, 336/1/1481, E3856/0, 144/14/75/.
Australian War Crimes Section. WC459, WC501.
Lt. Col. Sandy McCutcheon quote – *Japanese War Crimes*, page 21.

CHAPTER 16

Recollections – author's interview with Eiko Kajita, Naoetsu, October 2006.

General background and Capt Chisholm's evidence to War Crimes Tribunal from *Japanese War Crimes*, Alan B. Lyon.

Letter from Theo Leo to Naoetsu headmaster courtesy of Alan Lyon and Joy Lee.

'Row over Memorial to Diggers', Brisbane *Courier Mail*.

Shoichi Shimomura – courtesy of the Japanese–Australia Society and programme notes.

Prime Minister Tomiichi Murayama, statement by Murayama on 15 August 1995 on the occasion of the 50th anniversary of the end of the Second World War.

Prime Minister Shinzo Abe in address to Japanese Parliament at the beginning of October 2006.

EPILOGUE

Sandy Barrett references based on personal diary and memories of son Bruce.

Tom Henling Wade – interview with author.

Jimmy Houston – based on interviews with stepdaughter Pamela Nielsen.

Louis Zamperini – interview with author.

MAP OF SINGAPORE, 8–9 FEBRUARY 1942

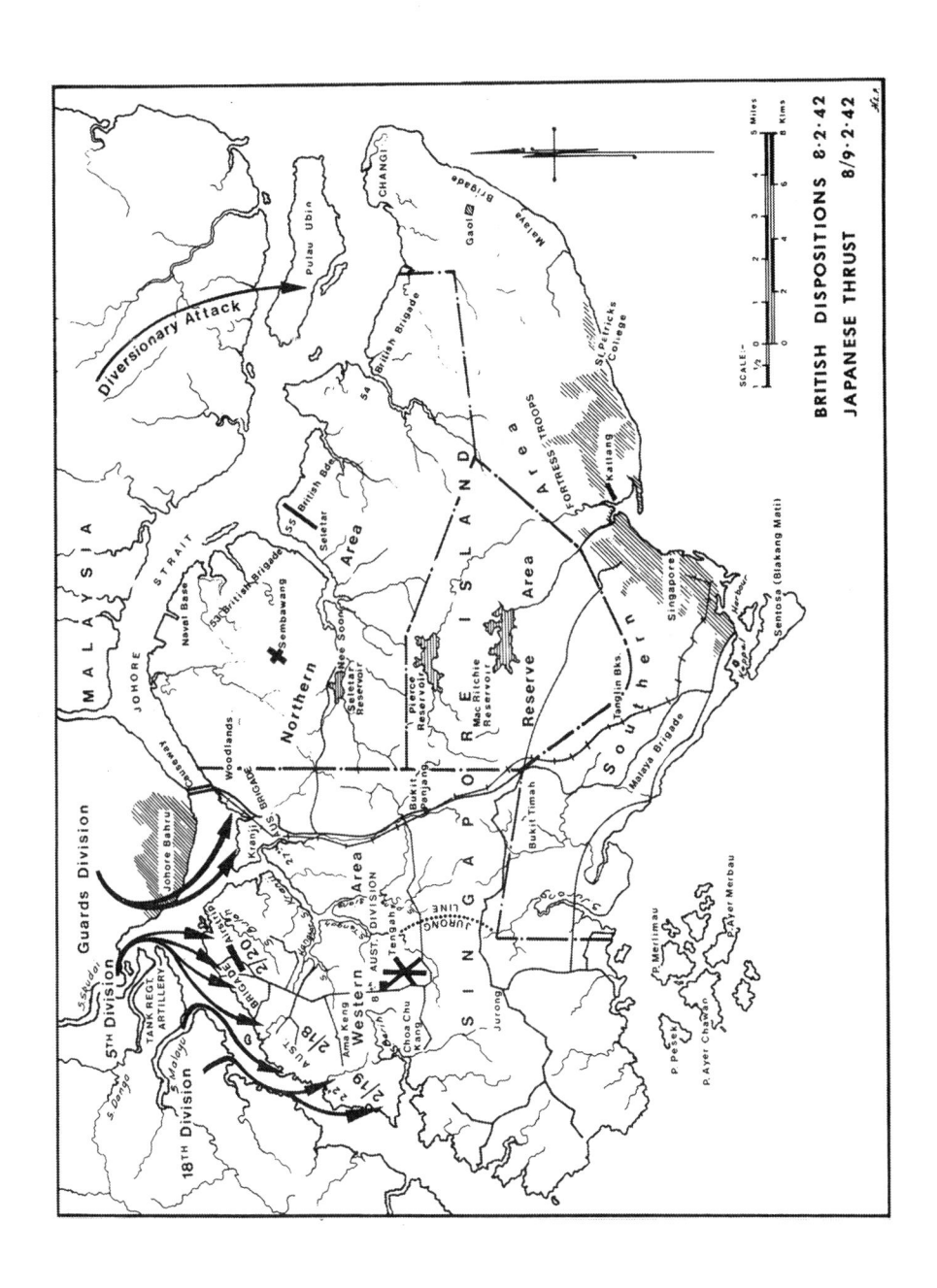

NAOETSU BOYS

The Naoetsu survivors interviewed by the author in researching this book (some of whom, sadly, have since passed away):

Don Alchin

Snowy Collins

John Cook

Joe Byrne

Cas Cook

Henry Dietz

George Daldry

Herb Lamb

Jack Mudie

Harry Julian

Mick McAuliffe

Kevin Timbs

Harry Woods

ACKNOWLEDGMENTS

I would like to acknowledge the following people for their help and guidance:

John Woods, who provided additional information and background about his father Harry; Eric Richardson, who was generous with his time on the phone from his home in Cairns; David Boughton and members of his family, including Anthony, Patricia and John, for their help in providing access to Dudley Boughton's diary; Jack Mudie's daughter Jenny; Terri Cook, John's widow; Deb Callaghan; Geoff Firth; The Australian War Memorial; Laura Hillenbra, Louis Zamperini's biographer; Joy Lee, Theo's widow; Kevin Nicol; David Thompson; Frank Hole's family, including Pat and daughter Jackie; Alan Lyon; Roderick Yates; James Keady, Battalion Secretary, 2/20th; Yoshikazu Kondo; Richard Wall, son of Don Wall, author of *Singapore and Beyond*; Lady Jean Griffin, for permission to quote from her late husband Sir David Griffin's memories of Changi; Ian Affleck, Curator of Photographs, AWM; Tom Henling Wade; *Mail on Sunday*, London; Lindy Cooper, Don Alchin's daughter; Carmel Ryan, for help in organising my visit to Japan; Fuyoka Nishisato; Bruce Barrett; John and Marjorie Robertson, children of Andrew Robertson; Tim Bowden for quotes from Merv Alchin, based on an interview he conducted with him about the experiences of prisoners of war; Phillip Alchin, for memories of his father; Paul Hennessey, for his help with Merv Alchin's family background and war experiences; Neil and John

MacPherson; David Rodda; Shoji Yamaga, President, Japan–Australia Society of Joetsu; Shoichi Ishizuka, ex-President, Japan–Australia Society of Joetsu, and his wife Yoko; Yoshiko Tamura, POW Research Network Japan; Nori Nagsawa, POW Research Network Japan; Kawakami Hiroshi; Pamela and Henning Nielsen, for access to Jimmy Houston's diary; Draggan Mihailovich, CBS News; Robin Brendle, CBS Sports; Kath Whiley, for her encyclopaedic knowledge of Singapore's military past; The *Straits Times* library, Singapore; and Singapore Airlines for their travel assistance.

I would also like to thank my agent Margaret Gee, who was instrumental in getting me started on this story, as well as my editors Jon Gibbs and Patrick Mangan, whose advice and contributions proved so valuable. Thanks also go to my publisher at HarperCollins, Amruta Slee.

Finally, thanks to my wife Vivienne for providing help with my research and spending so many long weeks transcribing hours of interview tapes.

If by some oversight I have omitted to mention somebody it is because so many people have offered their assistance over the past three years. My sincere apologies to anybody or organisation that I have inadvertently overlooked. My heartfelt appreciation goes to all of you.

Note: Attempts have been made to trace the copyright holders of material used in this book. Copyright holders are welcome to contact the author care of the publisher, so appropriate acknowledgment can be made in future reprints.

INDEX

A company, 20, 44, 53, 59, 61, 73, 75, 84–5, 88, 90
Ainsworth, Keith, 39, 133, 141, 198–9
Yonesaku Akiyama, 'horse head', 136
Alchin, Alec, 69
Alchin, Don, 4, 25, 32, 43–4, 59–60, 68, 75, 78–9, 100, 108, 111, 120, 134, 148, 155, 250, 257, 265, 316, 327
Alchin, Merv, 26, 43, 53–6, 60–3, 68, 74, 77, 87, 103, 111–12, 120–1, 213, 265, 327
Alexander, Doug, 148
Allanson, Geoffrey 'Scotty', 195
Anderson, Charles, 42, 73, 93, 115
Aoki, Yusu 'the Faith Healer', 136, 148, 155, 167, 171, 175, 183, 220, 281–2, 284, 289–93, 296
Ashford, Bill, 218
Assheton, Charles, 42, 73, 75, 83–5

Australian Imperial Force (AIF), 35
6th division, 9, 37
7th division, 12
8th division, 12, 30, 36, 38, 41, 45, 50, 64, 73, 96, 104, 125
9th division, 12
Australian Japanese Friendship Society, 321–2
Australian War Crimes Commission, 280
Axis powers, 10
B company, 20, 44, 59, 68, 72–3, 75, 84, 86, 108
Bailey, Irwin, 309
Baker, Jack, 183, 220, 291
Ball, Lloyd, 222
Barber, Albert, 222
Barber, Harry, 316
Barrett, Alex 'Sandy', 15, 132–3, 144, 148, 151, 153, 164, 166, 187, 195–6, 199, 201, 205, 211, 225, 228, 238–40, 246, 253, 275–6
Bathurst Army Camp, 20
Battalion Ball, 21
Battalion Concert Party, *All in Fun Revue*, 40

Bayliss, Slim, 190, 216, 218, 291, 296
Beale, George, 162
Beazley, Charlie, 87
Bell, Eric, 218
Bennett, Henry Gordon, 21, 45, 53, 59, 65, 76, 80, 88–9, 96–7, 100
Beri-beri, 150, 158, 161, 165–6, 173–4, 183–4, 190, 192, 194–200, 202, 205, 217, 220
Blackaby, Wally, 216, 218
Blamey, Thomas, 12
Boman, John, 216, 218
Borneo, 116
Boughton, Dudley, 17, 20, 43, 73, 92, 114, 127, 144, 147, 151, 170, 173–4, 210
diary, 110, 117–19, 135, 145–6, 157–8, 162, 165, 178, 182–211
Boughton, John, 17
Boyes, Arthur 'Sapper', 72, 90
Breavington, Rod, 117
British brigades, 71
British Far East Command, 45
Bronchitis, 145, 194

INDEX | 355

Brooke-Popham, Robert, 45
Brookes, Jim, 90
Buffett, Neville, 210
Bunnett, Frank, 216, 218
Burling, James, 155
Burling, Keith, 40, 155
Burma–Thai railway, 1, 115, 121, 213, 265
'burning pisses', 138, 169
Burns, Vince, 202, 296
Byrne, Joe (Harold Keith), 4, 24, 43–4, 58, 63, 73–4, 76, 100, 108, 123, 126, 140, 181, 243, 245–7, 272, 318, 326
C company, 20, 41–3, 47, 53–4, 57–8, 61, 72–4, 76–7, 83, 86
C force, 1, 4, 40, 112, 126, 131–3, 135–6, 150–1, 155, 221, 263
Campbell, Alan, 133, 151, 209, 218, 228, 244, 246
Carter, Bill, 42, 52, 73, 93, 109, 111
casualties, Allied, 60, 70
Chamberlain, Neville, 12
Chaney, Bob, 205
Changi, 1, 4, 5, 100
Changi barracks, 2
Changi prison camp, 104–8
  diet, 105–6
  entertainment, 113
  Japanese brutality, 118
  march to, 104–5
  Memorial to Allied dead, 114–15
  outside contact, 118
  overcrowding, 106
  prisoners educational scheme, 107, 109
  rations, 106
  Selarang barracks, 104–6, 109, 115, 117–18

Chapman, Martin, 22, 39, 133, 141
China, war against, 10
Chisholm, Jim, 15, 93, 132, 151, 153, 157, 159, 161, 164, 166, 217, 219, 225, 228–30, 240, 276, 286–8, 308–10
Chown, Robert, 133
Churchill, Winston, 51, 69–70, 99
Citizen Military Force, 12
Clavell, James, 117
Cleary, Leo, 191–2
Cleasby, Alan, 218
Clegg, Bill, 164
Clegg, Tom, 217
Cobban, Leslie, 209
Cohen, Ron, 189
Collins, Arthur 'Snowy', 4, 23, 43–4, 58, 74, 77, 90, 92, 105, 121, 143, 155, 181, 216, 243, 268, 326
Comerford, Tom, 190, 291, 296
'Composite Company', 94
Connor, Dennis, 218
Cook, Cas (John Eric), 24–5, 44, 74, 86, 96, 120, 134, 147, 180–1, 254, 273–4, 325
Cook, John, 3, 23–4, 44, 74, 86, 114, 122, 127, 136, 138, 160, 169, 171, 175, 180, 211, 274, 316–8, 324, 331–2
  diary, 172, 182–211, 220–1, 224–6, 236–7, 255–6, 258, 299
Cope, Captain, 52, 55–6, 61, 111
Corderoy, Ralph, 218
Cornforth, Roger, 22, 39–40, 84–5, 133

Crandall, John 'Jack', 186
Curtin, John, 27, 101
D company, 20, 41–2, 44, 52, 74, 81–4, 86, 163
Daldry, Charles, 16, 20, 82
Daldry, George, 4, 16, 18, 20, 24, 30, 33, 38, 44, 60–1, 74, 78–9, 82, 89–90, 103–5, 124, 140, 176, 179, 245, 250, 254, 266–7, 271, 328
Dalforce (Chinese guerrilla group), 74, 83–4
Dhobi itch *Tinea Cruris*, 44
diarrhoea, 147, 161, 165–6, 177, 183, 191–2, 194, 196–7, 200, 204–6, 209, 217, 220
Dietz, Henry, 4, 22–3, 30–1, 38, 43–4, 47, 53, 58, 73, 77–8, 82, 86, 90, 92, 100, 111, 122, 134, 147, 164, 176, 181, 251, 270–1, 284, 299, 329
diseases *see* by specific name
Distinguished Conduct Medal, 60
dog walloper *see* Naoetsu prison camp
Donaldson, Keith 'Donny', 53, 55–6, 61
Downie, James, 214–15, 285–6, 292
dysentery, 174, 183, 220
Eastforce sector, 52, 54, 59, 64
Eddison, Jack, 163–4
Edmonds, Tommy, 216, 218
Edwards, Alan, 87
Endacott, Eric, 169
Endau, 43, 47, 50, 52–4, 57, 63
Endau Force, 52, 57–8

Ewart, Archibald, 13, 20, 44, 75, 84, 116
Fadden, Arthur, 27
Fairley, John, 13, 20, 42
Farley, Robert, 146, 206, 214, 216, 218, 283, 286, 289, 291, 296
'Farmer, Larry', 79–80, 173, 332
Ferguson, 39
Firth, Ken 'Bluey', 16, 19, 20, 29, 38, 44, 75, 92, 133, 243, 270, 331
Fitzgerald, Lieutenant Commander, 244, 258–9
Fraser, Don, 26, 32, 80, 134, 144, 181, 187–200, 291, 296
Fukuye, Major General, 117–18
Gale, Victor, 117
Galleghan, Frederick 'Black Jack', 30–1, 72
Gaven, Frank, 22, 53, 73, 94, 109, 111
Geddes, Jim, 207
Gentle, Ted, 198
Gibbings, Cecil, 73, 132, 225
Goad, Dr, 218
Gorman, Mick, 171
Gray, George, 22, 39, 133, 141
Griffin, David, 109
Griffin, Robert, 222
Gronow, Merv, 203
Hale, William, 198–9, 291
Hammond, Mick, 237
Harper, Joe, 208–9
Hartley, George, 176
Hawkins, Frederick 'Pop', 185
Hayson, Wally, 159
Healy, Alan, 220
Henderson, John, 316

Hepburn, Jack, 132–3, 156
Herps, Merv, 205
Hickson, Robert, 283, 294–5
Hill, Laurie, 316
Hiroshima, atom bombing, 253–4
Hogarth, Jack, 200
Hole, Frank, 257, 316
Homer, Roy, 74, 77–8, 81–2, 91–2
Hopkins, Ronald, 279
Houston, Jimmy, 16, 20, 30, 38, 44, 66, 74, 82, 92, 103, 107, 116, 133, 144, 146, 155, 272, 299, 330–1
 diary, 110, 112–13, 157–60, 163, 165–8, 172, 174, 177–8, 182–211, 224–6, 235, 238–9, 257, 260
HQ Company, 44, 75, 82, 84
Hunter Valley Lancers, 23
Huntington, Jack, 199, 201–2, 205
Hurley, John, 204–5, 291
Hutchinson, John, 41
Ianna, Joseph, 218
Imperial garrison in Malaya, 11
Imperial Japanese Army *see* Japanese Imperial Army
Indian brigades, 71–2, 90–1
Indo-Chinese territories Japan's gains in, 10, 32, 42
Ingleburn camp, 19, 20
International Military Tribunal for the Far East *see* War Crimes Tribunal
Ishizuka, Shoichi, 322

Japanese
 advance, 47–9, 64–6, 96–7
 invasion plans, 46
Japanese Imperial Army, 49, 51, 57, 84, 96, 99
Japanese prison guards
 brutality, 1, 56, 61–2, 68, 96, 104, 135, 139–40, 155–6, 167, 174, 177, 183, 195, 214–15, 220, 224–7, 234–5, 238–9, 247–8
 civilian, 'the Dog Wallopers', 3, 136–7, 176, 190
 prosecution for war crimes, 280–98
Jeater, William, 13, 18, 19, 20, 21, 36–7, 39–40, 42
Jemaluang, 43
Johnstone, Albert, 210, 216
Jones, Thomas 'Peewee', 216, 218
Jono, Konjiro, 39
Judd, Garnett, 22, 193, 195, 286, 296, 310
Julian, Harold, 17, 19, 38, 80, 96, 122–3, 133, 148, 165, 182, 189, 235, 254, 272, 325–6
Kajita, Eiko, 307, 312–13, 321
Kamakura Maru, 120–5, 128
Katayama, Kongo 'the Cat', 136, 156, 282, 290, 296
Kerr, Alexander 'Jock', 174–5, 220
Kingham, Clarrie, 196
Kitchener, Jack, 37
Kluang, 43, 63
Kono, Hiroaki, 201, 227, 255–6, 282, 289–90, 296

Kota Bharu, 43, 46, 48, 51
Kuala Lumpur, 38, 51
Kuantan, 43, 50, 55
Kuriyama, Michio 'Snake Eyes', 126, 136, 143, 150, 156, 242, 282, 284, 289, 296
Lamb, Herb, 4, 15, 18, 20, 22, 30, 38, 41, 44, 74–5, 86–7, 124, 133, 141, 168, 180, 243, 267–8, 327
Laughton, John, 310
Lee, Theo, 15, 22, 30, 38, 40, 42, 73–5, 93, 107–9, 133, 149–50, 219, 225, 228, 239, 244, 255, 259, 274–5, 313–15, 331
Lewis, Wally, 40, 113, 156, 206, 218, 311
Lothian, William, 22, 39–40, 133, 141
Louis, Len, 209
Lowe, Jim, 22, 39
Lubey, George, 209, 291, 296
Lyon, Alan, 279, 281–3, 289, 292, 294–5, 297–8
MacArthur, Douglas, 280, 299–300
McAuliffe, Mick, 26, 32–3, 75, 86, 104, 106, 121, 134, 147, 171, 254, 271–2, 326
Macleod, Donald, 218
McCutcheon, Lieutenant Colonel, 283
Magin, John, 174, 284–5, 291
Malaria, 144
Malaysian brigades, 71
Martin, Alfred 'Jack', 184
Maxwell, Duncan, 18, 42, 72, 88

Meanjin, 109
Menzies, Robert, 9, 11, 12, 33, 45
Merrett, Ronald, 13, 20, 44, 75, 88, 90, 92, 116
Merrett Force, 90, 92
Mersing, 42–3, 45, 50, 53–4, 59, 61–2, 64, 68
Mihailovich, Draggan, 302–5
Military Cross, 54
Miller, Johnny, 204
Mort, Roger, 86–7
Moses, Charles, 13, 20, 42, 87, 100–1
Mudie, Eva, 14
Mudie, Jack 'Happy Jack', 4, 14, 18, 19, 22, 29, 30, 33, 39–41, 43, 46, 52, 54, 57–8, 73–4, 82–3, 90, 92, 94, 100, 109, 113, 122–3, 133, 149–50, 156, 161, 208, 225, 228–32, 235–6, 277, 316, 323–4, 330
Nakamiya, Yukio 'Baby Face', 290
Naoetsu Peace Memorial Park, 313–19, 323
Naoetsu prison camp, 1, 2, 3, 4, 113, 119, 133–78, 249
  American POWs, arrival, 222
  conditions, 132
  diaries, 2, 4, 17, 144, 157–78, 187
  diseases, 144–5, 147–51, 158, 161, 163, 165, 173–4, 177, 180, 183–6, 190–8, 204–8, 217, 220, 311
  food, 179–82, 188–205, 223–4
  hospital, 148, 166, 217, 219

liberation, 253–60
prisoners broadcast, 170
rations, 157–60, 167
roll call, 142–3
slave labour, 138
neuritis, 184
Nippon Stainless Steel, 131, 137, 139, 141, 149, 168–9, 214, 231, 239, 251, 260
Oakes, Major, 72
Obinata, Hiroshi 'Boofhead', 136, 309–12, 321
Obinata, Shizu, 321
Officer Cadet Training Unit, 42
Oota, Narumi, 155, 214, 281, 283, 294, 297
Oshima, Morimasa, 308–9, 312
Parry, Watkin, 310–11
Pearl Harbour, Japanese attack on, 48, 121
pellagra, 204
Percival, Arthur, 46, 50, 64–5, 69, 71, 73, 76, 94–5, 99
Perkin, James Ernest, 177–8
pleurisy, 145, 163, 206
pneumonia, 144, 148, 161, 163, 166, 184–6, 199, 205–6, 216–17, 220, 222
Pond, Samuel, 72
Port Dickson, 36, 38–9, 42, 44, 52, 85
Porter, Bruce, 227
Potts, Ray, 77
Power, Tommy, 218
prisoner of war (POW) camps *see* Changi prison camp, Naoetsu prison camp
  diseases, 106
  educational scheme, 107

overcrowding, 106
rations, 106
slave labour, 110
Puddephatt, John, 137
Punch, 41
Quinn, Daniel, 191, 194
RAAF *see* Royal Australian Air Force
RAF *see* Royal Air Force
Raffles, Sir Stamford, 35
Ramsbotham, Frank, 22, 41, 59, 116
recruitment drive, 12, 13
Red Cross, 147–8, 158, 166, 185, 197, 201, 206–7, 210, 223, 238, 287, 292, 296
Redman, Jack, 116
Reed, Norman, 194, 199, 202, 210
Richardson, Roderick (Eric), 13, 17, 20, 38, 42–3, 73–4, 83–4, 90–2, 134, 181, 218, 244, 254, 275, 329–30
Roberts, Jack, 220
Robertson, Andrew Esmond, 13, 38, 42, 52–3, 57, 85, 93–4, 106, 109, 112, 115–16, 120, 125–6, 132, 140, 146, 149–50, 153, 286
Rowe, Harry, 116
Rowe, John, 22, 90, 94, 116
Royal Australian Air Force (RAAF)
  No 1 Squadron, 49
Rudd, Ernest Steel, 209
Second Australian Imperial Force, 6th Division, 12
Sekihara, Masaji 'Fishface', 136, 191, 217, 309–10, 312
Selarang Barracks *see* Changi prison camp

Sembawang, 36
Seremban, 36, 38–9
Serong, Len, 108–9
Sexton, Padre, 40
Sheridan, George, 163
Shibano, Tadeo 'the Bull', 136, 149, 155, 214, 218, 238–9, 242, 246, 281, 285–6, 292, 296
Shicata, lieutenant, 139
Shin-Etsu Chemical Company factory, 131, 138–41, 158, 162, 168–9, 183, 198, 214, 220, 223, 243, 310
Simson, Ivan, 70
Singapore, 4
  attack on, 11
  bloody street battles, 5
  defences, 70–1
  evacuation, 98–9
  fall of, 64th anniversary of, 3
  invasion, 48, 88–98
  leave, 38–9
  pre-invasion society, 34–6, 38–9
  sport, 39, 46
  surrender, 99–101
  vulnerability, 64–5, 67–9, 73
  withdrawal from, 64
Singapore itch, 37
spinal meningitis, 150
Straits Times, 37
Susuki, Yoshihiro 'Hoppy', 136, 142, 178, 308, 310, 312
Sweet, Henry, 177
Sydney Morning Herald, 3, 10, 27
Taguchi, Yoshio 'the Germ', 136, 167, 282, 284–5, 297
Taylor, Harold, 13, 39, 72, 90, 94

Thomas, Sir Shenton, 35, 39, 95
Thumbs Up, 40–1, 133
Thunderbolt Fred Ward, 18
Thyer, James, 50, 52
Timbs, Kevin, 4, 17, 29, 38–40, 44–5, 47, 51, 74–5, 87–8, 100, 104–5, 108, 124, 133, 148, 155, 160, 180, 186, 219, 236–7, 250, 269–70, 328–9
Tokyo Guards, 104
Tokyo Trials *see* War Crimes Tribunal
Tracey, Slim, 209
22nd Australian Infantry Brigade, 2, 12, 22, 31, 34, 37–8, 41–3, 46, 48, 50, 52, 59, 62, 65, 70, 71–2, 76, 80, 83, 90, 92–3, 97
2/4th battalion, 70, 75, 82
2/10th Field Regiment, 64, 76
2/15th Field Regiment, 76
2/18th battalion, 2, 12, 20, 36, 52, 59, 64, 68, 73, 75, 80, 85, 88, 93–4, 112, 120, 125, 132, 146, 169, 209–10
2/19th battalion, 12, 36, 39, 41, 43, 46, 52, 54, 59, 61, 64, 72, 75, 85, 88, 94, 112, 117, 120, 125
2/20th battalion, 2, 5, 12, 15, 18, 22, 23, 24, 26, 29, 36–41, 43–4, 46, 50–2, 54, 60, 64, 66–8, 73, 75–6, 78, 80–7, 89–90, 93–4, 101, 105–8, 111–12,

115–16, 120, 124–5, 131, 133, 137, 146–7, 151, 155, 163, 193, 202, 209–10, 213, 263, 316, 318
  2/26th battalion, 72
  2/29th battalion, 59, 72, 83
  2/30th battalion, 30, 64, 72, 90
23rd Australian Infantry Brigade, 12
24th Australian Infantry Brigade, 12
27th Australian Infantry Brigade, 12, 42, 52, 65, 70, 72, 75, 83
Uishiki, Eiichi 'Whiskey', 136, 307–9, 312, 321
uniforms, inadequate, 37
Varley, Arthur, 18, 39, 43, 52, 54, 59, 64, 94, 115
Wade, Tom Henling, 244–7, 255, 264, 299

Wall, Don, 19, 37
Wallgrove Army Camp, 14, 18, 19, 20
Wannan, Eric, 219
War Crimes Tribunal, 279–98
Warren, Frank, 206, 210
Watanabe, Matsuhiro, 233, 241–3, 246–51, 256, 299–305
Wavell, Archibald, 64–5, 69, 71, 89, 94, 97, 99
Webster, Hayden, 108, 116
Westforce sector, 52, 59, 64
Williams, Dale, 39, 133, 215
Wilson, Francis 'Joe', 40–1, 60, 116
Woods, Harry, 14, 19, 20, 39, 74, 90, 92, 95–6, 108, 133, 149–50, 221, 225, 228–9, 273, 324–5
World War I, 11

X battalion, 90–3
Y battalion, 93–5
Yamashita, Tomoyuki (the Tiger of Malaya), 93–4, 99
Yanagizawa, Akira 'Gummy', 136–7, 140, 191, 217, 308, 310–12
Yates, Albert, 15, 109, 132, 156, 171, 199, 225, 228
Yokohama war cemetery, 4
Zamperini, Louis, 232–4, 241–3, 248–9, 251, 255–6, 276–7, 300–5, 332
Zentsuji, 228–30, 235